VICTORIAN MUSLIM

T0386359

JAMIE GILHAM
RON GEAVES
(*Eds*)

Victorian Muslim

Abdullah Quilliam and Islam in the West

HURST & COMPANY, LONDON

First published in the United Kingdom in 2017 by
C. Hurst & Co. (Publishers) Ltd.,
41 Great Russell Street, London, WC1B 3PL
© Jamie Gilham, Ron Geaves and the Contributors, 2017
All rights reserved.

Printed in India

The right of Jamie Gilham, Ron Geaves and the Contributors to be
identified as the authors of this publication is asserted by them in
accordance with the Copyright, Designs and Patents Act, 1988.

A Cataloguing-in-Publication data record for this book
is available from the British Library.

ISBN: 9781849047043

This book is printed using paper from registered sustainable
and managed sources.

www.hurstpublishers.com

CONTENTS

CONTENTS

GLOSSARY

Adhan	Muslim call to prayer
'Alim	Learned man; religious scholar of Islamic law and jurisprudence (singular of *'ulama*)
Amir	Title given to a military commander, governor or prince; leader
Ayat	Plural of *ayah*, or verse within a chapter of the Qur'an
Baraka	Lit. 'blessing'
Caliph	Lit. 'leader of the faithful'
Dar al-Islam	Lit. 'abode of Islam', territory that is under Islamic law or the geographical domain of Muslim faith and practice
Da'wa	Lit. 'call' or 'invitation' to Islam
Dhimmah	Religious minority under Muslim rule
Du'a	Free prayer, as opposed to the obligatory five daily ritual prayers
Eid	Muslim religious festival
Fatwa	Religious edict (plural: *fatawa*)
Fiqh	Lit. 'understanding'; Islamic jurisprudence, the personal understanding of a scholar organised into a disciplined body of knowledge achieved by deduction
Hadith	Report of the sayings/doings of the Prophet Muhammad
Hajj	Pilgrimage to Mecca; the fifth 'pillar' of Islam

GLOSSARY

Hajji	Prenominal title given to male Muslims who make the *hajj*
Harem	Women's quarters
Hudud	The part of *shari'a* law that deals with criminal law, with punishments including theft, adultery and apostasy
Imam	Religious leader
Insh'Allah	A commonly used phrase, meaning 'By the will of God'
Jihad	Lit., 'striving' or 'struggle'; the greater jihad is considered to be the struggle to overcome inner personal weakness, whereas armed struggle or 'holy' war is the lesser jihad
Juma namaz	Friday prayer
Koola-izzat	Hat of honour
Lascar	Maritime worker from South Asia and the Arab world
Li-lah	'For God'
Masjid	Lit. 'a place of prostration'; an alternative title for a mosque or place of worship
Maulana	Title for a religious scholar
Mu'min	Believer; a person who has complete submission to the will of God
Murid	Follower or disciple of a Sufi master
Nawab	'Prince'; Muslim nobleman/regional governor
Sadaqah	A good deed or voluntary payment of charity
Sadaqah al-jaariyah	An endowment, lit., 'charity in continuance'
Salat	Worship/prayer; the second 'pillar' of Islam
Shahada	Islamic testimony of faith, the first of five 'pillars' of Islam
Shari'a	Islamic law
Sharif	'Nobleman', chief
Shaykh	Tribal chief or religious leader; spiritual master in the Sufi tradition
Shaykh al-Islam	Effectively authority on Islam and leader of Muslims
Sufi	Follower of Sufism, or Islamic mysticism

GLOSSARY

Sunna	Custom, practice of the Prophet Muhammad and the early Muslim community
Sura	Chapter of the Qur'an
Tariqa	Lit. 'the way'; Sufi order
'Ulama	Religious scholars of Islamic law and jurisprudence
Umma	Worldwide Muslim community
Wahy	Revelation; the state of receptivity or openness in which Muhammad received and communicated the Revelation of the Qur'an
Zakat	Almsgiving or religious tax; the third 'pillar' of Islam

ABBREVIATIONS

ABM	Association of British Muslims
AIP	American Islamic Propaganda
AMI	American Moslem Institute
AOZ	Ancient Order of Zuzimites
APR	Ancient and Primitive Rite of Memphis
AQS	Abdullah Quilliam Society
BMS	British Muslim Society
CUP	Committee of Union and Progress
iERA	Islamic Education and Research Academy
LMI	Liverpool Muslim Institute
LMS	Liverpool Muslim Society
MRQCU	Mersey Railway Quay and Carters Union
MSGB	Muslim Society of Great Britain

NOTE ON QUOTATIONS AND SPELLING

To ensure that the sources retain their authenticity, all quoted material is verbatim unless otherwise stated. This accounts for the various spellings of the same word, for example 'Mahomedan' and 'Mussulman' for Muslim. Spelling of Muslim names, for example 'John Yehya-en Nasr Parkinson', and italics and capitalisation within quotations are also verbatim.

CONTRIBUTORS

Yahya Birt is currently writing a PhD at the University of Leeds on the social and intellectual history of British Muslim activism from the 1960s to the 1990s. He was previously a visiting fellow at the Markfield Institute of Higher Education in Leicestershire, and holds an MPhil in Social Anthropology from the University of Oxford. He has written over a dozen academic articles on aspects of Muslim life in Britain and is co-editor of *British Secularism and Religion: Islam, Society and the State* (Kube, 2011).

Patrick D. Bowen holds a PhD in religion and social change from the University of Denver-Iliff School of Theology Joint PhD Program. He is the author of numerous articles on American converts to Islam as well as the three-volume *A History of Conversion to Islam in the United States* (Brill). He also works on the history of organised esotericism in the United States and, with K. Paul Johnson, co-edited *Letters to the Sage: Selected Correspondence of Thomas Moore Johnson* (Typhon Press, 2015).

Ron Geaves is visiting professor in the Department of History, Archaeology and Religion, based in the Centre for the Study of Islam in the UK, at Cardiff University. He previously held chairs in religious studies at the University of Chester and in the comparative study of religion at Liverpool Hope University. His publications include *Sufism in Britain* (Bloomsbury, 2013); *Islam in Victorian Britain: The Life and Times of Abdullah Quilliam* (Kube, 2010); *Islam Today* (Continuum, 2010); *Aspects of Islam* (Longman, 2005); *Islam and the West Post 9/11* (Routledge, 2004); and *The Sufis of Britain* (Cardiff Academic Press, 1999).

CONTRIBUTORS

Jamie Gilham is honorary research associate in the Department of History at Royal Holloway, University of London. He has a PhD in modern history from the University of London and specialises in the history and politics of Islam and Muslims in Britain and the West since the nineteenth century. He is the author of *Loyal Enemies: British Converts to Islam, 1850–1950* (Hurst and Oxford University Press, 2014) as well as numerous articles about Islam and Muslims, especially converts, in the West.

Geoffrey Nash was associate professor in English at Qatar University (1992–2000) and since then has taught at the University of Sunderland, UK. He is a specialist in Orientalism, travel writing on the Middle East and Anglophone Arab writing, about which he has written and edited seven books and numerous articles. He is the author of *Writing Muslim Identity* (Continuum, 2012) and editor of *Postcolonialism and Islam: Theory, Literature, Culture and Film* (Routledge, 2014) and *Comte Gobineau and Orientalism* (Routledge, 2009).

Diane Robinson-Dunn is professor of history at University of Detroit Mercy and a fellow of the Royal Historical Society, UK. She has a PhD from Stony Brook University and studied Arabic at the Arabic Language Institute, American University in Cairo. She specialises in cultural encounter and exchange in the context of global, imperial networks involving Britain and the Islamic world during the nineteenth and early twentieth centuries. Her publications include *The Harem, Slavery, and British Imperial Culture: Anglo-Muslim Relations in the late 19th Century* (Manchester University Press, 2006 and 2014).

Mohammad Siddique Seddon is research associate at the British Muslim Heritage Centre. He has researched extensively on Islam and Muslim communities in Britain and is the author of *The Last of the Lascars: Yemeni Muslims in Britain, 1836–2012* (Kube, 2014) and co-editor of *Muslim Youth* (Continuum, 2012), *The Illustrated Encyclopedia of Islam* (Lorenz Books, 2012), *British Muslims Between Assimilation and Segregation: Historical, Legal and Social Realities* (Islamic Foundation, 2004) and *British Muslims: Loyalty and Belonging* (Islamic Foundation, 2003).

Brent Singleton is a faculty member at California State University, San Bernardino, where he also currently serves as coordinator for reference services at the John M. Pfau Library. His research interests and publications focus on late nineteenth-century Islamic movements in the United States and Britain, Islam in West Africa, and slavery. He is the editor of *The Convert's Passion: An Anthology of Islamic Poetry from Late Victorian and Edwardian Britain* (Borgo, 2009) and *Yankee Muslim: The Asian Travels of Mohammed Alexander Russell Webb* (Borgo, 2007).

PREFACE

Writing the history of Muslims into the history of Britain has been a lengthy and complex process. Like most historiographical enterprises, it has not been a straightforward linear exercise. In many ways, the subject for exploration—'British Muslims'—had to be tracked down and named, with this really only starting to happen once Britain's increasingly diverse Muslim communities had gained sufficient numbers to trigger questions about how they and their families and their religious traditions had become part of the fabric of British society. History, in this context, provided the ways and means to understand the present better, to make sense of both its neat and its messy dimensions, and to show that Muslim individuals and communities—whether long established or relative newcomers—formed part of a tradition that had been present in the British Isles for centuries. From as far back as the medieval period, Muslims constituted a presence, which over time rooted itself irreversibly across the country, spreading outwards first from port cities such as London and Liverpool and later from the northern mill towns to become part and parcel of Britain's everyday diverse reality. Key to this growing presence, of course, was Britain's global empire, which connected huge numbers of Muslims from around the world with the imperial mother country, and then, in similar fashion, the ending of that empire, which helped to trigger migration on a substantial scale. Again, understanding and appreciating the importance of these imperial and post-colonial connections has become central to the writing of British Muslim histories.

History, however, is often driven by the desire to recover a personal connection with the past, and likewise to identify human connections between people living now and then. Much writing about the history of Muslims in Britain has been spurred on by this ambition to identify earlier pioneering generations who carved out space for later Muslims to fill. Whether these were Ottoman or Persian plenipotentiaries paying court to British monarchs, hard-working lascars (maritime workers from South Asia and the Arab world) who made up a substantial proportion of the crews that kept the British empire afloat, or enterprising pedlars selling their wares in inter-war Scotland, pinpointing their predecessors in earlier times makes it easier to explain their presence now. Take the centenary commemorations of the First World War. The fact that hundreds of thousands of Muslim soldiers, mostly but not exclusively hailing from British-controlled India, fought and died in that conflict has connected Muslims in this country to Britain's wider history in ways that have been aimed at building confidence and trust across community divisions and misunderstandings. In this respect, history is not a neutral player, but rather testifies to the old saying that 'whosoever controls the past, controls the present'.

In the early years of the twenty-first century, the notion of a 'British Islam' has become more widely acknowledged. Not only are Muslims from diverse backgrounds engaging with the challenge of how to create a 'British Islam', there is also now much greater recognition of the role played by British converts in this story, albeit recognising that converts have come in a variety of metaphorical shapes and sizes. In any history of 'British Islam', however, Abdullah Quilliam stands out as a towering figure. From his conversion to Islam in 1887 to his departure from Britain in 1908, his leadership and activism in furthering the cause of Islam and forging a British Muslim identity were unmatched. But the role raises questions about how he was able to bring a Muslim community to life in the social and cultural environment of Britain at the turn of the twentieth century when bigotry, intolerance and antagonism towards Muslims were, as they arguably are in the early twenty-first century, rising sharply. In other words, why is he relevant today?

This volume provides us with answers to these kinds of questions. It illuminates the variety of innovative approaches that Quilliam adopted to communicate his unfamiliar ideas—his highlighting of the similarities of the three great Abrahamic faiths and their shared origins; his emphasis on the continuity between Christianity and Islam; his pursuit of 'good works' similar to those conducted by Nonconformist Christians—in an idiom that his audience readily understood. By adopting rituals, such as the singing of suitable hymns at Sunday services in his mosque, and celebrating Christmas as a way of conveying respect for Jesus as a prophet, we learn about how Quilliam sought to construct an indigenous British Islamic tradition, stripping it of its perception as an alien and unsuitable faith in the popular imagination. By building on existing studies, this volume provides a nuanced and cogent portrayal of Quilliam as a modern, rational, intellectual Muslim very much in tune with the latest rhythms of scientific, philosophical and political developments in European enquiry—in the process dissembling assumptions regarding Islam's supposed lack of progress from its medieval origins and its apparent incompatibility with 'modernity'. In the shaping of Quilliam's religious and political activism, his egalitarianism and ideas of social justice, in his championing of non-Muslim marginalised groups, we see at work here a profound ethically grounded engagement with the secular movements of the time, very similar to those of his mainstream counterparts.

But what, it seems, made him particularly attractive to his contemporaries was that he offered Islam in a style that had not been experienced in Britain ever before. It was precisely his unconventionality that enabled him to present new and often original perspectives and creative possibilities. This was particularly notable in his narrative regarding Muslim gender roles: he recognised contemporary feminist concerns challenging the dominant discourses in English society and offered feasible solutions to sexual injustices in Islamic laws and practices that could not be rejected as necessarily an affront to modern values. In this way, he defied popular Victorian and Edwardian understandings of Islamic gender relationships as oppressive and backward, and instead presented a version that promised to improve the lives of individuals as well as wider society. In this regard, his relevance today 'lies not so much in the specific version of Muslim gender roles that he advocated but rather in his willingness to cross established boundaries and engage with various ideas and influences'.[1]

Moreover, Quilliam's enduring relevance lies in how his thinking and practice resonate with current debates and controversies about roots, belonging, 'othering' and loyalty, with British Muslims as their focus. What this narrative offers is a deeply informed understanding of the resilience of British Muslims as they skilfully navigated the concerns and anxieties of wider society. By examining Quilliam's 'conflictual' loyalties that reflected the predicament of many of Britain's Muslim subjects before, during and after the First World War, we gain insights into how their successors have struggled to come to grips with similar issues that have resurfaced since 9/11 and the Western invasions of Afghanistan and Iraq. Examining Quilliam's career uncovers the challenges of being a Muslim and a citizen in a non-Muslim nation; and it enables us to evaluate the significance of the changing contexts in which British Muslims engaged socially and politically with wider society and how their attitudes and behaviour—acquiescence, accommodation, compromise and negotiation, but also resistance—were moulded and shaped. It is interesting to see that while his pronouncements urging Muslim imperial subjects to abstain from fighting against their co-religionists in Sudan called into question the ability of Muslims to be loyal to both Britain and their religion, at no point did Quilliam or his congregation call for the creation of a distinct 'Islamic state' for Muslims of the empire; nor did he or his followers advocate violent acts in pursuit of their aims. Indeed, allegations that his faith took precedence over his loyalty to the Crown ran up against evidence of his reverence for the monarchy (Quilliam offered special prayers on the occasion of Queen Victoria's birthday and celebrated her Diamond Jubilee at his Liverpool Muslim Institute in 1897) and, by extension (though with some reservations), the existing British empire. As Jamie Gilham has argued, with Britain pitted against the Ottoman empire at the end of 1914, he was more anxious than ever to demonstrate his loyalty to Crown and country and, in fact, repudiated his earlier rhetoric about religion taking precedence over patriotism ('our Holy Faith enjoins upon us to be loyal to whatever country under whose protection we reside').[2] Quilliam wrote to Sir Edward Grey, the foreign secretary, promising his unqualified allegiance to the British Crown and, moreover, offering his services to the government in promoting 'loyalty amongst the Muslims throughout the Empire'.[3]

Quilliam's life, works and practices, therefore, resonate today because we can identify parallels between the position and concerns of British Muslims then and now—how to be a Muslim in a hostile non-Muslim

PREFACE

environment, how to resist oppression nationally and defend the *umma* (worldwide Muslim community) transnationally. As this collection highlights, the complexity of Quilliam's life defies easy categorisation, and instead embraces the kind of variety nowadays found in contemporary British Islam. Interpretations of his legacy and significance may seemingly lie at opposite ends of the spectrum of current debates. On the one hand, he is appropriated as an exemplar of an integrated and moderate Muslimness, a bulwark against extremism, while on the other some see him as a radical Islamist threatening to unleash a jihad against the crusading British. But as Yahya Birt, a contributor to this volume, once put it succinctly: 'in a way, [Quilliam's] mixture of local public service and global political concern makes [him] an oddly resonant figure for young British Muslims today—a marionette for our anachronistic fears and hopes'.[4]

Professor Humayun Ansari OBE
Royal Holloway, University of London

INTRODUCTION

Jamie Gilham and *Ron Geaves*

The rise and fall of Abdullah Quilliam's reputation and influence is quite remarkable: from high-flying provincial lawyer and civic figure, first Briton to actively propagate Islam, founder of the Liverpool Muslim Institute and leader of British Muslims endorsed by the sultan of Turkey, to discredited solicitor who abandoned his Institute and Muslim community to live out his life away from the public gaze under the pseudonym 'Henri de Léon'. Unsurprisingly, the headlines upon Quilliam's death in 1932 pointed to what was a truly 'extraordinary' life.[1] By the time of his passing, he had successfully dissociated himself from his public role as the Shaykh al-Islam of the British Isles, effectively supreme authority on Islam and leader of Muslims in Britain. Notably, the renewed but short-lived press interest in 1932 focused more on the fact of Quilliam/de Léon's 'double identity' than his accomplished Muslim life and work for Islam.[2] Quilliam then slipped into almost total obscurity for half a century.

It is little wonder that a resurgence of public and scholarly interest into this 'extraordinary' life has gathered momentum in recent years. If now it is indicative of post-9/11 Muslim and non-Muslim interest in the history of Islam in Britain and the West, it was initially prompted

1

by two of Quilliam's surviving grandchildren in the 1970s, who believed that their grandfather's 'flamboyant' life and legend would make for a riveting biography.[3] As Yahya Birt outlines in his contribution to this volume, Quilliam was also rediscovered by a small number of British Muslims during the 1970s and 1980s.[4] In Liverpool, interest in Quilliam led to the foundation of the Abdullah Quilliam Society in 1998, which acquired the former Liverpool Muslim Institute premises at Brougham Terrace. In 1997, Quilliam's granddaughter, Patricia Gordon, who had set to work on researching the (aborted) biography of her grandfather more than twenty years earlier, unveiled a plaque at Brougham Terrace to commemorate Quilliam's Institute and Muslim community.[5] The Abdullah Quilliam Mosque and Heritage Centre was officially opened at Brougham Terrace by the Society in 2014.[6] Academic interest in Quilliam and his Institute increased alongside this Muslim community engagement during the 1990s and early 2000s. Symbolically, Quilliam made it into the *Oxford Dictionary of National Biography* in 2004,[7] while, in 2008, his name was appropriated by former Islamists who launched the 'counter-extremism' think-tank 'The Quilliam Foundation', today known simply as 'Quilliam'.[8]

Substantive academic research into Quilliam's life and times conducted in the early 2000s culminated in Ron Geaves' biography of Quilliam, which was published in 2010. Circumstances had brought Geaves to Liverpool Hope University where he was approached by Akbar Ali, the founder of the Abdullah Quilliam Society, to establish a series of lectures on the history of Muslims in Britain. Professor Geaves agreed. A friendship developed between the two, leading to Akbar Ali's suggestion that Geaves research and write the biography of Abdullah Quilliam. The biography appeared at a time when many second- and third-generation British Muslims were beginning to become aware of the earlier presence of Islam in Britain, a phenomenon that offered not only opportunities to study their history but also cemented Islam and Muslim identity as located in Britain for a much longer period of time than the economic migrations occurring in the decades following the end of the Second World War. For British Muslims, Quilliam and his community of Muslim converts revealed a story that had nothing to do with migration, but which showed Victorian and Edwardian British men and women embracing Islam for religious reasons. The publication of the biography attracted the attention of the mainstream media, with both radio and television producing major documentaries. The interest was to extend into Jordan and Malaysia. Today, significant numbers of British Muslims are aware of the mosque in Liverpool from the last decade of the nineteenth century and the man who created it.

Though comprehensive, Geaves indicated that his biography was not definitive, for 'there remain enough gaps in the narrative [of Quilliam's life] for further research'.[9] Geaves pointed to where further research was required, such as Quilliam's well-known but little-understood association with Freemasonry.[10] Subsequent research has produced further insights into Quilliam's publications and Muslim community.[11] But glaring gaps remain, and this book fills some of these by shedding new light on and offering fresh interpretations about Quilliam, his life and work as arguably the most influential British Muslim of the nineteenth century and, despite his death in the interwar years, one of the most important of the twentieth.

The first two chapters of this book consider specific influences on Quilliam's life and thought. Much has previously been inferred about Quilliam's Methodist upbringing, but Mohammad Siddique Seddon delves further, interrogating both the religious and political (and religio-political) influences that shaped Quilliam's Muslim missionary activities, philanthropic work and scholarly writings to help explain his political convictions. Seddon argues that Quilliam's religious and political activism, although primarily inspired by his conversion to Islam, was also shaped and influenced by revolutionary socialism. Patrick D. Bowen offers a long-overdue in-depth analysis of Quilliam's life-long association with Freemasonry. Bowen shows that Quilliam again bucked the trend by joining several 'fringe' Masonic lodges that were not recognised as legitimate by mainstream Freemasons. These lodges possessed exotic foundation myths and emphasised their affiliation with non-Christian religious traditions, including Islam, which connected Quilliam to an international esoteric Freemasonry. Bowen argues that Quilliam's identity and activities as a Muslim must be understood within the context of this international esoteric Masonic phenomenon.

The next three chapters focus on aspects of Quilliam's intellectual endeavours, discourse and thought. Ron Geaves considers Quilliam's vast published work, which, he argues, informs us about Quilliam the journalist, the geologist, the campaigner for social justice and, above all, the defender of Islam in a non-Muslim society. Geaves also shows that Quilliam's writings reveal that he was the quintessential Muslim convert engaged in a heroic effort to reposition Islam as an accomplished civilisation with a lasting influence on Europe. Geaves argues that the common themes in Quilliam's writings have resonance today, and therefore have parallels with those of contemporary literate Western Muslim converts. Diane Robinson-Dunn subjects one of Quilliam's core themes—that of gender and gender relations—to close scrutiny. She argues that, in defiance of popular Victorian and Edwardian understandings of Islamic gender relationships, which were usually understood in terms of the 'oppressive' and 'backwards' *harem* (women's quarters), Quilliam instead presented a version of Muslim gender roles based on Islamic virtues and limited polygyny, which, if adopted in the West, promised to improve the lives of individuals and wider society. Robinson-Dunn explains that, by having a foot in both 'West' and 'East', Quilliam was able to create a discourse and lifestyle that went against the grain of each, while simultaneously incorporating elements from both. Geoffrey Nash focuses on Quilliam's relationship with the 'East', specifically Ottoman Turkey, by situating his discourse on Christendom, Islam and Turkey's position in the world alongside that of his English Muslim contemporary, Marmaduke Pickthall. Although they differed over its leadership, Quilliam and Pickthall championed the Ottoman empire, and Nash focuses on how, as international Muslims, they imagined Turkey in relation to European Christendom. He shows that both men argued for the validity of Ottoman Turkey as the historical leader of the worldwide Sunni Muslim community, proclaiming the universality of Islam's message, decoupling Europe from Christendom, and projecting a modernity in which Islam not only fitted but could lead.

The two penultimate chapters consider Quilliam's status and importance in his lifetime. Jamie Gilham offers a detailed examination of Quilliam's role as the first—and only—Shaykh al-Islam of the British Isles. He argues that, though honorific, the role was strategically important for the Ottoman Turks, who rightly believed that Quilliam could be trusted to work in the interests of their empire at a time when the European powers were threatening its dismantlement. Gilham shows that Quilliam took the role equally seriously and that the 'office' of the Shaykh al-Islam enabled him not only to represent the Liverpool Muslim community at civic events but also, to some extent, to lead and speak on behalf of Muslims and for Islam nationally and internationally. Brent D. Singleton interrogates Quilliam's international status, focusing on his connections with Muslims primarily in the United States and West Africa. Singleton argues that, as a well-placed Muslim convert in the heart of the British empire, Quilliam symbolised different things to different Muslim communities worldwide, with varied results: for some Muslim converts in America, he was a model, mentor and mediator; for many Muslims in the British empire, particularly West Africa, he provided material and spiritual support and a morale boost, a legitimatisation for holding on to their religion and culture in the face of colonialism.

It is well documented that some of Quilliam's fiercest Muslim critics were to be found not in the United States or West Africa, but in India.[12] Yahya Birt takes a rare contemporaneous Muslim critique of Quilliam from the Indian politician-to-be, Mian Fazl-i-Husain (who met Quilliam in Liverpool in 1901), as a provocation, to re-evaluate the received picture that British Muslims today have of Quilliam as a charismatic, outspoken leader of Muslims in the face of adversity. Birt rightly warns us that the main sources for Quilliam's life are his own publications, primarily the Liverpool Muslim Institute periodicals the *Crescent* and *Islamic World*, which need to be treated with caution because Quilliam self-consciously promoted himself, his message and Muslim community. Birt argues that, in the absence of accounts from contemporaries like Husain, the roles projected through Quilliam's surviving publications and lectures feed directly into the various 'afterlives' that he now enjoys among Muslims, and that the complexity of this inherited portrait allows for quite different interpretations of his legacy and significance. Birt concludes that Quilliam's 'afterlives' are actually in 'rude health', encompassing much of the variety to be found in contemporary British Islam. Indeed, it is not difficult to detect and elicit contemporary relevance from the essays in this book: in Quilliam's striving to be Muslim in a non-Muslim and generally hostile environment; in his efforts to promote and propagate Islam in Britain and the West; in his defence of Muslims, the *umma* and its leadership; and in his championing of other marginalised groups, including the working classes and minority faiths. Quilliam's was an unconventional life well lived: he was, of course, certainly not beyond reproach, and he made some poor judgements; yet it was this unconventionality that enabled him to offer new and often original perspectives and possibilities, especially in terms of Muslim–Christian relations.

Cumulatively, the essays in this book deepen our understanding of Quilliam's life and work for Islam in the West. Not least because Quilliam shrouded his later life in mystery, there is undoubtedly more to be uncovered and new perspectives to be cast; moreover, other contemporaneous voices and sources, especially non-Western (Ottoman, African, Indian), need to be discovered, presented and interpreted. From rise and spectacular fall to resurrection: Quilliam's life, work and legacy is set to continue to inspire and provoke debate through the twenty-first century.

1

ABDULLAH QUILLIAM

A MUSLIM REVOLUTIONARY SOCIALIST?

Mohammad Siddique Seddon

Introduction

Surprisingly, there are relatively few contemporaneous accounts of
Abdullah Quilliam that merit serious consideration beyond those in
John J. Pool's *Studies in Mohammedanism* (1892) and Sir Thomas
W. Arnold's *The Preaching of Islam* (1896). When Pool wrote his work,
he included a chapter entitled 'Islam in England', which focused on
Quilliam's new, distinctly British Muslim community. In Pool's obser-
vations of this nascent community, he offers very little hope of their
success or acceptance by the wider society. However, had it not been
for the impact of local and national hostilities and global politics, we
can only speculate about what might have developed from their missionary exploits. Arnold's study contains only a brief and vague portrait
of Quilliam and records his conversion to Islam while travelling in
Morocco in 1884, noting that Quilliam was struck by the sobriety and

good manners of the Muslims he encountered. Arnold also notes that Quilliam thereafter returned to his home city of Liverpool to establish his 'Muslim mission'. Unlike the overwhelming majority of writings recording Quilliam's activities in the same period (including Pool's), Arnold is objective and non-judgemental. While noting a hybrid form of Islam with a distinctly British identity whose indigenous adherents were 'profoundly ignorant of the vast literature of Mohammedan theologians', Arnold explains that 'they have introduced into their religious worship certain practices borrowed from the ritual of Protestant sects, such as the singing of hymns, praying in the English language etc.'[1] But Arnold does not see Quilliam's innovations as an abrogation of Islam—rather, he considers them to be the defining features of a religion able to 'adapt itself to the particular characteristics and the stage of development of the people whose allegiance it seeks to win'.[2] However, according to Ron Geaves' account of Quilliam's life as an important English Muslim leader, we might conclude that Quilliam was obsessed with class and social mobility.[3] Given his comfortable middle-class Victorian upbringing, this might be a fair observation. Conversely, the 'hard evidence' of his religious egalitarianism, philanthropic and social welfare endeavours—including fee-free legal representation for the poor, and his position as honorary president and legal advisor for the Mersey Railway Quay and Carters Union (MRQCU)[4]—appears to suggest that Quilliam had clear socialist political convictions, possibly influenced by the Bolshevik socialist revolutionary uprisings in Russia. This extremely important event of the period does not feature in many of the accounts of Quilliam's life and the working-class struggles of industrial Liverpool. This chapter explores the religious and political influences that shaped Quilliam's Muslim missionary activities, philanthropic work and scholarly writings in an attempt to shed light on his particular political convictions as manifest through his unique religio-political endeavours.

Methodism, temperance and 'mission'

Quilliam was born into a respectable middle-class, Nonconformist Wesleyan Methodist family that had strong ancestral links to the Isle of Man dating back some 300 years. Quilliam's father, Robert, was a successful watchmaker, and the family resided in a reasonably affluent part of Liverpool. The young William was educated at the prestigious Liverpool Institute, whose former pupils also include Sir Paul McCartney. Quilliam appears to have been a very bright and applied student, winning a number of prizes for his efforts, including the Queen's Prize for Geology, an interest he sustained throughout his life.[5] His ancestry to the Isle of Man made Quilliam a proud 'Manxman' who eventually became the president of the Liverpool Manx Society. Sir Robert Quilliam was granted a family crest by Elizabeth I in 1571 and a number of Quilliams had held high office on the Isle of Man for centuries. The most notable was Abdullah Quilliam's great-uncle, John Quilliam, who had also been a member of the House of Keys (the island's directly elected lower branch of parliament), and served with Lord Nelson at the battles of Copenhagen and Trafalgar as first lieutenant of HMS *Victory*.[6] Quilliam used his Manx heritage and Manx Club connections, as well as Masonic lodge networks (see Chapter 2), to travel around Britain addressing non-Muslim audiences to proselytise Islam.[7]

In 1872, Quilliam studied law, taking his articles with the Liverpool firm of solicitors William Radcliffe and Smith a year later, while also carving out a career as a writer and journalist for various magazines and newspapers, including the *Liverpool Albion*, as a means of financing his studies. When he passed his exams in 1878, he immediately began his own practice and, after establishing a number of unsuccessful business partnerships, he eventually formed the legal firm of Quilliam, Heaton and Moore in 1894.[8] Quilliam's professional life seems distinctly shaped by his religious convictions and social relations. Jamie Gilham has asserted that Quilliam was '[l]iving and working as a "poor man's lawyer" in Liverpool' and that his membership of the Liverpool Alliance Masonic Lodge was largely driven by '[t]he Masonic ideals of non-sectarian fraternity, faith and charity [that] especially appealed to Quilliam'.[9] Added to Quilliam's firmly established beliefs regarding equality and philanthropy was his life-long commitment to alcohol abstinence through the temperance movement, which Quilliam joined at the tender age of seven when he was taken by his grandmother to a Methodist evangelic meeting where he signed the total-abstinence pledge. By the age of fourteen, perhaps inspired by his grandfather's many public lectures in favour of temperance, Quilliam was secretary of the Russell Street Temperance Society and was already an accomplished public orator.[10] Quilliam would continue to preach the virtues of sobriety throughout his life. After his conversion to Islam, he also used his connections in the temperance movement to proselytise his new faith through numerous lectures on how the social evils associated with alcohol abuse were absent in Muslim societies. In the Preface to the second edition of his *Fanatics and Fanaticism* (1890), Quilliam wrote that:

> W[hen] some years ago I first renounced Christianity and embraced Islam, I found that I was looked upon as a species of monomaniac, and if I endeavoured to induce people to discuss the respective merits of the two religions, I was either laughed at or insulted. I then determined that I would promulgate the tenets of Islam in an indirect way, and for this purpose whenever I was asked by my old temperance friends (with whom for all my life I have been humbly endeavouring to combat the evils of intemperance) to deliver a lecture on Total Abstinence from intoxicating drink I invariably introduced in some form or another a reference to Mahomedansim [*sic*]. By this means I drew public attention to the matter, and caused enquiry upon the subject.[11]

Quilliam's publication was well received, running into three editions in English and further translated into many languages, introducing him as an English Muslim intellectual to many parts of the Muslim world.[12] His commitment to the temperance movement was constant and loyal. Geaves has noted Quilliam's close association to the various temperance movement organisations, locally and nationally, and Quilliam's increasing role and position within them.[13] Quilliam's mother, Harriet, was an avid church evangelist who joined the Good Templar Order in 1872 and established the 'Fairfield Lodge', which was based at the family home.[14] Gertrude Himmelfarb asserts that, in the developing Nonconformist Christian denominations of the late Victorian era, a clear distinction can be made 'as Evangelicalism was the primary bearer of those [Victorian] values among the middle classes, so Methodism was among the working classes'.[15] Perhaps the downside of Nonconformist denominationalism was, at least in its nascent stages, that it merely reinforced industrial capitalism's rigid classism. As T.B. Bottomore ironically opines, 'it produced also the snobbery of the middle classes, the "religion of inequality" as Matthew Arnold called it, which maintained fine but strict social distinctions at which foreign observers marvelled[!]'.[16] For Quilliam, his disaffection with the theological disputes and moral contradictions in late Victorian Christian society created a deep disillusionment that, by his open admission, was only resolved by his discovery, study and then acceptance of Islam.

Although Quilliam was respectfully married to Hannah Johnstone in 1879, at the Fairfield Wesleyan Chapel, he appears to have been a confirmed polygamist well before his conversion to Islam. It is assumed that his marriage to Hannah, who bore him four children, was an unhappy one and Quilliam continued a long-term liaison with a local chorus girl, Mary Lyon.[17] Mary bore him five more children and lived at Moscow Drive, in fairly close proximity to the Quilliam home. Quilliam's apparent 'double life' appears to run in stark contradiction to his respectable, middle-class lawyer profession and Methodist evangelist beliefs. No doubt Quilliam's lengthy affair with Mary was seen as an eccentric display of non-conformity libertarianism in late Victorian Britain. Nevertheless, the staunch liberalism associated with the Methodist church in Liverpool had manifested itself in their political resistance to the slave trade in the city.[18] As Geaves asserts, 'In this period of his life, Quilliam could be marked out as a Liberal in a number of other significant ways.'[19] These particular political convictions included his passionate opposition to capital punishment, outspoken views on anti-slavery and the treatment of American 'negroes', and his notable campaigning for the rights of the working class as leader of numerous trade unions in Liverpool.[20] Quilliam was the legal representative of a number of trade unions, including the Operative Bakers' Union, and the Upholsterers and Coppersmith Societies. From 1897 until 1908, Quilliam remained the elected president of the 8,000-strong MRQCU.[21] It is fair to assume that Liverpool's burgeoning trades union movement, inspired by strong socialist values of equity, fairness and workers' rights, was collectively expressing a clear vote of confidence in Quilliam's legal abilities and political convictions in his continued appointment as president of the MRQCU, an important and well-subscribed labour organisation. Added to this was his reputation as 'the poor man's solicitor' because, in the words of his English Muslim contemporary, Khalid Sheldrake, Quilliam regularly 'fought cases for men who were penniless and charged no fee'.[22]

Colonialism, conformity and class

At the height of imperial Britain, when state and church hegemony was spread far and wide across the globe, as both an entrepreneurial and civilising project, Anglican Christianity was beginning to fracture and wane in the British empire's metropolises. As Geaves rightly asserts, 'Victorian Christianity was not without its problems [… the] Church was too often associated with political conservatism and the many denominations of Protestantism were consequently linked to class-divisions and dissent against the status quo.'[23] By the end of the nineteenth century, ideas about the colonised and subjugated 'Other' were not merely underpinned by imperial hegemony but supported by pseudo-scientific racism inferred through social Darwinism and eugenicist theories, which, as Humayun Ansari states, provided an ideological framework for much of the British population, whose 'prejudices were based on their confusion of cultural and biological evidence'.[24] In this pervading social climate, Quilliam sought to accommodate and adjust his Muslim proselytising activities to the existing and familiar institutions and cultural practices of British society. This process of 'indigenising' Islam into a particular socio-cultural context in which Muslim values and identities were generally perceived to be 'in conflict with the established norms of the majority population made the task facing Muslim communities in Britain difficult'.[25] Despite the hostilities and indignations Quilliam and his community of Muslim converts faced, they were convinced that 'a successful propaganda of Islamic principles in the British Isles can only be conducted by those who are "Britons, born and bred"'.[26] However, the differences among the British social classes appear to have been quite stark and contradictory in their responses to Quilliam's proselytising.

The working classes seemed generally more accepting of their Muslim counterparts, as witnessed by an increasing occurrence of marriages between indigenous white women and Muslim settlers. Such marriages were usually frowned upon by the 'higher' classes as grossly inappropriate because they 'closed the social gap between the ruler and the ruled', and therefore seriously compromised both the racial and imperial domination of the British.[27] Yet, as Ansari further observes, 'Even at the height of imperial power, some people felt that an attraction for "Oriental" men "pervaded" ladies of "all classes of society"—from "the smartest peeresses" to "English women of the housemaid class".[28] The 'upper' classes, whose encounters with Muslims were usually limited to Indian nobility or intellectuals who had accepted the reality of British rule, enjoyed almost 'equal terms' liaisons with those Muslims with whom they came into personal contact. These relationships implicitly acknowledged a reciprocal regard for each other's imperial/colonial status, while the lower-middle and working classes were generally less convivial. Ali Köse further asserts that, by the end of the nineteenth century, 'there were a substantial amount of Muslim students and professionals' in Britain who came from 'a high class' in their societies of origin and had a good command of English.[29] They therefore 'easily moved among British middle and upper classes' and were able to engage the interest of their indigenous British counterparts more effectively than the lascars, settled in the docklands of Cardiff, Liverpool, Manchester and South Shields. Both Geaves and Gilham confirm that the overwhelming majority of Quilliam's convert Muslim community were working-class people from Liverpool, and Gilham observes that 'Because Quilliam deliberately sought to attract local working-class folk, many of the converts were indeed, as [the Scottish convert, John Yehya-en Nasr] Parkinson noted, working men and women.'[30] Geaves further asserts that 'Quilliam's converts came from all walks of life. In this, the Liverpool Muslim community differed from Woking, as the latter was formed predominantly of upper-class English men and women and their South Asian equivalents.'[31] Gilham's analysis of the occupations of members of the Liverpool Muslim Institute (LMI) reveals that 'the majority of the sixty British Muslims whose occupation is known were of working-class origin' and that 'a minority were from the "old" middle-classes … a few were, as Quilliam claimed, well-educated and widely travelled'.[32] In fact, the majority, working-class socio-demographic of Quilliam's community was derided and undermined by Christian missionaries who visited the LMI as 'very ordinary people … drawn, generally speaking from the lower ranks of life—persons, as a whole, neither of education nor position'.[33] It was perhaps this spiritual arrogance from the clergy that drew Quilliam, as a Muslim, nearer to those less well positioned socially than himself.

Added to the differentiated reception of Muslims in Britain across the social classes were the political and religious tensions that were emerging through developing British government policy towards the Ottoman sultanate, dubbed 'the sick man of Europe'.[34] High on the agenda of anti-Ottoman activities was an increasing pro-Armenian lobby, which consistently overlooked any atrocities committed by the Armenian *dhimmah* (religious minority under Muslim rule) during the uprisings of the 1890s and instead argued that Britain had a duty both to defend and support its Armenian Christian 'brothers' against the 'uncivilised' and 'despotic' Ottomans. As a result, Ansari asserts, 'the negative views of Islam and Muslims generally continued to generate hostility and resentment towards Muslims in Britain'.[35] Possibly as a means of counteracting the hostile and negative reception of Islam among the British public, Köse observes that 'Quilliam undertook social work in the interest of spreading Islam and he founded a house called *Medina House* [*sic*].'[36] The Medina Home for Children, originally established at 68 Sheil Road, Liverpool, was officially registered with the local authorities in 1896. This project saw the Muslim community in Liverpool providing an orphanage for the homeless children who where often born out of wedlock or abandoned by their impoverished parents. The Medina Home housed, clothed, fed and educated the orphans of Liverpool, providing a great civic and social service to the city. The orphanage also operated among the homeless, illegitimate street-urchins of Liverpool's docklands, an unfortunate by-product of the prostitution 'trade' so familiarly connected with nineteenth-century dockland life. Exactly how many children passed through the orphanage is not known, but Quilliam and his co-religionists were not completely altruistic in their philanthropic efforts, as 'foundlings who [were raised in the orphanage] were brought up as Muslims', and mothers who gave up their infants to the orphanage were required to sign a special clause stating that the children would be raised as Muslims.[37]

Anti-imperialism, Turcophilia and treason

Quilliam's ingenious strategy of introducing an indigenised Islam as a primary missionary activity meant that he was able to present a 'new' faith that bore in mind the background of the people he was addressing. The organising of morning and evening Sunday services was an attempt to make potential converts 'feel at home' while they were subtly exposed to *da'wa* (lit. 'call' or 'invitation' to Islam).[38] Concerning this activity specifically, Quilliam later wrote that: 'These [British] people had to be brought gradually into the faith: consequently to make them feel more at home at the missionary meetings, we held a service something like the one they had been accustomed to.'[39]

Services were held at the LMI. Morning services at the Institute were devoted to prayer and meditation, and the evening congregational worship consisted of singing 'Muslim hymns' and a reading from the Qur'an, followed by a sermon on the tenets of Islam. Quilliam's hymnbook was titled *Hymns Suitable for English-Speaking Muslim Congregation*, and many of the hymns were taken straight from evangelical poets and divines, with others adapted to conform to Islamic beliefs.[40] As Quilliam's missionary activities began to draw more converts to the faith, his Institute attracted both local and national antagonism. In the *Islamic World*, the Institute's monthly international journal, Quilliam claimed that the increasing hostilities were a direct result of his ability to attract a significant number of converts.[41] Muhammad Mashuq Ally attributes Quilliam's condemnation in part to his open criticism of the church and its missionary activities in Muslim countries.[42] However, Quilliam was also seen as 'anti-British' as a result of his infamous *fatwa* (religious edict) to Egyptian soldiers in 1896, which openly criticised British colonial policy in Sudan and urged Muslim soldiers in the British army to refrain from taking arms against the Muslims of Sudan.[43] In adopting his pro-Ottoman, anti-British political stance, Quilliam allied himself with some of his Muslim convert peers, which included the writer Muhammad Marmaduke Pickthall and Lady Evelyn Zeinab Cobbold.[44] 'Turcophile' English Muslims like Quilliam and Pickthall were subjected to close scrutiny and surveillance by the British intelligence services, and in contemporary terms they would be described as 'political Islamists'. As European countries were aligning to 'square-up' to and finally defeat the failing Ottoman empire, pro-Ottoman British Muslims were gravitating together, forming a number of active associations, such as the Islamic Information Bureau and the Anglo-Ottoman Society, in defence of their caliph, the Ottoman sultan. British intelligence services were increasingly afraid of the political influence of revolutionary socialism or Bolshevism from Russia taking root among what they considered to be subversive groups such as the pro-Ottoman Turcophiles. Gilham observes that:

Pickthall and his associates [which included Quilliam, now living under the pseudonym Henri de Léon] were taken seriously. Pickthall was no Bolshevik, but a glance of the [Islamic Information] Bureau membership and a perusal of the [Muslim] Outlook [the Bureau's pro-Ottoman bulletin] led the India Office to suspect that the group was, 'to some extent anti-British'.[45]

Quilliam was unlike other 'high-profile' converts such as his contemporary, Lord Headley, who, after his conversion in 1913, became president of the British Muslim Society, an 'apologist' organisation established 'to propagate Islam in Britain'.[46] The British Muslim Society was centred at the Woking Mosque and appears to have appealed largely to the aristocracy and the middle class, many of whom had colonial experiences in India or other colonised British territories. Ally claims that both the Society and Lord Headley presented Islam 'in a very delicate way ... to show that Islam was not "antagonistic or hostile" to Christianity'.[47] Köse also confirms that Headley was 'very careful about politics. He would not involve himself in politics as Quilliam of Liverpool did.'[48] Unlike Quilliam, Headley made it quite clear that, as president, he would not allow the Society to be involved in politics, particularly given that, at the time, Britain was actually at war with the Ottomans.[49]

Quilliam's and Pickthall's political affiliation ran contrary to most of their English co-religionists, with Headley and many of his British Muslim Society members preferring to remain distinctly apolitical and instead present themselves as 'loyal' and 'faithful' British Muslim subjects. In his review of R.G. Corbet's book, Mohammedanism in the British Empire, published in 1902, Quilliam was quite candid in his largely positive critique of Corbet's monograph, concluding that:

There are two other sides of the question, however, which Mr. Corbet possibly has not seen. One is, the potentiality which Islam has inherent within itself for not only aiding, but at some (Inshallah! [Insh'Allah, 'by the will of God']) not very distant date, of controlling the destinies of the mighty British Empire; and the other is, the fact, too often forgotten by English writers, that all Muslims, however loyal they may be to the reigning sovereign of the country in which they dwell, yet have a veneration and an affection for and a loyal feeling to the occupant for the time being of the seat of the Caliph of the Faithful. 'All Muslims are brothers' is no mere catch phrase; it is a reality, a truth. Injure one Mussulman [Muslim] and you injure all. Be discourteous, be unjust, to the Emir-al-Moomeneen [caliph, lit. 'leader of the faithful'], and at once you are placing yourself in a false position towards the Muslim world.[50]

At a time when the British empire claimed to have more Muslim subjects than Christians, Quilliam was bravely drawing a line in the sand with regard to what he believed represented fidelity of faith and allegiances in the British imperial context. His bullish response to Corbet's thesis on what the loyalties of Britain's Muslim subjects should be—which included open praise for Quilliam and his Liverpool Muslim community for their 'modernist', rational and contextualised understanding of Islam in a British, minority faith context—manifests itself as a clear edict to his adherents and all British imperial Muslim subjects at large by responding that:

> If Great Britain desires to realise and to utilise the mighty power, and to preserve the brilliant loyalty of its Islamic subjects, the first steps towards the attainment of that object are a good understanding and a firm friendship with the Caliph of the Faithful, His Glorious and Imperial Majesty Ghazi Abdul-Hamid Khan, Sultan of Turkey (may Allah long preserve him!) and an official discountenancing [sic] of the scurrilous attacks upon Islam and Muslim rulers which from time to time appear in the British press.[51]

Quilliam consistently claimed to be a loyal and faithful Muslim subject despite his stark criticism of government foreign policy towards the Balkans crisis, Sudan military expedition and hostilities towards the Ottomans. But his forthright, outspoken and often controversial views caused many to charge Quilliam with 'treason'. Gilham asserts that Quilliam's political views were no more than 'a minor irritation for local politicians' and that it was more likely that 'his general activities' as Shaykh al-Islam (effectively the authority on Islam and leader of Muslims; see Chapter 6) that both subjected him to official scrutiny and made his life in Britain difficult.[52] However, his religious appointment by the Ottoman sultan, Abd al-Hamid II, as the 'Sheikh-ul-Islam of the British Isles' (Shaykh al-Islam) was also implicitly a political role. In addition, Quilliam's further 'appointment' as Persian vice-consul, and that of his son, Robert Ahmad, as Turkish consul-general at Liverpool, had received no previous permission or recognition by the British government.[53] It can therefore be argued that Quilliam's religious and political agitations were certainly causing some measured degree of consternation among British officials, locally and nationally.

As enquiries were increasingly made into Quilliam's 'irregular' and 'illegal' marriages, mostly conducted at the Institute without 'conforming to English law' or without a special licence, officials concluded that the marriages were so infrequent and few in number that it would not be 'in the public interest' to force prosecution.[54] Ultimately, as Gilham argues, it was not Quilliam's 'anti-British' activities that brought about his flight to Turkey, but the charge that he had conspired to 'fabricate evidence' in a divorce case he was handling. It was further claimed that he had also induced the case respondent to 'commit misconduct' with a woman in Glasgow in order to secure a *decree nisi* for his client, Martha Thompson.[55] Quilliam was, later, to fervently deny all charges in a letter to the *Liverpool Daily Post*, sent from Istanbul. He stated that 'my name has been unwarrantly [*sic*] associated with matters of which I had no knowledge or connection ... wrong conclusions were drawn and erroneous constructions put upon what were perfectly innocent, although, as subsequent events proved, injudicious actions'.[56] But it was already too late, as Quilliam was found guilty *in absentia* in 1908, and the press had enjoyed a field day speculating on his culpability and, more importantly, why he had 'spirited away' to Turkey before the trial.

Reform, revolt and revolution

In late Victorian society, the impact of the Industrial Revolution, rise of the empire, de-traditionalisation of state (Anglican Protestant) religion and the focus on rationalism, science and technology transformed Britain into a leading capitalist economy that divided the population into clearly defined socio-economic classes: upper, middle and working. Quilliam, as an educated and comfortable middle-class religious leader and lawyer, would have been well aware of the spiritual and political consequences of an increasingly divided society. The reality of the effects of these stark divides was at once collectively comprehended and most debated in the social reforms of the century: the Poor Law Amendment Act of 1834. The 'New Poor Law', as it was called, sought to make legal distinctions between provisions for the poor through what were termed 'outdoor' and 'indoor' relief. Outdoor relief was administered in the form of dole or food, clothing, medical help or whatever the administrating parish deemed appropriate. Indoor relief meant the workhouse or poorhouse, best captured in Charles Dickens' novel *Oliver Twist* (1837).

The New Poor Law sought to reaffirm the institution of poor relief and, more importantly, the legal right to relief. Further, the amendment established legal definitions of those eligible for relief.[57] However, a Royal Commission, ordered to produce a report on the Poor Law two years before the introduction of the New Poor Law, protested against 'the mischievous ambiguity of the word poor'.[58] It clarified that the laws were not intended for the 'poor'—a word that was commonly misunderstood as the 'labouring class', who, although 'poor', were self-sustaining and not 'indigent' or 'paupers'; the latter, on the other hand, were unable to support themselves and were, therefore, the given recipients.[59] The Commission's report therefore implied that the law should be titled 'The Pauper's Law'. 'Paupers' were newly identified as 'impotent' and 'able-bodied'. The 'impotent' (sick, aged, widowed, orphaned) were unaffected by the reforms, but the 'able-bodied', the intended targets of the amendments, would receive relief, but only so it would encourage them to remove themselves from 'pauperism'. Effectively, the legal distinction between 'poor' and 'pauper' allowed a further distinction of 'less eligibility' or the idea that able-bodied paupers would be 'less eligible'—desirable, agreeable, favourable—than that of the 'lowest class', namely (self-supporting) labourers.[60] The result of this new distinction was the 'workhouse principle': that relief to the able-bodied pauper (and his/her family) should be given in the workhouse, as it was only there that the requirement of 'less eligibility' could be fulfilled. Therefore, under the New Poor Law, to be identified as an 'able-bodied, less eligible pauper' meant a 'sentence' in the workhouse 'prison'. Himmelfarb argues that 'confinement to the workhouse, being a loss of liberty and status, was itself the primary attribute of less eligibility'.[61] What the amendments to the Poor Laws did was, in effect, to immediately lower the numbers of poor/paupers, as recipients would automatically be referred to the workhouse, cut-off from society and required to undertake long, repetitive and menial work. Thus, the overall result was actually *more* poor/paupers in need of genuine relief but too terrified to surrender their liberty to the workhouses. This new social reality in turn caused uproar among the middle classes who absolutely opposed the rationale of the amended laws. Advocates for the reforms argued in favour on 'humanitarian' grounds because the distinction between the 'poor' and 'pauper', they claimed, elevated the poor as it stigmatised the pauper. Conversely, their opponents condemned the reforms both on the grounds of their derogatory distinction and the distinction itself.[62]

Given that the poor relief was both administered and dispensed through the parish unions of the state church, and that most of the middle-class objectors were Nonconformists, the response to the New Poor Law Act manifested as an act of rebellion. That said, John Westergaard and Henrietta Resler opine that Methodism actually prevented proletarian revolution in Britain by diverting it into politically harmless channels, allowing the working class in Victorian industrial capitalism 'to express some kind of equality and reform without engagement in revolution'.[63] Yet, the social philosophies associated with the various strands of Wesleyanism 'extended beyond respectful liberalism, in some variants at least, to radicalism and militancy; even perhaps to active subversion'.[64] Quilliam's organised religio-political activities were certainly viewed in this way by the British intelligence services. A.H. Halsey asserts that, in industrial Britain, Nonconformists were not only the leaders of religiosity but also of a radicalism that schooled more than one generation of radicals, claiming that capitalism was not just un-Christian, but actually 'anti-Christian'.[65] Again, Quilliam appears to have subscribed to this view, as did his sometime LMI *imam* (religious leader), Moulvie [*maulana*, or religious scholar] Mahomed Barakat-Ullah, who, along with the pan-Islamist, Mushir Hussain Kidwai, was particularly influenced by Bolshevik ideas, and advocated revolutionary socialism as being entirely compatible with the achievement of Muslim aims.[66] There is little evidence to suggest that Quilliam was opposed to the ideas of socialism. In 1895, for example, the Institute's Young Man's Debating Society hosted an event discussing the merits of socialism.[67]

What actually emerged from the rebellion of the New Poor Law Act was a strategic response that might be described as ideological philanthropy. This response both improved the conditions of the working class and witnessed 'the enormous surge of social consciousness and philanthropic activity on the part of the middle and upper classes'.[68]

Industrial capitalism, the phenomenon ironically responsible for the rise and wealth of the middle class, was abated by a religious and revivalist tone in the accession of social consciousness. Himmelfarb states that 'It is not surprising to find Methodists and Evangelicals prominent in the founding of orphanages, schools, hospitals, friendly societies and charitable enterprises of every kind' in late Victorian society.[69] To varying degrees, this manifest ideological philanthropy gave rise to a multitude of reform movements, humanitarian societies, research projects, publications and journalistic ventures that enlightened the last quarter of the nineteenth century. Most of these were overtly religious, not least the Christian Social Union and the Salvation Army.[70] Even expressly secular, socialist organisations such as the Fabian Society and the Marxist Social Democratic Federation imbued this quasi-religious spirit.[71] A distinct combination of rationality and religiosity permeated the social consciousness of late Victorians like Quilliam and his co-religionists. As an exceptionally intelligent and visionary man, Quilliam may have possibly been influenced by such ideological philanthropic models like the Toynbee Hall project in the East End of London when conceptualising and establishing his Liverpool Muslim Institute.[72]

By employing the term 'ideological philanthropy', I am suggesting a clear distinction between acts of relief and charity motivated by a dual purpose to serve others while in the same instance fulfilling a personal moral need against what the social reformer Beatrice Webb identified as 'pharisaical self congratulations':[73] that is, the self-serving nature of philanthropy that assumes an elitist authoritarianism in which the act of giving becomes something that satisfies the guilt association of those who 'have' over the 'have nots'. Conversely, Nonconformist and Methodist philanthropy was founded on John Wesley's maxim, 'Gain all you can … Save all you can … Give all you can', what Max Weber has termed 'Protestant aestheticism'.[74] The ideology behind this religious benevolence is that it is essentially a two-way interaction in which both recipient and benefactor gain. It is this ideological philanthropy that revolutionised the concept of charity in the Victorian era. Quilliam's philanthropy was informed by both his Wesleyan past and his new Muslim belief in the concept of *zakat*, one of the five basic compulsory duties of Islamic faith. Because of his proficiency in Arabic, Quilliam would have understood the etymologi-

cal, conceptual and ideological implications of *zakat*. The word, which
has no equivalent in English, means, 'to purify, cleanse, bless or
increase' and, as an obligatory duty, it requires a portion of one's
wealth to be distributed among the needy.[75] Ideologically, it is also
meant to serve as a reminder to the faithful that wealth is ultimately a
trust bestowed by God. Politically, *zakat* is a fiscal policy through
which social justice can be secured because Islam aims to produce an
egalitarian society in which the social and economic gap between the
rich and poor is reduced through the payment of *zakat* and its non-
compulsory equivalents: *sadaqah* (good deed or voluntary payment of
charity), *li-lah* ('for God') and an endowment known as *sadaqah
al-jaariyah* (lit., 'charity in continuance').

Conclusion

Geaves rightly reminds us that we must view Quilliam in his own particular historical and social context: as a product of late Victorian imperial society.[76] As a modern, rational, scientific, religious intellectual,
Quilliam was certainly a man of his time. His personal library, said to
have housed over 2,000 books, is evidence of his open and enquiring
spirit. Quilliam the 'modernist' would have kept abreast of all new
technological, philosophical and political trends and would have
engaged with modern developments in the spirit of objective enquiry
and self-advancement. As a 'rationalist', he was pragmatic and empirical—if something made sense and had proven results, he would
endorse it. The 'scientist' in Quilliam was willing to engage with the
empirical facts and scientific evidences of archaeology, geology (his
specialist subject) and biological evolutionism as espoused by Charles
Darwin. As a 'religious intellectual', Quilliam emerged as the first *bona
fide* Shaykh al-Islam of Britain. This achievement should not be dismissed on the grounds that the title was merely 'honorific'; his vast
bibliography on matters of religion alone is as yet to be surpassed by
any British Muslim scholar. But Quilliam was not just a man of literary
and oratory eloquence: he was a missionary activist, egalitarianist, phi-
lanthropist, reformist, socialist and political agitator, much to the
annoyance of the British imperial establishment.

While Quilliam's ultimate objective of establishing a 'British Islam',
complete with indigenous Muslims, was never fully realised, his legacy

remains with us today. The model, for anyone wishing to emulate it, to establish a micro-Muslim community, complete with institutions and infrastructures, is an accessible 'blueprint' preserved in his collected writings, journals and magazines and, luckily, in the very building, the Liverpool Muslim Institute (now the Abdullah Quilliam Heritage Centre) at Brougham Terrace, where he undertook his ambitious endeavours. This chapter asserts that Quilliam's religious and political activism, although primarily inspired by his conversion to Islam, was also shaped and influenced by the then newly emerging proletariat, revolutionary socialism. His continued commitment to the burgeoning working-class trades union movement, both as a leading member representative and legal advisor, coupled with his reputation as the 'poor man's lawyer' because of his frequent fee-free representations for the impoverished, clearly demonstrates his empathetic proximity to working-class struggles. Added to this are his associations with Pickthall and their pro-Ottoman activities that raised the suspicions of the British intelligence services that they might be 'Bolsheviks', but were definitely 'anti-British'. Quilliam's other close association with Barakat-Ullah, a self-proclaimed 'revolutionary socialist' who declared it to be compatible with Muslim aims to rid India of British imperialism,[77] and the apparent facilitation of discussions and debate on socialism at the Institute suggest that Quilliam was at least accommodating of, if not wholly committed to, the ideals of socialism. Finally, there is Quilliam's unrelenting religious stand against British imperialism in Sudan, and his opposition to British hostilities against the Ottomans, manifest through his controversial *fatwas* that were certainly instrumental in, if not wholly responsible for, his exile to Turkey in 1908.

2

ABDULLAH QUILLIAM AND THE RISE OF INTERNATIONAL ESOTERIC-MASONIC ISLAMOPHILIA

Patrick D. Bowen

Introduction

Despite playing an important role in Abdullah Quilliam's life from the mid-1870s until the early 1910s, Freemasonry has received relatively little attention in studies of this influential convert to Islam.[1] Quilliam was a member of over a dozen Masonic and para-Masonic organisations during his lifetime, receiving numerous honours and serving as a leader in these groups. In addition, through his influence, several Muslims joined a para-Masonic order that he headed, further cementing his position as the most prominent British Muslim in the late nineteenth and early twentieth centuries.

Quilliam's Masonic life, however, was not a typical one. Besides being the only well-known Muslim Mason on British soil, he was also a member of a handful of 'fringe', or irregular, Masonic lodges that were not recognised as legitimate by the mainstream, or regular, Masonic bodies. These groups, most of which were led by a Manchester merchant named John Yarker, possessed exotic foundation myths and were often known to emphasise their affiliation with non-Christian religious traditions, most notably esotericism, Hinduism and Islam. In fact, within the context of fringe Masonry, Quilliam's embracing of Islam was not as radical as it is often perceived. Indeed, as it turns out, through British fringe Masonry, Quilliam was connected with a growing, broader current of an international esoteric Freemasonry that contributed to the growing Euro-American identification with Muslims in the late nineteenth and early twentieth centuries. This chapter examines Quilliam's Masonic career with this connection in mind and argues that although Quilliam's Islamic and Masonic identities were very much distinct from those of others within the esoteric Freemasonic current, they still give valuable insight into the influence and spread of the international esoteric-Masonic Islamophilia of the period.

Early Masonic career

The scholarly consensus on the beginnings of Freemasonry is that it developed in Europe around the early seventeenth century.[2] Freemasons were originally English and Scottish gentlemen who were interested in ancient, non-Christian knowledge and occult powers. The fascination with secret—esoteric—knowledge was therefore a central element of the Craft. However, after the movement went underground during the second half of the seventeenth century, it re-emerged in the early eighteenth on more humanistic, political and Deist-focused bases. Although members continued to teach the ancient myths of the society's founders and held on to esoteric interpretations of many of the group's symbols, Masonic lodges were increasingly serving the role of mere meeting-places for men with shared interests. Esotericism-focused orders were very rare, particularly in England, where Freemasonry was now commonly restricted to the upper classes. In the nineteenth century, although British Masonry did undergo a democratisation, largely propelled by the rise of a middle class that sought both new voluntary associations and access to the country's power brokers, British Freemasons continued to place little importance on esotericism.

It appears that a concentrated, sincere interest in esotericism and 'Oriental' knowledge within the English-speaking Masonic world did not re-emerge until the late 1860s and early 1870s, when a handful of esoterically-inclined Masons joined a new Masonic research group, the Societas Rosicruciana in Anglia.[3] Backed by a wealthy Masonic regalia manufacturer, these Masons not only began researching and writing about esoteric and non-Christian religious topics but also started creating numerous eccentric Masonic and para-Masonic orders—so many, in fact, that the period was eventually referred to as a time of an 'occult revival'.[4] Of course, most of these new orders were not accepted as 'regular' by mainstream Freemasonry, making the Mancunian merchant John Yarker, an honorary member of the esoteric Theosophical Society and a leader in several of these Masonic groups, one of the most influential figures in this fringe Freemasonic current.[5] As we will see, Yarker would in fact turn out to be the key link between Quilliam and the esoteric-Masonic world.

Available records concerning Quilliam's Masonic and esotericism-connected activities from before 1895 are few; however, those that do exist provide great insight into his identity as a Freemason and how this possibly related to his identity as a Muslim.[6] One of the earliest dates associated with Quilliam being in a Masonic lodge is November 1877. According to a 1902 article, in 1877 a twenty-one-year-old Quilliam was one of the founding members of Liverpool's Royal Oscar lodge of the Swedenborgian Rite of Freemasonry, a Yarker-led fringe organisation that focused on the writings of the eighteenth-century spiritualist Emanuel Swedenborg.[7] Although Quilliam was verifiably involved with this Rite by 1901,[8] whether he was actually a member at this early date is difficult to say; fringe Masons were occasionally known to falsely attach early dates to the enrolment of prominent members, usually to increase their own legitimacy by suggesting such people had been involved from the beginning.[9] In any case, Quilliam did not wait long to start his mainstream Masonic career, gaining his initiation in Liverpool's Alliance Lodge, no. 667, on 15 July 1879, just two weeks after his wedding to Hannah Johnstone.[10] Still, it took barely one year for Quilliam to move on (or back) to the fringe, when he joined two more Yarker-led groups: the Royal Oriental Order of Sikha and the Sat B'hai—a Hindu-focused order generally referred to simply as the Sat B'hai—and the Ancient and Primitive Rite of Memphis (APR).[11]

Of the three fringe Yarker orders in which he was enrolled, the APR was the largest and possibly the most important for Quilliam. The APR was a faction of the fringe Rite of Memphis, which itself was an off-shoot of another non-mainstream group, the Rite of Misraim.[12] The latter organisation, which claimed to be imparting ancient Egyptian knowledge through an unprecedented ninety degrees of initiation (levels of spiritual development), was formed in Milan in 1805 and quickly spread to France. In the early 1830s, one Jacques-Etienne Marconis joined the Misraim Rite but soon broke off on his own to start what he called the Rite of Memphis. Marconis's organisation was basically an imitation of the Misraim group, but with an additional six degrees of initiation and an elaborated new foundation myth, which claimed that the rite had been imported to Europe from an Egyptian 'separhic' priest 'who purified the doctrines of the Egyptians according to the tenets of Christianity'.[13] Unsurprisingly, the Misraim lodge was not pleased with Marconis's imitation, and eventually forced him to shut the lodge down—but not before he had ensured his legacy by establishing a few branches outside of France.

One of Marconis's longest-lasting branches was one started in the United States in 1857, which, in 1862, officially adopted the name Ancient and Primitive Rite of Memphis.[14] In 1872, John Yarker received from the American APR a charter for a 'Sovereign Sanctuary of the Ancient and Primitive Rite of Freemasonry according to the Rite of Memphis for the United Kingdom of Great Britain and Ireland', making him in charge of the movement in his home country, and eventually all of Europe. Bolstered by its high number of degrees, which appealed to distinction-seekers and esotericists alike, the order was quickly able to find success. By 1881, it was publishing a journal, the *Kneph*, and had numerous lodges throughout Britain and a few in southern Europe.[15] In addition, since Yarker had a penchant for collecting Masonic affiliations, he also began associating his APR with other factions of both the Rite of Memphis and the Rite of Misraim. By the early 1880s, then, the APR was connected with such a high number of lodges—some of which were even in Muslim-majority regions, like Tunis and Egypt, and possibly Turkey[16]—that in 1881 this international coalition decided to officially formalise their association by adopting the name Ancient and Primitive Rite of Memphis-

Misraim and creating a position for the head of the entire order, the grand hierophant general 97°.[17]

The same year that the APR officially went global, its *Kneph* began publishing two sets of items directly related to Quilliam. The first was reports concerning Lily of the Valley, no. 7, Liverpool's branch of the APR, for which Quilliam became the head in April 1881.[18] The second set of items concerned a group called the Ancient Order of Zuzimites (AOZ), which, in its first *Kneph* appearance in April that year, announced that the order's leaders had decided to make the *Kneph* its official organ.[19] According to a Quilliam-authored history of the group, published in the June issue of the *Kneph*, the AOZ was:

> a secret society analogous but in nowise antagonistic to the Masonic Order … The [AOZ] is supposed to have been founded in the early part of the second century (Anno Mundi). Authentic chronicles mention the Zuzimites in the year of the world 2079 (1918 years before the Christian era …).[20]

The namesake of the order was the Zuzim of Genesis 14:2, which Quilliam described as 'a race of giants and warriors, who lived in the fertile valleys of Palestine and waged war with the kings of Sodom and Gomorrah'.[21] Although the AOZ's ritual also made reference to the Zamzummim of Deuteronomy 2:20,[22] according to the group's 1881 'Liturgy', the AOZ's mythology was not strictly biblical, as it claimed both Greek and Egyptian gods as early members and made references to medieval occult ideas.[23] Furthermore, Quilliam noted in his history of the order that several of the 'superior' of the group's twenty-one degrees were added by various individuals from different backgrounds at different points in history, such as when Peter Di Murone in the thirteenth century created the Celestine Degree.[24] Consistent with the order's penchant for mixing sources from different ethnic communities, the group made its first 'principal object' to be 'the creation and perpetuation of an international fraternity and universal brotherhood without distinction of race, colour, or creed'.[25] Quilliam, it seems, would long adhere to this liberal AOZ principle.

What should we make of this strange organisation and its obviously fabricated origin story? One might be inclined to say, since the AOZ was led by Quilliam, who was known to indulge in other less-than-believable fringe Masonic narratives, such as that of the APR, that there can be no doubt that this was entirely his invention. We cannot, how-ever, assert this with absolute certainty, since in 1908 it was reported that the order was old enough and active enough to have been exported to New York as early as 1868, when Quilliam was only twelve years old.[26] There are clues, nevertheless, that point to the group being started by Quilliam in 1874. It was, first of all, only in 1874 that the AOZ reportedly began holding annual sessions,[27] and it was also that year that an eighteen-year-old Quilliam—who was not even old enough to join most other Masonic lodges, and by the AOZ's 1881 rules would have been three years too young to even become a mem-ber of that very order—was supposedly installed as the AOZ head, a position he would not relinquish for over twenty-eight years.[28] It is hard to imagine that the AOZ's members, most of whom, if the group was indeed established in the 1860s or earlier, would have presumably been middle-aged, would have allowed this exclusive reign of such a young man. It is also notable that the order's Liverpool lodge (called a 'tent') just so happened to be the first AOZ lodge formed, and when the group held a convention in January 1881, all its 'representatives', with the exception of one man from Manchester, were Liverpudlians. If the order was indeed over thirteen years old by this point, and had already set up a branch in America, one would think that it would have been organised and popular enough to have been able to gain at least one additional branch outside of northwest England.[29] In fact, it was only at this 1881 meeting that the AOZ first decided to establish a grand body ('Tabernacle') to unite its different representatives—another fact that is surprising given its supposed age.[30]

Although it is possible that the AOZ was an old Liverpool association that Quilliam simply brought to prominence, given the above evidence it is more than likely that the order was, as many have assumed, a cre-ation of Quilliam, perhaps originally as an informal teenage club that merely imitated—in a very imaginative, if not immature fashion—the adult Masonic lodges to which his father and grandfather belonged.[31] It is hard to say if anything official had actually been established in 1874,[32] but, regardless, once Quilliam became involved in Masonry he seems to have been inspired to try to transform his club into something more respectable, something along the lines of a full-fledged para-Masonic order. Yarker's fringe movement, then, offered a useful path for this: by gaining recognition from Yarker's community, especially from his better-established APR, Quilliam would secure for his group the legitimacy it would have lacked had it tried and inevitably failed to obtain approval from mainstream Masonic bodies. In fringe Masonry, Quilliam had apparently discovered a path for bringing to life his creative, liberal daydreams about organisations with exotic identities—daydreams that surely included having himself as his order's exulted leader. The experience surely taught Quilliam that even if the Zuzimites project failed, there was still the possibility that he could organise people to follow other unique types of identities that exemplified his liberal views. There should be little doubt, then, that Quilliam had this lesson in mind when he converted to Islam and established the Liverpool Muslim Institute.

Islam—Masonic ties

Unfortunately, very little is known about Quilliam's Masonic and para-Masonic activities between 1882 and 1895. Later discussions about his Freemasonic career imply that during this period he maintained membership in most of the groups that he had first become involved with between 1874 and 1880, but sources from the period to prove this are scarce. The lack of evidence suggests that his Masonic commitments may have suffered somewhat, perhaps due to Quilliam devoting a significant amount of time to his new interest in Islam. We know, for example, that during the first six years of this period, Quilliam appears to have made a number of trips to North Africa.[33] Still, despite his travels, he was able to serve in a high office in the local APR in 1883 and establish the Vernon Temperance Hall in 1886.[34] Surprisingly, though, despite the *Kneph* being the official organ of the AOZ, the group is not discussed in the magazine's 1882 or 1883 volumes, nor is it mentioned in other available records from the 1880s through the early 1890s.[35] After publicly announcing his conversion and forming the Liverpool Muslim Association in 1887,[36] Quilliam's free time for Masonry must have been even more limited, which might explain why we can only verify a single Masonic event for Quilliam between 1887 and 1894: his taking the role of treasurer in the APR in the latter year.[37]

During this period, Quilliam may have been putting to use his Freemasonic ties to help spread Islam. We know that at least one convert to Islam under Quilliam, James B./Djemal-ud-deen Bokhari Jeffery, had reportedly been a member of the AOZ since 1874 or 1876,[38] and that Quilliam regularly used his involvement with voluntary associations to promote Islam[39]—so it is likely that he spent some of this period recruiting converts from the Masonic organisations with which he was connected. Also, in 1892, Quilliam had two Islam-themed essays appear in the first two issues of *La lumière d'Orient: revue bi-mensuelle de L'Islam*, a short-lived journal published by the famous French Mason and esotericist Papus (Gérard Encausse).[40] Papus, who was in several of the same esotericist groups as Yarker, and would later become a high-ranking transmitter of the APR, was desirous of fostering universal brotherhood through his various activities and had started *La lumière* to promote a more educated, sympathetic understanding of Muslims among Europeans.[41] For his efforts, in January 1893, Papus was awarded the fourth class of the Ottoman Imperial Order of the Mejidieh decoration by the Ottoman sultan.[42] He soon was even able to export his main esotericist interest, Martinism, to Muslim-majority regions.[43] The source of Quilliam's connection with Papus is not yet known; it is possible that Yarker had put the two men in touch, but it is also possible that the men's Ottoman ties served as the link.[44]

Whatever the circumstances were for Quilliam and Papus connecting, from that point forward Quilliam's Masonic and esotericist ties would be increasingly publicly linked to his identity as a Muslim—a reality that is reflected in the fact that the vast majority of information we have about Quilliam's Masonic interest comes from it being mentioned in his Islamic journal, the *Crescent*. The first mention of anything related to Masonry in the *Crescent* appeared in an article in a January 1895 issue, and it shed further light on Quilliam's connecting of Islam and Freemasonry. This piece describes Quilliam's installation as the head of the Tabernacle of Concord of High Priesthood, 'one of the higher degrees of masonry'.[45] As the *Crescent* observed, in his acceptance speech Quilliam explained that: 'one of the reasons he so admired Freemasonry was that it taught its members to believe in the one, true, and only God, and gave Him no partners in His inheritance. That was pure Islamic doctrine.'[46] It seems, then, that between 1881 and 1895 Quilliam had found, if not an organisational path for his Islamic movement to gain prominence, at least an ideological connection that could be promoted.

Perhaps Quilliam's passion for Islam and its ties to Masonry were partially outgrowths of his early foray into Yarker's fringe. Yarker himself would have been a good resource for developing an interest in the religion. As early as 1869, he had expressed belief in the theory that Muslims had been responsible for transmitting Freemasonry to Europe, and that evidence of this could be found on buildings in France.[47] In a version of the APR ritual that he edited, furthermore, a few Islamic themes were emphasised.[48] Yarker's fringe Masonic friends were also interested in Islam, including F.G. Irwin, who told British Masons the theory, which he had learned in Gibraltar, that Muslims had brought Freemasonry to Europe via Spain, and Kenneth R.H. Mackenzie, who in his writings sometimes expressed sympathetic views of Muslims.[49] Mackenzie had even established a para-Masonic rite that emphasised Islam, the Order of Ishmael, in which both Irwin and Yarker were officers, and, after Mackenzie died in 1886, Yarker became its leader.[50] Given his closeness to the fringe scene generally and to Yarker in particular—who, it should be mentioned, was made an officer in the AOZ[51]—it is easy to see how Quilliam might have interpreted and become attracted to Islam through the lens of the fringe Masonic Islamophilia.[52]

Quilliam's commitment to the idea that there was a historical link between Islam and Freemasonry was made explicit in an article that ran in his second periodical, the *Islamic World*, in 1901.[53] In this piece, which was written by either Quilliam or Yarker, the author asserts that Masonic ceremonies undoubtedly come from Islam, and that, philosophically, Freemasonry and Islam are very close, especially the form of Islam that is followed by Shi'i Sufis in Turkey and Egypt—a claim that had previously received traction among some Anglophone esotericists.[54] Not surprisingly, the essay stresses the influence of a 'Muslim societ[y]', Egypt, on the development of the APR in particular, and proudly notes that the group had Egyptian Muslim members. Appended to this article is a list of Yarker's Masonic honours, several of which are degrees conferred upon Yarker by Egyptian and Turkish Masons, including some in the APR.[55] Given the prevalence of these connections between Islam and Freemasonry, Quilliam must have indeed been honoured to receive from the Ottoman sultan the Masonic-like Order of the Osmanlieh decoration for rendering 'great service to the Ottoman Empire' in 1898.[56]

Another Masonic affiliation Quilliam probably had during the last years of the nineteenth century was with Albert L. Rawson, an American fringe Mason with ties to both Yarker and the American white converts to Islam.[57] Rawson, whose relationship with Quilliam was probably instigated by the latter's becoming involved with the schisms in the American Muslim movement at the time, was a prominent member in two Islamophilic para-Masonic orders, the 'Shriners'[58] and the 'Sheiks of the Desert'.[59] Interestingly, in the early 1900s, Yarker (who was made an honorary member of the latter group in 1887) would insist that those two orders, along with Mackenzie's Order of Ishmael, had all sprung out of the same original Islamic secret society.[60] Whether Quilliam was directly connected to any of these groups, however, is unknown.

Despite this perceived compatibility between Quilliam's new religion and Freemasonry, however, the *Crescent*'s mentions of Quilliam's name in Masonic contexts would still be fairly rare in the second half of the 1890s, and were usually limited to references to 'regular' lodges to which he belonged. In 1898, Quilliam was identified as a member of the Good Templars, and in 1899, besides being noted for joining the mainstream West Kirby Lodge, no. 2690, he was listed as a member of both the Grand Council of the Allied Masonic Degrees and the Liverpool Lodge, no. 1547.[61] Little else concerning Freemasonry was mentioned in the journal during the decade.

In the autumn of 1901, after more than a year of silence on Masonic matters, the *Crescent*'s approach to Masonry completely changed. That year, the journal revived public discussions of the topic, and for the next half decade Freemasonry would have a consistent presence in both the *Crescent* and, apparently, in Quilliam's public activities. In September, the journal ran an announcement by Yarker concerning Quilliam's recently having received an APR decoration called the Grand Star of Sirius 'for his eminent services to General Literature, and coupled with his zealous services to Masonry in general'.[62] Immediately next to this article, on the same page, it was announced that the APR had recently made Egypt's Prince Mohamed Ali Pasha an honorary member; and accompanying this was a commentary, presumably written by Quilliam, arguing for the right of Muslims to become Masons.[63] The *Islamic World* piece on Freemasonry's connections to Islam was published around this time as well. In October, the *Crescent* duly discussed Quilliam's reception that month of the Sat B'hai's highest honour, and it began running occasional briefs about Masonic events and trivia.[64] Quilliam's 1901 Masonic activities were topped off in November with his helping to found the Masonic Birkenhead Temperance Lodge, which he would soon be using to promote his religion.[65] The following year's volume contained four pieces of Masonic trivia,[66] a discussion of Quilliam being made the regional (Ireland and the Isle of Man) head of the APR (95°),[67] an article on the Swedenborgian Rite,[68] and four mentions of the AOZ.[69]

The revival of things Masonic in the journal may have been stimulated by an increased interest on Quilliam's part in the possibility that Masonry could be used to support his Islamic activities. In his 1902 discussions of the AOZ in the *Crescent*, Quilliam repeatedly noted that the AOZ had significant Muslim participation, with twelve out of twenty of the order's officers being Muslim.[70] Then, in May the following year, the journal began sporadically running advertisements for the AOZ, emphasising that the group had Christian, Jewish and Muslim members, a trait that was consistent with its first 'principal object', as discussed above. That year, the *Crescent* also published multiple mentions of Freemasonry in Egypt, one of which was contained in a summary of a speech that Quilliam had delivered at the local Masonic Literary Society.[71] Quilliam's interest in international Muslim–Masonic connections was surely stimulated further in 1904 and 1905, when visiting international Muslims—a Tunisian, a Turk and a man from Hong Kong—either joined or became officers in the AOZ, and a British Muslim convert was made head of a Masonic lodge in Kolkata, India.[72] Between 1904 and 1906, the AOZ's meetings, which were often held at the Liverpool Muslim Institute, were attracting larger crowds than anyone could remember, and the order was undergoing relatively rapid expansion: by late November 1906, the AOZ had established its eleventh 'tent'.[73] Muslims undoubtedly contributed significantly to this growth.

Although during this period the *Crescent* was especially committed to regularly discussing the AOZ's activities, these years also saw Quilliam's other Masonic interests receiving an increase in attention from the journal. In addition to the several pieces of Masonic trivia, there were multiple mentions of Liverpool's mainstream lodge, the

Temperance lodge at Birkenhead, Quilliam's Good Templars group, the local Council of Concord, the Grand Council of the Allied Masonic Degrees and the Royal Arch Masons (for which Quilliam had been installed as an officer in 1903).[74] Quilliam stayed active with the APR too,[75] and in 1907 Yarker, who by this time had been elevated to the head of the international APR body (97°) and was awarded by the Ottoman sultan the medal of Iftihar,[76] had multiple essays on Freemasonry, including two discussing Muslim-connected Masonry, published in the *Crescent*.[77] Interestingly, Yarker was now claiming Islamic roots for Kenneth Mackenzie's Order of Ishmael, which, since such a claim does not appear in extant Mackenzie-authored documents on the group, may have been largely due to an influence from Quilliam and Yarker's excitement over receiving his Iftihar medal.[78]

For some unknown reason, in 1907 and 1908 this wave of promoting Masonry in the *Crescent* slowed down considerably. Besides Yarker's articles and a few mentions of the AOZ, almost nothing else Masonry-related ran in the journal's final volumes. Over the next few years, Quilliam appears to have withdrawn from Freemasonry, apparently even allowing the AOZ to peter out.[79] The next and last set of evidence for Quilliam's connections with Masonry comes from 1913, and it is probably significant that it is associated with the death of John Yarker. In the summer of 1913, after having left Liverpool and eventually settling in London where he would assume the identity of Henri de Léon, Quilliam was corresponding with the notorious occultist and APR member Aleister Crowley concerning the fate of the rite after Yarker's death the previous March.[80] Quilliam, whose title in the order was now 'patriarch grand keeper general of the golden book' (probably a ninety-fourth or ninety-fifth degree position), aligned with Crowley in choosing the rite's new successor, Henry Meyer.[81] Meyer, however, soon abandoned the group and—although the head position was quickly passed from person to person, even briefly going to Papus before ending with Crowley—the APR appears to have soon become inactive.[82] Crowley, interestingly, became more and more fascinated with the Islamic world after this point, but he does not seem to have maintained contact with Quilliam. In fact, we know nothing more about Quilliam's possible Masonic ties after 1913; apparently, as Henri de Léon, he never joined any Freemasonic order. It seems, then, that since Quilliam's Freemasonic activities had been so closely tied to his relationship with Yarker and the Masonic fringe, when this link was severely weakened by Yarker's death, Quilliam lost his passion for Freemasonry generally.[83]

The spread of esoteric-Masonic Islamophilia

In the spring of 1922, a black man appeared in New York City claiming to be a ninety-six-degree Sudanese–Egyptian Muslim Mason with important connections to British Freemasonry.[84] Over the next year-and-a-half, this individual, one Abdul Hamid Suleiman, attempted to win influence over African American Masons, black nationalists and the general black masses. By April 1923, he had either set up or taken over an organisation known as the Canaanite Temple, in which its African American members identified as Muslims and apparently adhered to Suleiman's esoteric beliefs and rituals.[85] Suleiman's Canaanite Temple is one of the earliest known African American Muslim organisations, and it is rumoured to have been connected with the more well-known Moorish Science Temple of America, which was embedded with multiple esoteric Masonic elements and, after gaining prominence in the late 1920s, had connections with the famous Nation of Islam (est. 1930). Considering that ninety-six-degree Freemasonry was almost exclusive to the APR, if Suleiman did indeed have ties to Egypt and England—claims he had been making since the first decade of the twentieth century and would continue to make into the late 1920s—this raises the possibility that his Temple, and thus through it some of the most influential African American Islamic groups in history, had ties to the esoteric-Masonic Islamophilia to which Quilliam was connected. Suleiman may have even come into direct or indirect contact with the liberal Quilliam, who happily associated with black Muslims, including Dusé Mohamed Ali, a British Muslim of Egyptian–Sudanese descent,[86] whom Suleiman met at a special Masonic gathering in New York in 1922.[87]

Other forms of American Islamic and Sufi (Islamic mysticism) currents also had connections with esoteric-Masonic Islamophilia. In 1887, leading members of the American branch of the Theosophy- and Papus-connected Hermetic Brotherhood of Luxor created a 'Sufic Circle' to study and apply Sufism's occult knowledge.[88] Although at the time this group did not have significant Masonic ties, one of its most prominent members, S.C. Gould, was a very active Mason with ties to Theosophy and Papus's Martinism, and it appears that he was responsible for reviving the group in the late 1890s and early 1900s under the name 'Order of Sufis'.[89] Fascinatingly, one supposed member of this new group, C.H.A. Bjerregaard, had a history of interest in Sufism, and was in fact one of the first Americans to join up with the prominent Sufi and associate of Quilliam, Inayat Khan, and therefore possibly influenced Khan's teachings at the time.[90] Gould's revival of the Order of Sufis may have been connected with his gaining ties to prominent white Muslim converts, including Quilliam and Mohammed Alexander Webb, both of whom had pieces published in Gould's various journals in the second half of the 1890s and the early 1900s.[91] Webb, a Theosophist and Martinist like Gould, had led an Islamic movement in the United States between 1893 and early 1896, and his efforts were at first strongly supported by Albert Rawson, members of the Islamophilic para-Masonic Shriners, and even Quilliam himself.[92] However, schisms emerged and both Rawson and Quilliam turned against Webb for a time (see Chapter 7).

Europe had its own collection of individuals with esoteric-Masonic Islamophilic backgrounds. In the early 1900s, Rudolf von Sebottendorff, who may have been a Muslim convert, first became seriously interested in Sufism while studying occultism and, apparently, just after having joined a Masonic lodge, possibly the French Rite of Memphis.[93] In 1924, he wrote a book on the Bektashi Sufis entitled *Die Praxis der alten Türkischen Freimaueni* (*The Practice of Ancient Turkish Freemasonry*), apparently after having become interested in the nineteenth-century theories known to esotericist Masons. The Swede, Ivan Aguéli, also connected Sufism with esotericism, but his efforts in this area had much more historically significant results.[94] A painter, in the early 1890s Aguéli entered the Parisian cosmopolitan scene where he embraced both Theosophy and anarchism, the latter of which, in 1894, led to his going to prison, where he first read the Qur'an, which duly led to his becoming a Muslim. After moving to Egypt, Aguéli joined up with anti-colonial efforts through which he befriended a Sufi Muslim who initiated him in the Shadhiliyya Arabiyya order and gave him permission to initiate others. Aguéli returned to Paris where, in 1910, he joined the

Universal Gnostic Church, a break-off group from Papus's Masonry-and Theosophy-influenced Martinism. It was in this organisation that he came into contact with René Guénon, an esotericist and a former follower of Papus, and initiated Guénon into Sufism. Although Guénon would not start practising Sufism until the 1930s after having joined a different Sufi order, his initiation by Aguéli seems to have been what first set Guénon on the Islamic path. When he later became the leading Traditionalist intellectual, Guénon insisted that only certain 'traditions' were valid expressions of the 'perennial' religion, and he included both Sufism and Freemasonry among those.[95]

The fact that most, if not all, of the prominent Western promoters of Islam and Sufism in the late nineteenth and early twentieth centuries possessed connections with the European esoteric-Masonic community tells us that this was a single, if only mildly cohesive, historical force reshaping Western religiosity. Esoteric Masonry offered at once both a place of experimental creativity and a semi-legitimised institution in which to form boundaries for new identities. Pure liberalism by itself may not have been able to organise people into stable communities. Communities require ground rules upon which multiple people can agree; and the unrestricted freedom of thought of pure liberalism militates against such a process. With the 1860s and 1870s emergence of the esoteric-Masonic occult revival, then, liberals (and later, conservatives) now had the perfect means for publicly uniting people under highly unorthodox identities.

Quilliam's own identity and activities as a Muslim should therefore be understood within the context of this international phenomenon. Not only was he an acquaintance of esoteric-Masonic Islamophilic leaders and an exponent of some of their theories but his very identity as a Muslim and his desire and ability to form the liberal Liverpool Muslim Institute appear to have emerged at least partly out of his experience in Orient-focused fringe Masonry. It appears, then, that through his attaining relatively great success in spreading his message of Islam, Quilliam became one of the figures most responsible for rechannelling the limited potential impact of esoteric Freemasonry into a truly culture-changing religious movement.[96]

3

THE SIGNIFICANCE OF ABDULLAH QUILLIAM'S LITERARY OUTPUT

Ron Geaves

I have no wish, oh Allah, but Thy will;
I have no chart but Thy unerring word
Which in the cave the Holy Prophet heard
That blessed night upon bleak Hira's hill.
I trust in Thee, I wait in patience still
For the reward for all that I have wrought,
For good deeds done, for battles grimly fought
'Gainst passion's might and all the hosts of ill.
My inmost heart, my very thoughts are known;
There is no secret hidden, unconfess'd,
For Thou dost search, Oh Allah, every breast,
That power is Thine, and only Thine alone.
So let me live, Oh God, so let my life be passed,
That when I die, I rest with Thee at last.[1]

Abdullah Quilliam, 'Islamic Resignation'

41

Introduction

Writing in the *Review of Religions* in 1912, the English Muslim convert Khalid Sheldrake describes Abdullah Quilliam's efforts to promote Islam in Liverpool with both pride and nostalgia. Quilliam had left Liverpool for Constantinople in 1908 and Sheldrake bemoans the absence of a similar venture to organise Islamic activities in Britain. In praise of Quilliam, Sheldrake mentions that he was the 'author of *The Faith of Islam*, *Footprints of the Past*, *The Religion of the Sword*, *Studies in Islam*, and many others'.[2] He goes on to note that this was in addition to editing the *Crescent* and the *Islamic World*. Sheldrake is right to point out 'and many others'. The most comprehensive listing of Quilliam's literary output can be deduced by combining the lists contained under his own name and that of Henri de Léon[3] in *Who's Who*. From 1902 to 1908 under the name of Abdullah Quilliam, the literary output is listed as *Faith of Islam* (1887); *Fanatics and Fanaticism* (1888); *Religion of the Sword* (1889); *Polly* (a novel) (1891); *The Wages of Sin* (a novel) (1894); *Moses, Christ and Muhammad* (1897); *Studies in Islam* (1898);[4] *Manx Antiquities* (1898); *The Balkan Question from a Turkish Standpoint* (1903); *Az-Nazir-ud-deen* (1904); and *King Bladud of Bath* (1904). Under Henri de Léon listed from 1926 to 1932, the output is more varied, probably reflecting the eclectic interests of the Société Internationale de Philologie, Sciences et Beaux-arts, of which Quilliam/Léon was president in London. These include *Bache* (*The Garden*), a collection of Turkish poems (in Turkish) (1904); *Kanli Katil Kanjalos* (Turkish drama) (1907); *Some Ancient Jewish Philologers* (1912); *English-Manx-Gaelic Etymologie*s (1914); *Geology of the Isle of Man* (1915); *Sheikh Haroun Abdullah: A Turkish Poet and his Poetry* (1916); *The Haggadah* (1916); *Pipe Fishes* (1917); *The Chellonia, or Shield-Covered Reptiles from Palestine* (1917); *Two Sussex Parishes* (1918); *Memory Scientifically Considered* (1919); *The Excellent Name of God* (1920); *Ionization* (1921); *Influenza* (1922); *Asbestos and Asbestiform Minerals* (1922); *The Curiosities of the Calendar* (1922); *Sleep and the Psychology of Dreams* (1923); *Herbal Theurapeutics* (1925); *The Psychology of Oriental Peoples* (1926); *Der Prophet gleich Moses* (1927); *Arabian Poets* (1928); *The Folklore of Herbal Theurapeutics* (1928); *Medicine and Physiology among the Arabs* (published in India, 1927–28); *The Celtic Discovery of America, 300 Years before Columbus* (1929); *Pukkto, the*

Language of Afghanistan (1929); *Memory* (1929); *A Great Arabian Astrologer* (1930); and *The Diffraction of Light* (1931).

Leaving aside the fact that *Bache (The Garden)*, *Kanli Katil Kanjalos* and *Some Ancient Jewish Philologers* were probably written by the real Henri de Léon before Quilliam took up his identity after the death of the physician somewhere between 1908 and 1912, it is still a remarkable output; and this has to further take into account the large collection of articles, poems and serialised novels that appeared in the *Crescent* or elsewhere, especially those that deal with Islamic themes, and could be broadly described as part of Quilliam's strategy to promote Islam in the British Isles between 1887 and 1908.

In my biography of Abdullah Quilliam, first published in 2010, one element of Quilliam's achievements was left relatively unexplored. Quilliam has bequeathed to us a significant body of writings: although mostly articles and journalism, from the above list it can be seen that it also consisted of short books on Islam, poetry and fiction. The writings inform on Quilliam the journalist, the geologist, the campaigner for social justice, but above all as the defender of Islam. Most significantly, they speak to us of his efforts to promote Islam in a society whose view of it was distorted by colonialism and historic Christian/Muslim rivalries in Europe and the Middle East. Colonialism was turning aggressive during the decades that Quilliam was establishing a Muslim community in Liverpool, and Muslims were bearing the brunt of it in Saharan Africa and the North West Frontier. Resistance against the Ottoman empire was growing apace in the Christian-dominated Balkans and resurrecting old Christian stereotypes concerning the bloodthirsty 'Turk', religion spread by the sword, the Crusades and the sexual profligacy of the Prophet compared to the divinely bestowed celibacy of Jesus. Secondly, but closely linked, Quilliam's writings reveal him as the quintessential convert to Islam engaged in a monumental effort to reposition Islam, not as a decadent and warlike superstition of the 'native' but as an accomplished civilisation whose history had influenced the development of Europe, and, above all, as the latest revelation and renewal of the Abrahamic religions, applicable to all humanity. To accomplish these two aims would require all the focus of a powerful intellect, and the skills of a legally trained journalist.

Perhaps it is not surprising to find that many of Quilliam's writings touch upon the same themes as we find among literate Western Muslim converts today. This may well be because the challenges of arguing for Islam as a viable religious option in modern Britain remain similar to those of the late Victorian era. Quilliam's writings demonstrate:

1. Efforts to present Islam as a religion of reason (not anti-science or dependent upon emotional appeals to miracles that illogically confront the laws of nature). Quilliam's conversion testimony published posthumously in *Islam: Our Choice* (1961) shows his conviction that Islam is a religion of reason as opposed to Christianity.[5] His articles on geology and the dating of rocks on the Isle of Man were used to show that Islam was not opposed to evolution, nor did it have a problem with the age of the earth;

2. attempts to present Islamic civilisation as not inimical to the West but rather a major contributor to European development, especially in the fields of science, maths and astronomy;

3. that Islam is not the religion of the foreigner, that is, the conquered backward 'native', but has deep historic roots in both British and European thought. Examples of this include his articles on the minting of King Offa's coin and the Islamic civilisation in Andalusia, especially its multicultural tolerance;

4. that Islam is not a tyranny, but has developed peaceful, harmonious ways of multi-faith living that contrast with Christianity's persecution of minorities (Jews, Black Africans). In this respect, he promotes the *millet* system in the Ottoman empire, and surprisingly argues that Jews could be rehomed in Palestine;

5. that the Ottoman empire should be courted as an ally against Russian expansionism and that the attempts by Christians to break away were illegitimate rebellions against a just rule that through the *millet* system permitted an enlightened self-autonomy;

6. that Muslim women were not chattels of men but had been given rights by the Islamic Revelation, even defending polygamy and the more equitable divorce laws;

7. that Muhammad had to be reappraised as one of the great historical religious figures.

Quilliam's writings show that he was not an apologist for Islam, but took a forthright position that demonstrated the logic of polygamy, Islam's divorce laws, its religious objections to alcohol, and even *shari'a*

(Islamic) law (including *hudud*, or criminal punishments such as theft, adultery and apostasy). Controversially, in the context of modern interfaith dialogue, Quilliam was aggressive towards Christianity. It was the religion that he had become disillusioned with and broken away from. His reasons for this are clear in his writings and demonstrate the contemporary disenchantment that many felt at the time, especially with regard to the doctrines of Atonement and Trinity. Thus we find him writing on advances in biblical scholarship that undermine the divine status of the Bible; scientific advances that demolish Christian myths concerning the origins of human beings; the benefits of temperance; doctrinal differences; inequalities; and sectarian divisions within Christianity. In all these writings, Islam was presented as the correction for these errors, and the errors themselves as the proof of Christianity's decline.

Proselytising Islam

In 1889, Quilliam published *The Faith of Islam*. Two thousand copies were printed, and in the Preface to the second edition, published in 1892 and which went to 20,000 copies, Quilliam notes that the original 1889 print run had sold out in eight months.[6] Consequently, a further 3,000 were printed in 1890. Quilliam states that he based the book on three lectures delivered at Mount Vernon, the first location he used to promote Islam in Liverpool after his conversion.[7] However, it is also argued that the work was based on a series of letters that he wrote to Elizabeth Francess Murray (later Fatima Cates), and which were instrumental in her conversion.[8] Quilliam was proud that Queen Victoria personally requested a copy of *The Faith of Islam* shortly after its publication and ordered a further six copies for her children a month later. One of these had been presented to the Prince of Wales, Edward, who became king in 1901.[9] However, the book's real significance is that it formed one of the central planks in Quilliam's efforts to promote Islam. The work was sent out to Australia, Canada and the United States to assist fledgling Muslim presences in their attempts to organise an Islamic mission. It was also translated into thirteen languages including Burmese, Persian, Hindustani and Arabic.[10] It formed the standard text that Quilliam would use in Britain in his efforts. Quilliam begins the book by declaring:

When we consider that Islamism is so much mixed up with the British Empire, and the many millions of Moslem fellow subjects who live under the same rule, it is very extraordinary that so little should be generally known about this religion, its history, and that of its followers; and consequently the gross ignorance of the masses on the subject allows them to be easily deceived, and their judgment led astray by any pretender striving to raise up an excitement against those of that persuasion …[11]

In addition to providing a biography of the Prophet, the core teachings of the faith and an overview of the contents of the Qur'an, Quilliam is keen to show the superiority of Islamic monotheism over the Christian Trinity, the authorship of the Qur'an as opposed to that of the Bible, and the need for a new revelation in the Abrahamic tradition to revise, reform and supplant Judaism and Christianity. Interestingly, Quilliam argues that the 'civilising' morality attributed to Christianity under the British empire is actually more readily achieved through Islam: 'The virtues which Islam inculcates are what the lower races can be brought to understand—temperance, cleanliness, chastity, justice, fortitude, courage, benevolence, hospitality, veracity, and resignation. They can be taught to cultivate the four cardinal virtues, and to abjure the seven deadly sins.'[12]

He is keen to show how Islam has been distorted in European accounts of the religion, especially the position of women, divorce laws, polygamy and slavery. He is eloquent and persuasive with regard to equality and compares Christian hierarchical structures unfavourably with Islamic egalitarianism:

> The Christian *ideal* of the brotherhood of man is the highest; but Islam preaches a *practical* brotherhood—the social equality of all Moslems. This is the great bribe which Islam offers. The convert is admitted at once to an exclusive social caste; he becomes a member of a vast confraternity of 150,000,000. A Christian convert is not regarded as a social equal, but the Moslem brotherhood is a reality.[13]

The Faith of Islam was written while Quilliam was operating out of the rented Mount Vernon address, but we know from his own accounts that direct proselytising of Islam met with evangelical Christian and other more racist or Islamophobic reactions. As a consequence, he was asked to vacate the premises.[14] The experience led to much soul-searching and the seeking of a strategy that would make Islam appear acceptable to a British public. Quilliam's next publication would show the results of his deliberations. He decided to go for a more subtle message. *Fanatics and Fanaticism* was published in 1889 and carried Quilliam's misgivings in the Preface of the second edition. He explains that his first strategy had been to compare the shortcomings of Christianity with the strengths of Islam, but that he had been treated as a 'species of monomaniac'; and when he tried to persuade people to discuss the 'respective merits of the two religions', he was maligned or ridiculed.[15] In 1887, Quilliam had been invited to deliver a lecture to the Mount Vernon Temperance Society.[16] The lecture was entitled 'Fanatics and Fanaticism', and it became part of Quilliam's 'stock in trade' to interest people in Islam. Quilliam states:

> I then determined that I would promulgate the tenets of Islam in an indirect way, and for this purpose whenever I was asked by my old temperance friends (with whom for all my life I have been humbly endeavouring to combat the evils of intemperance) to deliver a lecture on Total Abstinence from intoxicating drink I invariably introduced in some form or another a reference to Mahomedanism.[17]

'Fanaticism' is introduced by Quilliam as commitment or dedication to a right cause when most people are opposed. He draws upon the anti-slavery movement, the invention of the railway and the steamship, and the introduction of the penny postage system as examples of such commitment by passionate campaigners or inventers. His final example is Muhammad who, he explains, was:

> an uneducated, illiterate man, and who, with the rest of his nation had been brought up among the grossest forms of superstition and idolatry, received what he believed was an inspired message from the Almighty God to denounce the worship of idols, and proclaim the Unity of the Deity, and call the world to the worship of the Most Merciful, Compassionate and Just God.[18]

It was probably the first time that Muhammad had been compared with William Wilberforce, George Stephenson and Rowland Hill. After a short history of Muhammad's efforts, Quilliam returns to the theme of alcohol and its negative impact on society, though not without drawing his audience's attention to Islam's view on alcohol:

> Another thing I should mention about the Prophet of Arabia is, that he was a total abstainer from intoxicants, and gave that law to his followers. It is

nearly thirteen hundred years since the prophet fled to Medina, and for all these centuries every sincere Moslem has abstained and does still abstain from all alcoholic beverages.[19]

In the Preface, Quilliam explains that this lecture delivered in Mount Vernon Hall gained his first convert to Islam. Within a year of its first publication, *Fanatics and Fanaticism* had sold out and went to a second edition in 1890. If Quilliam's passion for the temperance movement could be used to successfully introduce Islam, so could his interest in geology, self-reliance, travel and numerous writings on comparative religion. In all these writings, Quilliam was content to introduce Islam obliquely. Quilliam was a keen amateur geologist with a special interest in the rocks of his family's place of origin, the Isle of Man. He had won the Queen's Prize for Geology while at school, and in 1903 was elected as vice-president of the Liverpool Geological Association, an organisation he had joined in 1878. In 1907, the Geological Society of London, the oldest geological association in the world, made Quilliam a fellow in honour of his lifetime commitment to the subject. His two key works in this respect were *Manx Antiquities*, published in 1898, and *Geology of the Isle of Man*, published in 1915.[20] Both works and the many lectures delivered on the same topic were about the task of dating rocks and only at the conclusion would he express how his discovery that certain rocks that he had examined on the Isle of Man had been dated to five million years deepened his faith in a Creator-God rather than diminishing it. Geology and Darwin threatened biblical accounts of the origins of life and the creation of the world, but Quilliam could argue that Islam did not conflict with his life as a scientist.

In his writings on comparative religion, which included Confucianism, Judaism, Zoroastrianism and Buddhism,[21] Quilliam would gently indicate that the morality found in such faiths culminated in Islam, or that all religions were part of universal quest for truth, completed in Islam. He would argue that the belief in an eternal, omniscient, omnipotent and all-wise Deity carries logically with it the fact that God's religion and rule of life must have been the same in all ages. This primal religion is given the name of Islam. In all these writings, Quilliam demonstrated that he was a man of his times, grasping the intellectual zeitgeist of the Victorian era. Perhaps the essay that most demonstrates his ability to integrate Islamic doctrine with Victorian values is 'Self-reliance' (1906),[22] based upon sura (chapter) 53 of the Qur'an, An-Najam (the Star).[23] Quilliam states that he has chosen the passage because, in his words, 'I wish to enforce upon your minds that important teaching of our Holy Faith, that from each person is required a record of labour and of good works, and that each individual must work out his own salvation by acts done while he is in the flesh.'[24] This strategy was used successfully in Quilliam's extensive lecture tours and the regular Sunday afternoon lecture delivered at the Liverpool Muslim Institute. As a lawyer, he was often invited by the Law Society to lecture on various criminal cases that he had been involved in as a defence advocate and invariably would take the opportunity at some point to compare British law with some element of *shari'a*.

Islam and reason

The central plank of Quilliam's strategy for presenting Islam to a British audience was to reposition the religion as in tune with rationality and reason. There were two strands to this media exercise to transform attitudes. The first was to demonstrate that Christianity, or at least the version that had developed since the time of St. Paul, was not rational, and the second was to show that while Christianity was out of kilter with modern scientific discovery, Islam was not. The truths of science revealed the mysteries of creation and could not be in contradiction to the revealed truths of religion. If there was a discrepancy between the two bodies of knowledge, then the religion must be at fault, unless the science was wrong.

The rationality of Islam is a recurring theme of Quilliam's writings as a missionary for Islam, and he described this as a paramount reason for his own conversion.[25] For Quilliam, the teachings of the Qur'an support the discoveries of science; and, in turn, the discoveries of science and the improved knowledge of the nature of creation led to an increase in awe for the Creator of such complex wonder. We have already seen this kind of writing in his scientific articles, where the emphasis is on scientific discovery. He also comes at it from the opposite direction, focusing on the Qur'an, the character of Muhammad and Islam's historical openness to scientific discovery:

> Science is the garden from whose prolific soil the tree of knowledge, with its ever functifying [*sic*] branches, has sprung, and has thus been the foun-

tain of inspiration from which social good has come. The Prophet Muhammad taught this great truth when he instructed his disciples that 'He who leaveth home in search of knowledge walketh in the path of God,' and again when he said, 'To listen to the words of the learned, and to instill into others the lessons of science, is better than formal religious exercises,' and his noble declaration that 'The ink of the scholar is more holy than the blood of the martyr,' should be inscribed in letters of gold over every seat of learning in the world.[26]

Often, these claims for Islam's harmony with scientific discovery are compared unfavourably with Christianity's antipathy for science. In such writing, Quilliam would seek examples of church persecution in the Middle Ages, for example Galileo. Comparisons of Islam's rationality with Christianity's lack of reason and reliance on appeal to emotions are part and parcel of Quilliam's critique. In the chapter 'Philosophy of Religion' in *Studies in Islam* (1895), he writes that 'a true religion must be reasonable', and goes on to say that 'Islam, therefore, appeals in all cases to the reason, while Christianity, by the narration of the affecting account of the life of Jesus, and his pathetically painful death, endeavours to influence the feelings and emotions.'[27]

In *Studies in Islam*, Quilliam also explores all his theological issues with Christianity, pointing out that Islam does not require a belief in miracles that strain credulity or in supernatural theologies concerning the humanity of the founders of Judaism, Christianity or Islam (a theme he returns to in *Moses, Christ and Muhammad*, written in 1897). He was aware that conventional Muslim doctrines concerning the formation and inviolability of the Qur'an and the critique of Christian and Jewish scriptures as being tainted by human error were supported by modern biblical scholarship, and that the knowledge of this was contributing to doubt among Western Christians. Quilliam was something of an amateur theologian and biblical scholar, and often lectured in Liverpool and the northwest of England on the latest controversies arising from German scholarship. Quilliam was also reflective about theology and morality. Although his conversion to Islam did not challenge his beliefs in hell, which were strongly emphasised by evangelical revivalist preachers of the period but worried liberal sensitivities, he was more vigorous in his concerns about the doctrines of the Atonement and the Incarnation. The traditional Christian doctrine of Atonement—which may be expressed as: 'all human beings deserved to suffer in hell for their sins, and God's justice demanded that this should be so. But in his mercy God accepted the death of one sinless man, Jesus Christ, as a substitute for fallen humanity'[28]—worried many educated Victorians. Rational thinking found the idea that the human race was condemned through inheriting a burden of sin from primal ancestors to be anathema, and many felt that the concept of one person standing in for another was morally offensive. Such ideas are crucial in the Christian doctrines of the Incarnation and the Trinity. Critiques of Atonement, Trinity and Incarnation are foundational elements of all Muslim missionary endeavours in the nineteenth and early twentieth centuries and are used by Quilliam at every opportunity. These critiques form part of a concerted campaign to convince his readers that Islam is a faith more in tune with reason than Christianity and are most fully developed in *Studies in Islam*. However, the endeavour to present Islam as reasonable and rational faced massive challenges to shift public opinion. On the whole, with few exceptions, Victorian views of Islam and the Muslim world had been shaped by the historic clash of rival civilisations, culminating in the conquest of the Western European empires over most Muslim territory, and the Christian missionary enterprise that expanded along with the imperial enterprise. To defend Islam as a religion of reason would require changing public and media perceptions of Islam as savage, warlike, foreign and backward, especially concerning issues of gender. In the chapter 'How Errors as to Islam Originate and Are Perpetuated' in *Studies in Islam*, Quilliam declares that:

> It is really astonishing to hear from the lips of educated English people the most ridiculous and erroneous statements with reference to the supposed doings and sayings of the prophet Mahomed, and the tenets they imagine the followers of Islam to hold. Frequently one is absolutely wearied at the number of times stupid and manifest errors, such as that the prophet's coffin hangs in mid-air in a cave, retained in this position by a complex system of loadstones, that Muslims believe that women have no souls, or other similar absurdities, are reiterated, and have again for the one thousandth time to be contradicted.[29]

Quilliam's strategy is straightforward. He highlights a number of ludicrous beliefs concerning Islam and Muhammad, identifies the authors and destroys their logic. He then shows examples of Western writers, such as Thomas Carlyle, for example, who have been more considered. His logic is simple: the lack of knowledge is more than ignorance; it is part of a deliberate attempt to blacken Islam, and once this is understood, by demonstrating the more outrageous beliefs held by members of the public, it is possible to call into question all misunderstandings of Islam.

Islam is misunderstood

In the following examples of Quilliam's writings, he attempts to redress, in his view, some of the more substantial misunderstandings or common misperceptions of Islam. In 1891, he published *The Religion of the Sword* to clarify the Islamic understanding of just war and *jihad* (lit., 'striving' or 'struggle') but also to put to rest the common Christian critique of Muhammad as blood-thirsty and warlike, as compared with Christ's pacifism.[30] The work argues that Islam was not spread by the sword but primarily by the efforts of its missionaries. *The Religion of the Sword* is supported by numerous essays and lectures that compare the treatment of religious minorities in the Muslim world with persecutions that took place in Christendom, for example 'Jews under Christian Rule'. In the short essay 'The Philosophy of Persecution', published in the *Crescent* in 1896, Quilliam asserts that Christianity holds a unique place among the religions of the world with regard to a history of persecution: 'The Christian religion is peculiarly a persecuting religion. Every branch and sect of Christians has persecuted to the exact extent to which it has had the power to persecute.'[31] In these articles, Quilliam proclaims the *millet* system[32] used in the Ottoman empire to be a form of equality and interfaith harmony. He even goes to the extent of arguing that Jews persecuted in Christian lands could be given Palestine by the Ottomans, an argument he presented in several synagogues throughout Britain.[33] One of the challenges is contemporary rather than historic. The British media were continually writing on the attempts of Christian minorities in the Balkans to break free from the Ottoman empire. Generally, the tone was one that condemned the tyrannical Turks and called upon the Western powers to support the valiant efforts of fellow Christian Europeans to free themselves from a despot. The campaign was picked up by Christians throughout Britain, including those in Liverpool. In 1903, Quilliam refuted the bishop of Liverpool's allegations concerning Turkish atrocities in Macedonia, in a packed meeting in the Town Hall, presided over by the lord mayor. Quilliam's speech was reprinted in the national press of several European nations and became part of his literary output as *The Balkan Question from a Turkish Standpoint* (1903). The full text was also published as 'The Macedonian Question' in the *Crescent*.[34] The article goes way beyond the contemporary crisis in the Balkans and again explores the ideal of the Ottoman *millet* system as an exemplary Islamic practice based on religious tolerance and equality.

However, support for the Turks raised issues of loyalty that would dog Quilliam's efforts to present Islam as a universal faith readily adaptable to British life. It was essential that Quilliam, as spokesperson for British Muslims between 1893 and 1908, demonstrate that Islam is not a foreign religion. In addition to positioning Islam as the completion of Judaism and Christianity, and placing the Islamic revelation as a universal monotheistic faith as opposed to an Arab or Oriental phenomenon, Quilliam attempts to show its relationship with European civilisation and its contribution to its development. Quilliam is, for example, one of the first writers to comment on Offa's coins, writing an erudite piece on the Anglo-Saxon king's minting of gold coins with the Islamic testimony of faith (*shahada*) printed on one side in Arabic. Under the title 'An Anglo-Saxon King Proclaims the Unity of Allah and that Muhammad is His Prophet', the article appeared in the Woking Muslim Mission's journal, the *Islamic Review and Muslim India*, in 1916.[35] Quilliam resists the obvious explanation that Offa was a convert to Islam as 'untenable', but rather focuses on the interconnectivity of the early Muslim world and Europe. However, his most common example of Islam's impact on Europe is reserved for writing on Andalusia and the role of the Moors in maintaining a society of interfaith harmony and contributing to European thought and culture, possibly even triggering the Renaissance.[36]

The final challenge for Quilliam would be gender, and a number of essays were written on the topic (see Chapter 4). Perhaps the most controversial is his defence of polygamy, published in the *Crescent* in 1907.[37] Quilliam does not use the arguments employed today in Muslim apologetics, that the Qur'an invokes a preference for monogamy, but offers a full-scale justification, even preference for polygamy on moral grounds. After exploring the common practice of polygamy historically, he argues that multi-marriages in Victorian society would overcome the common convention of middle- and upper-class men possessing mistresses and would legitimatise the children of such illicit liaisons.[38] It is apparent that Quilliam considered it his Islamic right to have more than one wife. As a lawyer, he worked extensively in divorce cases, often defending women who could not free themselves from abusive marriages. He campaigned for changes in the divorce laws and vigorously argued that Islam's divorce laws were more equitable. Quilliam regarded the issue of gender to be a paramount issue in Western misunderstandings of Islam, writing that, 'Probably Islam has never been more misrepresented as to its teaching than it has been and still is with regard to the mode and manner in which the inspired messenger of Allah, Sidna Muhammad (Eternal Peace and every blessing be upon him!) regarded the female sex.'[39] In an essay entitled 'What Our Holy Prophet Muhammad and Other Great Men Have Said about Women', written in 1905, Quilliam adopts a simple strategy. He highlights a number of favourable sayings by Muhammad on women and compares them with enlightened statements of equality and value by famous contemporary and historic European writers.[40] In 1903, he wrote his most developed treatise on Muslim women and the rights given to them by the Islamic revelation. Based on the first *ayah* (verse) from the fourth *sura* (An-Nisa) of the Qur'an,[41] Quilliam lays out his intention as follows:

> This assumed debasement of females under Islamic rule has been seized and enlarged upon with avidity by all kinds of theorists, social, political and theological. It is, therefore, desirable and advisable to point out in a brief survey of the legal, social and religious position of Muslim women how completely at variance is such an assumption from the facts.[42]

One of Quilliam's pet hates was the focus on the horrors of the *harem* in Victorian travelogues, but nothing enraged him more than claims by Christian clergymen that Islam taught that women do not possess souls. In 1905, he directly addressed the issue after an article appeared in the *Liverpool Courier*.[43] Following a comparison with Christian theological and biblical statements on women and an overview of Qur'anic divorce laws as compared with Victorian restrictions on female divorce, Quilliam argues that:

> Any unbiased student of Islamic and Christian law on this subject, will have to declare that the rules laid down by the Muslim legists are far more humane and just towards women than those of the most perfect Roman law matured and developed in the bosom of the Christian church.[44]

Conclusion

The limited space in this chapter does not allow for a full coverage of all Quilliam's extensive writings ether as Abdullah Quilliam between 1889 and 1908 or as Henri de Léon between 1910 and 1932. I have concentrated on a selection chosen to illuminate his method of promoting Islam to a deeply sceptical British public. Quilliam delivered countless lectures, and usually deployed the strategy of turning lectures into essays or vice-versa. The essay was his stock in trade, but he also wrote some longer books such as *Faith of Islam*. I have not touched upon his poetry or his novels that were serialised in the *Crescent*, but all of his writings reveal his conviction. A summary of his presentation of Islam throughout his writings is best revealed in his own words:

> There is no imperialism in religion. Each man and each race must see God as they can. Islam, or, as these bigots in their ignorance term it, 'Muhammedanism,' is based on an idea which does not belong to any one nation, but is common to all mankind. The comprehensiveness and grandeur of the fundamental idea pervades and influences the whole structure. It has for its object the sanction and consolidation of old usages and traditions rather than the introduction of new ones. It invites all races in Asia and in Africa, aye, throughout the world, to worship the One God, and to practice [*sic*] charity and benevolence. It abolishes the monopoly as well as the class distinctions of the priestly caste with all its fantastic ceremonies. In place of these it establishes and maintains a worship by simple prayer. It believes in no atonement, no bloody sacrifices to appease an offended Divinity—a sanguinary creed now being eliminated from the theology of the most enlightened part of Christendom. It enjoins distributions of alms to the poor and the exercise of kindness to every human and animal creature. Vice in every shape and amongst all classes was and is condemned and stigmatized as an offence against Allah. It suppresses intoxicating liquor-drinking and gambling, while justice and benevolence are made the keys of paradise.[45]

The task of convincing Victorian and Edwardian readers that this was the true reality of Islam was gargantuan but, as noted by Jamie Gilham, Quilliam's combination of a background in Nonconformist preaching and Victorian polymath learning, used to the lecture theatre, produced 'a unique means of proselytising'.[46] Added to this were the skills of his two professions, journalism and law. Quilliam's writings went hand-in-glove with his lecture hall activity and leave historians with a record of the key components of his methodology. The themes chosen by Quilliam were those that would be repeated by the equally successful Woking Muslim missionaries, who first came from India to Britain in 1912. They would survive as the main method of introducing Islam to the British public and to attract converts until the middle of the twentieth century, when economic migrants would arrive *en masse* from South Asia and change the face of Islam in Britain dramatically. Humayun Ansari notes that Islam was presented as a 'progressive moral force', adopting an approach with which their audiences could be familiar. He states that 'Islam needed to be made indigenous, as it had been elsewhere. It could not expand if it was perceived as an "alien" or "exotic" religion practised by people whose traits the majority population regarded as inferior.'[47] Quilliam had discovered a new way of communicating Islam that departed from the traditional arguments and style of *fiqh* (Islamic jurisprudence) and was more familiar to educated Western audiences. His train of thought, along with the missionaries for Islam that followed him, was more likely to be supported by Western writers, scientists and philosophers than Islamic scholars. In critiquing the validity of the Christian scriptures; the doctrines of Incarnation and Atonement, seen as out of kilter with the spirit of reason that was the zeitgeist of the era; and challenging common misconceptions of Islam, especially gender issues, slavery, polygamy and *jihad*, Quilliam discovered a successful formula, one that still echoes with those that convert to Islam even today.

4

'FAIRER TO THE LADIES' AND OF BENEFIT
TO THE NATION

ABDULLAH QUILLIAM ON REFORMING BRITISH SOCIETY BY
ISLAMISING GENDER RELATIONSHIPS

Diane Robinson-Dunn

Introduction

During the late nineteenth century, when Islamic gender relationships, usually understood in terms of the *harem*, a concept that had become a familiar trope in British culture, signifying all that was oppressive, backwards and in need of reform, Abdullah Quilliam took the opposite tack. Through his words and actions, he presented a version of Muslim gender roles, which, if adopted by the people of the United Kingdom, promised to improve the lives of individuals and the larger society. He believed that combining Muslim virtues with the limited or restricted polygyny of the Qur'an would put an end to some of the most glaring gender-based injustices of the time while simultaneously encouraging emotionally and spiritually fulfilling bonds. In addition, polygynous families would strengthen the race and nation by producing greater numbers of healthy children, thus preventing or even reversing any tendency towards degeneration and decay. According to Quilliam, the British empire as a whole would benefit if the beliefs and domestic arrangements associated with its peripheries, in Africa, the Middle East and India, served as a model for the people of the metropole, not vice-versa.

Islam to remedy gender-based injustices

Even before discovering Islam, Quilliam was aware of gender-based injustices existing in his own society and how the Victorian era's sexual double standards contributed to the intertwined social ills of prostitution and poverty. His mother Harriet, who had been an important influence in his life, particularly with regard to his early political and intellectual development, was herself an activist and reformer, who, in addition to other causes, had joined the campaign to repeal the Contagious Diseases Acts. This legislation, first passed in the 1860s, when Quilliam was still a boy, gave police the authority to conclude, without further evidence, that any female who happened to be alone in public was a prostitute. Not surprisingly, poor women and those without friends or relations tended to be arrested most often, but this legislation made all females vulnerable. Once labelled, the women and girls in question became social outcasts with very little hope of respectable occupation. In addition, they had to submit to a dehumanising regulatory regime or else face prison. Men who solicited prostitutes, however, experienced no similar scrutiny, and continued to do so freely and legally. While these acts were eventually repealed in 1886, as the result of activists and concerned citizens such as Harriet, the sexual double standard remained,[1] and Quilliam, like his mother before him, called attention to it by seeking to remedy the injustices it caused.

In 1897, Quilliam brought this issue before an audience at the Liverpool Muslim Institute, explaining that because of the Victorian sexual double standard, seduction occurred 'almost daily' in Britain, ruining the lives of girls who previously occupied 'fairly respectable positions'. Once pregnant and unmarried, prostitution or poverty often remained their only future options. Drawing upon knowledge from his work as a solicitor, he related how each year over 200 women and girls petitioned the Liverpool courts in hope of obtaining 'orders of affiliation' to force the fathers of their children to assume some responsibility for them. Yet these cases represented only the tip of the iceberg of a much larger social problem, as nine out of ten females who found themselves in such circumstances did not seek justice through the legal system. Quilliam caused a 'sensation' in the crowd when he estimated that Liverpool, 'the second city of the British Empire' and 'centre of Christendom', was, in fact, the home to 2,000 'illegitimate children'.[2] However, this otherwise bleak situation created an opportunity for Quilliam's Muslim community to come to the aid of British people by providing a means through which unwed mothers could 'retrieve their character' and return to the path of 'virtue and respectability'. As announcements for the Institute's new Muslim orphanage, the Medina Home, explained:

> it is unfortunately the case in England that while society forgives the man any transgressions of this nature, it remembers for ever a woman's slip. The way for a woman to return to virtue is made difficult, while the way for a man to commit indiscretions of this character is facilitated.[3]

While the Medina Home provided immediate assistance to mothers unable to raise their children and in need of a fresh start, Quilliam understood that philanthropy alone would not solve the underlying problems that created such difficult circumstances. Like other reformers of his day, he believed that substantial changes were necessary, both in terms of individual values and social structures. Unlike his fellow Victorians, however, he looked to the spread of Islam and the legalisation of polygamy, or more specifically polygyny, for answers. It is important to note that Quilliam did not imagine that these changes would lead to a Britain in which all or even most men would have more than one wife. As he emphasised repeatedly in his writings and speeches, Islam only allowed a man to be married to more than one woman at a time if he could afford to do so and treat each wife with absolute equality, which usually meant providing a separate home for each.[4] Since only a small minority of men would have the emotional and financial resources as well as the willingness to support two or more families, the number of polygynists would necessarily be limited.

As Quilliam explained to an audience in Liverpool's Alexandra Hall, even in the Ottoman empire and India, where polygyny was legal and socially acceptable, only a small percentage of Muslims actually practised it, 7 per cent in the former and 5 per cent in the latter.[5] In addition, because he understood human nature to be essentially the same in both the East and the West, he believed that if polygyny as sanctioned by Islam was introduced into English society, it would have the effect of making the majority of men like their Eastern counterparts, resulting in husbands who were more faithful to their wives and, in fact, more monogamous in practice than currently. Under the influence of Islam, British men would be more likely to check their impulses and practise restraint, while the women of the country would be protected from the negative consequences of a romantic dalliance. As Quilliam explained, the 'story of seduction is much the same the world over. The man lies, and the woman believes him.'[6] Yet, if British men knew that they would be committing themselves to supporting a wife and children, perhaps in addition to an already-existing family, when acting on a temporary attraction, then there would be fewer incidents of seduction. Men would be far less likely to take mistresses, and the morals of the community would improve overall.[7] Quilliam's followers could imagine the transformation of their own society as they read of domestic bliss in Muslim lands where homes were 'sacred', mothers devoted, and even the young men behaved in a manner 'as shy and chaste as maidens'.[8]

Based in part on his own travels, Quilliam pronounced polygyny as practised according to Islam 'fairer to the ladies' than the laws and customs of his own country. Because all females had a legal protector, nowhere in Muslim lands did he encounter large numbers of 'abandoned women' wandering the city streets, as was the case in London or Liverpool.[9] In addition, a mother in that part of the world did not have to be the first or only living wife in order to be entitled to acceptance and respect, both for herself and her offspring. A second wife was considered a legitimate role, the rights of which were recognised by religious authorities and the courts. In contrast, the closest equivalent in the British system, a mistress, was not acknowledged by respectable members of society and certainly had no legal status. In Muslim lands, even the concubine had a place, unlike her British counterparts who lived on the margins, 'outlawed' and 'ostracized'.[10]

Perhaps the greatest injustice of the British system, which turned so many women into social outcasts, was suffered by the children who had nothing to do with the circumstances surrounding their births. As Quilliam explained in a lecture on the topic of polygyny, in Britain innocent children were treated as 'sinners' who must go through life stigmatised and 'handicapped' by 'legal degradation and disability'. In addition, most lived in poverty, as single mothers struggled to survive and feed their families, sometimes on as little as twelve shillings a week.[11] Even in the rare event that a mother would be willing and able to take the father of her child to court and obtain a favourable ruling, she would receive a pittance, if that. As Quilliam put it, according to 'Christian law', if 'some scoundrel' seduced a woman and fathered her child, he was obligated to do no more than give her five shillings a week.[12]

Such dismal prospects for the future combined with factors such as isolation or desperate circumstances could drive some women to commit infanticide, a crime that Quilliam considered to be a direct result of a system that outlawed polygyny. While most reports of this practice were isolated incidents, often of frightened girls who abandoned their newborns, the *Crescent* reported a particularly horrific story of an individual who saw an opportunity to profit from the large number of unwanted infants in her area. A Mrs Dyer of London began offering to take them into her care, presumably to find families interested in adoption. She collected ten pounds for each, only to murder her new charges after the mothers had left. The authorities discovered that, in the twelve-month period before her arrest, she had killed at least fifty babies.[13]

While the above case would seem to have had little relevance for Muslim converts in Liverpool, it was included in the *Crescent* most likely because of the shocking way in which it called attention to social ills that neither Christianity nor the country's secular institutions had been able to cure. Yet, Quilliam's followers would have understood their faith and its laws, principles and gender roles as providing the means to prevent both unwanted children and the infanticide that sometimes resulted when they came into the world. In addition to Quilliam's arguments about the benefits of polygyny, Muslim readers would have been reminded of the passages in the Qur'an forbidding parents from killing their own offspring, either because of poverty or because an infant happens to be born female.[14]

Just as the article on the Dyer case dramatised gender-related social ills in England, so too did Quilliam's poem, 'Which of Them Was Neighbour unto Her?' In it, he focuses on the 'outcast' or 'abandoned' woman and the indifference of the Christian middle class to her plight. As with the previous article, the context of the poem meant that readers would have had little difficulty in recognising the spread of Islam as the implied solution. He wrote:

> I saw a woman beg in the street
>> On the Christmas day, for bread to eat;
>> And loud the church-bells were chiming then,
>> The refrain of 'Peace and Goodwill to men'
>
> I saw a Christian, sleek and well-fed,
>> Pass the woman and turned his head;
>> The crumbs that under his table fell
>> That day, would have fed the beggar well
>
> Following the Christian churchman came
>> A woman whose brow was stamped with shame;
>> Out from her purse, a coin she cast,
>> And the beggar blest her, as she passed.
>
> To the Church the sleek man went his way;
>> The woman of shame, she blushed to pray;
>> Yet which of them, the more blest will be
>> Magdalene scorn'd, or proud Pharisee.[15]

It is particularly appropriate for the prostitute, identified as a 'woman of shame' and 'Magdalene scorn'd', to come to the aid of the beggar. For these two roles, as Quilliam and his followers would state repeatedly, were often the only ones available once a woman had lost her respectability. Therefore, neither judges the other. They share mutual sympathy and a common bond, expressed in the poem through the giving of a coin and a blessing. The Christian gentleman, in contrast, ignores both, confident in his moral superiority despite the fact that he benefits from an unjust social and religious system.

Given the negative portrayal of Christians in Quilliam's writings and speeches and in the pages of the *Crescent*, the reader may very well be left with the impression that the 'churchman' is in some way responsible for the debased condition of the poem's other two characters, who occupy the same general space in the city or town within earshot of the church bells. For in this publication and Quilliam's writings and speeches, Christian leaders typically appear as the villains and oppressors of women from the 'cowardly and despicable' ecclesiastical authorities who condemned Joan of Arc to be burned at the stake to the Elizabethan bishop who pronounced the greater part of womankind as 'doltified with the dregs of the devil's dunghill', to the contemporary vicar found guilty of improper conduct towards females in his employ.[16] The fact that the man in the poem turns his head when passing the woman begging for bread could be interpreted as a sign of his guilt, shame or attempt at denial.

While the outcast woman in the form of the beggar or prostitute may have presented the most glaring examples of female hardship for the Victorians, Quilliam also took an interest in other contemporary feminist causes such as the reform of property and child custody laws. He maintained the position that the advances for women, which British people were only in the process of discovering and integrating into their legal system, had existed in the Islamic courts for thirteen centuries. For example, in the event of divorce, the Muslim woman automatically assumed custody of any children under a certain age; yet, not until 1886, did the courts in Britain begin to grant mothers even partial guardianship of their infants.[17] Similarly, while the Muslim female could count upon receiving a dowry at the time of marriage, which remained her personal property to manage as she pleased, the British wife legally owned nothing, not even the purse she carried, until 1882.[18]

When Quilliam addressed these topics in his writings and speeches, he drew from his own knowledge of family law in Britain as well as some thirty-five years of professional experience with the country's legal system. He took particular interest in the issue of divorce and, not surprisingly, maintained that, just as with regard to property and child custody, Muslim courts had been far more just and humane towards women in need of a divorce than had Western ones. In one of his lectures at the Liverpool Muslim Institute, he emphasised the advantages of Islamic over both Roman and Christian law, noting that in the former, a wife could obtain a divorce for a number of reasons including ill usage, want of proper maintenance, or habitual neglect. Yet, it was not until 1895 that British women began to gain similar rights.[19]

Despite the liberalisation of the law, however, many British people, both men and women, still could not obtain a divorce in the early twentieth century due to practical difficulties. The requirement that all parties travel to London, for example, created a significant obstacle because of the inconvenience and expense. As Quilliam related during one of his lectures at the Institute, he had been involved professionally in a divorce case in which the client needed twenty-three witnesses but could not afford to provide transportation and lodging for them. One would imagine that issues of childcare and lost wages would be of concern as well. Quilliam drew attention to the inconsistency of a legal system that allowed serious crimes such as murder to be tried in the local assize courts, but still forbade their use for divorce cases.[20] He described such a state of affairs as 'a disgrace to us all in a civilized nation'[21] and agreed with the famous radical and legal expert, Earl Russell, whose article on the religious roots and 'grotesque absurdities' of British divorce law appeared in the *Islamic World*.[22]

Given Quilliam's low opinion of the divorce laws in his country combined with his concern for justice, the poor and the rights of women, it is perhaps not surprising that he took extraordinary measures in order to obtain a divorce for one of his penniless clients, Martha Thompson, in 1908. Employing a trick not unknown in the legal profession, he hired one of his former clerks to pretend to meet her husband by accident only to lure the man to a brothel so that evidence of adultery could be used against him in court. While this particular case erupted in scandal, beginning Quilliam's undoing as a leader of Muslims in Britain,[23] it reflects his reputation: he was known for his chivalry and coming to the aid of struggling women whose husbands had left them with mouths to feed, making him popular among 'certain classes' whom he represented 'earnestly and fearlessly'.[24] A contemporary Liverpool publication depicted him as riding a white stallion through the city streets, while women of the slums threw flowers at his feet, an image that may have inspired the modern caricaturist to refer to him as a champion of 'poor pregnant flower girls'.[25]

Chivalry as a model for Muslim masculinity

The ideal of chivalry served as a model of Muslim masculinity for Quilliam and his community, not despite but because of its medieval associations. Rapid urbanisation and industrialisation had left many

Victorians nostalgic for the past, and contemporary aesthetic and intellectual movements, most notably those associated with the gothic revival and the pre-Raphaelites, tended to idealise this era in history, presenting it as a time of honour and nobility, when true artists and craftsmen flourished and gallant knights saved beautiful damsels in distress. In addition, as Quilliam and other educated Victorians understood, Islamic civilisations flourished during the Middle Ages, when most of Europe still remained undeveloped by comparison, and Muslim leaders such as Salah-al-Din were known even in the West for chivalrous virtues such as bravery, kindness and generosity. One article in the *Crescent* related that the status of women was higher in Moorish Spain than after the Christian conquest. [26]

Echoes of medieval troubadour poets, the embodiment of chivalry, with roots in Islamic Spain and Sufi mysticism, could be found in the pages of the *Crescent*. Quilliam and a number of his followers wrote in the tradition of courtly love verse, a genre that had developed originally from Sufi poets who expressed the soul's longing for God as a lover yearning for his beloved. According to some among them, a man's love for a woman brought him closer to God as long as he did not lose sight of the true spiritual, as opposed to more earthly, nature of his feelings. Elaborating upon this tradition, the troubadours of southern France and northern Italy imagined themselves as becoming ennobled when they experienced a deep, heartfelt and all-consuming love for a woman and expressed it through poetry and music. In keeping with the lofty ideals of the mystics, the woman in question had to remain physically unattainable. [27]

A perfect example of this particular style is the poem, 'I Love Her,' by the Scottish Muslim convert, John Yehya-en Nasr Parkinson. Even the title reveals the author's inability to address directly the woman with whom he has become enamoured. Rather than professing his love to her, he speaks of it to a third party. In this work, Parkinson puts his beloved on a pedestal, admiring her beauty or 'presence fair' and comparing her to Helen of Troy. Fury consumes his soul, and flames of passion burn within him, yet he embraces this inner torment as an end in and of itself: he has no desire to return to his previous emotional state and remains content to love from afar. While he may dream of a day when their eyes will meet, he is satisfied simply knowing that the two share the same sun, concluding with the line, 'It is enough to know the sunbeams warm, That kiss my lips, before had kissed her hair.'[28]

The relationship between the woman in question and the rays of the sun, through which the poet feels connected to her, is particularly important given the tradition in Sufi mystical poetry in which the beloved is understood to be like a gossamer veil between the individual human soul and God, as represented by the sun. When the lover turns a pure heart longingly towards the radiance of his beloved, he begins to orient himself towards the light of the divine countenance, which would be overwhelming if experienced directly.[29] Along the same lines, another of Parkinson's poems describes a scene in which the historical figure Abd-al-Rahman, ruler of Islamic Spain during the eighth century, gazes upon the beauty of his beloved and, realising that it comes from Allah, becomes so overcome with emotion that his hands, the very ones that remained steady in battle as he conquered foes, begin to shake. The poem concludes with al-Rahman saying that he would give his heart to bask in the 'light of her countenance'.[30]

Quilliam also wrote a number of poems expressing his feelings of yearning and longing for his beloved. For example, in one he calls the object of his affections 'the Queen of my soul' and relates the 'ecstasy' he experiences just being in her presence.[31] An issue of the *Crescent* describes him as a chevalier or knight who serves the cause of Islam, not as a warrior but as a poet 'courteous and refined' and wielding a 'pen of fire' more noble 'than the sword of a king'.[32] As if to ensure that the reader makes the connection between this contemporary Muslim man of letters in Liverpool and the troubadour knights of the age of Islamic Spain, the above poem is followed immediately by another entitled 'The Last Great Moor', which refers to the splendour and beauty of Grenada before its fall when the 'knightliest knights' were hers.[33]

Quilliam's family life

In 1907, Quilliam wrote several poems that depart from the courtly love tradition in that they seem very much like proposals of marriage. While they never use that word, in the first, he professes a passion 'deep, profound, sincere and lasting' and asks his beloved to reflect on the 'question' he has asked her, so that the two of them might have 'years of joy and bliss' together.[34] In the second, he assures her that his love is firm, unchanging and will last for life.[35] The third presses her to say the words, so that from this day forward she will belong to him and he to her 'until we die'.[36]

It is unclear to whom these poems were written. While it is possible that he could have been reminiscing about his younger days when he first proposed marriage to Hannah, his wife of almost thirty years, there is no obvious reason for him to become suddenly preoccupied with this theme. It also seems unlikely that a fifty-one-year-old man would reflect upon his youth and decide that the most appropriate label for his teenage self is that of the 'philosopher',[37] as in his second poem entitled 'The Maiden and the Philosopher'. A more plausible explanation would be that Quilliam sought a third wife. For, in 1907, he already had two wives, according to Islamic, if not British, law: Hannah, his legal wife, and Mary Lyon, who married him in a Muslim ceremony most likely in the Liverpool mosque. These poems may have been written for Edith Miriam Spray, who would later marry him according to Islamic rites as well, and with whom he was in a relationship by 1910.[38] Then again, perhaps Quilliam had become enamoured with yet another woman not interested in becoming one of several wives or who simply did not return his feelings.

Clearly, Quilliam considered himself to be of the small percentage of men who were constituted in such a way that they could not commit to one woman alone and for whom the Islamic tolerance of polygyny applied. Yet he did not believe that having more than one wife prevented him from being a dedicated and loving husband. As he explained in one of his lectures on the topic of Islam and polygamy, God finds nothing 'more delightful' than a happy marriage, yet men and women differ in how they love. He maintained that while men are able to love more than one wife with perfect equality, women cannot ration their emotions in such a way. Bolstering this argument by paraphrasing the Anglo-Scottish Romantic poet Lord Byron, Quilliam stated that 'Love is of man a thing apart; 'Tis woman's whole existence.'[39]

The importance of happiness and love within marriage appears as a reoccurring theme in the discourses of Quilliam and the Liverpool community. For example, one *Islamic World* article considers the issue of 'true marriage' and describes the love within it as 'a very delicate and sensitive plant' in need of care from both the husband and the wife.[40] Similarly, an article in the *Crescent* states: 'As the trial by fire is the only absolute test of pure gold, so marriage, with its varied experiences, is the only infallible proof of true love.'[41]

The author then goes on to discuss how hardships either bring a couple closer together or drive a wedge between them.[42] Other speeches and writings give husbands and wives advice for marital bliss.[43] When conducting weddings at the Liverpool mosque, Quilliam often expressed his wish that the couple would love each other and live in happiness like the Prophet Muhammad and Khadija (his first and only wife for over twenty years), or like Fatima, Muhammad's daughter, and Ali, her husband and later Muslim leader.[44]

One wonders if Quilliam's marriages were, in fact, happy ones. Discerning the true feelings of historical actors is a difficult task even under the best of circumstances. In the absence of any records such as letters and diaries and over a period of years when feelings, no doubt, change, it becomes impossible. All that can be said with any degree of certainty is that his wives knew of each other and had some sort of agreement regarding the large polygynous family of which they were a part.

Abdullah/William and Hannah Quilliam were married for thirty years, from 1879 until 1909, and had four children together.[45] Because she was his only legal and publicly acknowledged wife during this period, she attended civic and social functions with him.[46] While William was still married to Hannah, however, he met Mary, who was working as a 'showgirl' in Liverpool, and the two were married according to Islamic rites. Mary, who often used his surname as well, had five children with him. Although she and her offspring lived in a separate residence from Hannah and hers, whenever Mary's children appeared in public with their father, they did so as Hannah's in order to avoid a scandal.[47] Given the oftentimes sad, or even tragic, fate of Victorian showgirls who became pregnant by married men, Quilliam, no doubt, thought of his own family when he made the previously discussed argument that polygyny, as allowed according to Islamic law, was more just to women and children than the alternative and far too common practice among Englishmen of taking temporary mistresses.

After Hannah died from cancer in 1909, Mary and Quilliam finally were able to have an official, public marriage, an issue of no small importance as it legitimised their five children in the eyes of the law and society.[48] However, by this time, Quilliam had met Edith, who either already was or soon would be married to him according to Islamic rites. Just as Hannah and Mary had been able to come to an agreement regarding their shared husband, so too did Mary and Edith. In fact, Edith served as a witness when Mary and William wed in the Preston Registry Office in 1909.[49] Quilliam spent the last years of his life legally married to Mary but living with Edith in London, under the name Henri de Léon. As he had ceased to be a public figure by that time, they had no reason to worry about a scandal. Both Mary and Edith mourned together at their husband's funeral, along with Mary's and Hannah's children and many grandchildren.[50]

The descendants of Quilliam's wives were not strangers to one another, nor to him. In 1903, Quilliam had purchased Woodland Towers, a house in Ochan on the Isle of Man, large enough to accommodate the children and later the grandchildren, who played there together as one family.[51] They must have looked forward to these holidays where they could take a break from their regular routines in Liverpool and enjoy the fresh country air of the small island; perhaps they explored the nearby Douglas promenade, then in its heyday as a destination for seaside tourism. One of the grandchildren shared fond memories of family gatherings, describing Quilliam as compassionate, courteous and a source of 'comfort and strength', noting his love for children and animals as well as his colourful and entertaining manner.[52]

Quilliam placed a high value on having children and grandchildren and seems to have believed that, regardless of the difficulties that might arise from sharing a husband, the system of polygyny ultimately benefited women by giving more of them the opportunity to become mothers. British Muslims, both in Liverpool and those associated with the mosque in Woking, had made the point that during that particular time in history, females outnumbered males in Britain. Therefore, as long as monogamous marriage remained the only socially and legally acceptable way to procreate, many women would have no choice but to remain childless. This state of affairs they considered a great injustice: one letter to the editor of the *Crescent* posed the rhetorical question: 'what have these superfluous five million females done wrong that they should be deprived … of enjoying that which is every woman's birthright, the joys of maternity?'[53]

In addition, Quilliam believed that the love a woman experiences when she has a child is more profound and fulfilling than any feelings she could have for a man, even her husband. In his poem 'When Does a Woman Truly Love?', Quilliam considers the different stages in a woman's life, from infancy, to adolescence, to the first years of marriage, explaining how in each one she feels a type of love which at the time she believes is true and whole, yet each is lacking in some way. It is not until the birth of her first child when she holds her new-born baby to her breast that she discovers a 'love so pure, so good, so true' that it could only have come from paradise itself.[54] Along the same lines, in another of his poems, entitled 'A Mother's Lullaby', Quilliam imaginatively puts himself in place of the mother who is so filled with love for and pride in her infant son that when she looks into his eyes they seem 'almost divine'.[55]

According to him, and a number of his followers who expressed themselves in the *Crescent*, this special bond between a mother and her newborn continued beyond the infant stage and through childhood, shaping the next generation of adults. A piece entitled 'The Sheikh's Passing Thoughts' begins with Quilliam emphasising the importance of that parent as a role model, stating that 'what the mother does the child thinks'.[56] Another article, entitled 'How Women Mould Men', explains that, during infancy, it is the mother who lays the foundation stone of character in her offspring. She then builds upon it by educating and inspiring her or him over subsequent years.[57]

Perhaps not surprisingly, Quilliam's mother Harriet had much to do with his development. She devoted herself to educating young William, bringing him to lectures, encouraging his interest in literature, and discussing issues of religion, politics and social reform with him.[58] Mother and son even campaigned together in the cause of temperance, on occasion speaking alongside one another at events.[59] In a poem praising his mother, Quilliam describes her central role in his life, beginning with the very first time she cradled him in her arms. He goes on to relate how, as a grown man, when he looks upon the lines of her 'dear face', he can see his own history etched into them.[60]

The close relationship between Harriet and her son, and Quilliam's belief that the role of a mother was more important to a woman than that of wife, are especially interesting in light of his association with the

Ottoman empire and his frequent praise of Ottoman politics and culture. For in that dynasty, the political alliance and emotional bond between mother and son trumped that of husband and wife. Sultan Abd al-Hamid II began life as the son of a slave concubine, with a number of half-brothers and other male relatives who hoped to assume the throne one day. The fact that he had survived and triumphed despite the dangerously, sometimes fatally, competitive politics of the imperial *harem* had much to do with his mother's ability to educate him, promote him and protect his interests. When he became sultan, she continued to advise him and took the well-earned title of valide sultan, a formal office that carried with it a higher status, more power and a larger stipend than any of her son's concubines or wives would receive.[61]

Polygyny and 'mixed marriages' to invigorate race, nation and empire

Quilliam also would have admired the fact that the reproductive practices of the Ottoman dynasty encouraged the creation of multiracial offspring generation after generation.[62] For, as he explained at one of his Sunday talks at the Institute, there were certain 'well-defined truths' regarding the evolution of the species and its physical development, and those applied to human beings as well as other animals. Just as ranchers purposely crossbred cattle in order to improve the stock, peoples needed an 'infusion of new blood'.[63] While there were, no doubt, any number of ways of encouraging additions to the gene pool, polygyny was one of them.

African readers wrote to Quilliam in praise of polygyny as a traditional way of strengthening a people. In one letter to the editor of the *Islamic World*, Ismail Ibn Dawood, an Egyptian, stated that, as long as African men had multiple wives, as sanctioned by the laws of Islam, they produced healthy children. However, those who had converted to Christianity and then limited themselves to monogamous marriages only, found their families unable to survive past the third or fourth generation.[64] Similarly, a man from Liberia contacted Quilliam to commend him for his lectures on the topic of Islam and polygyny. He went on to emphasise the need for Africans to begin turning inward so that they might better know themselves, value their own heritage, and thus prevent the spread of monogamy from 'sapping the very life out of us as a race'.[65]

A writer for the *Sierra Leone Weekly*, whose article appeared in the *Crescent*, extolled the virtues of polygamy in African society and in general, pronouncing that form of familial and social organisation far superior to European marriage customs with their 'evil effects'. According to that writer, the 'practically polygamic' conditions accompanying slavery in the American South and Caribbean produced offspring superior to the children born since emancipation. The writer maintained that the most vigorous men, both in body and mind, of the African diaspora resulted from unions between black slave women and white fathers, for example Frederick Douglas and Booker T. Washington. In addition, because of the availability of black female slaves to white men, white mothers did not have to worry about satisfying their husbands sexually after giving birth and could instead observe a period of 'rest and reserve which African mothers [in polygynous marriages] enjoy'. After emancipation, however, white women lost this privilege and, as a result, have become 'tired', causing them to produce children who are also 'tired', or lacking in competence and ability.[66] It should be noted that Quilliam was a staunch abolitionist, egalitarian reformer, critic of racism and believer in promoting the rights and wellbeing of black people throughout the world. This article was included in the *Crescent* not because of but rather despite the fact that its arguments could be used by apologists for slavery.

This superior system of polygyny, if adopted in Britain, would reverse the declining birth-rate and strengthen the nation and empire, at least according to Quilliam's good friend and fellow convert, Henri de Léon.[67] In 1904, Léon maintained that the English people were in danger of committing 'race suicide': the country's birth rate had dropped from 36.3 per cent in 1876 to 28 per cent in 1901, and 'physical degeneration' could be expected to follow, as 'depopulation and decay' went hand in hand. Yet, as he explained, Muslim countries where polygyny was practised had growing populations. If the people of the United Kingdom wanted to remain an imperial power and 'among the virile countries of the world', then, presumably, they needed to look to the Muslim example. Following this logic, polygynous marriages would produce more children who, when grown, could then maintain and possibly even extend the empire by populating the settler colonies and filling the ranks of the military, government and trading companies, or, as Léon put it, 'sending forth sons strong and numerous'.[68]

Léon's choice of words reflects the familiar gendered discourses of empire, which associated colonisation with masculinity. In fact, Léon was not so much presenting new ideas as he was offering an alternative solution to problems that would have been well known by others of his time. Fears of degeneration and decay, which remained a constant source of anxiety for the Victorians, had in no way subsided in the early twentieth century. In fact, the term 'race suicide' was not uncommon and was employed by others concerned with the falling birth rate in England and the British Isles, such as Bishop Ripen of Leeds, whose meeting to discuss this issue was covered in the *Islamic World*. During that meeting, Ripen warned his audience that in London the number of births was declining 'in fearful proportion' to the number of marriages performed, which meant that in that city, roughly 500 fewer babies came into the world each week. As anxieties over degeneration intertwined with class politics, it is not surprising that he understood this problem as especially prevalent among the 'wealthy and well-to-do' as well as religious people, upon whose procreation he, no doubt, believed the good of society depended. While Léon focused specifically on population decline in England and its consequences for the British empire, Ripen considered this issue as a European-wide phenomenon. As the latter explained, in the past two decades, the decreasing birth rate had become of concern not only in England and Wales but also in Scandinavia, France and Austria. He feared the global consequences of the diminishing power of the 'civilised countries' of the world.[69]

In this context, amid fears of racial degeneration, British decline and the future of Western civilisation, one group of people was presented as a model of what could be achieved, even by Christians of European descent, when they decided to embrace polygyny: the Mormons.[70] While that denomination began as a mere offshoot of mainstream Christianity, it continued to grow, thrive and spread even in the face of persecution. According to the publications of Quilliam and his community, much could be learned about imperialism by observing the Mormons, from the futility of trying to impose the inferior system of monogamy on a people who knew better, which was as true in Africa as it was in the American West, to the colonising power of polygynous family relationships. As one article in the *Crescent* explained, 'the numbers of their children with their vigorous bodies and healthy minds, are subduing the wilderness, turning the forests into smiling fields of grain'. It goes on to relate how Mormon fecundity, in terms of cattle, corn and human beings, so impressed President Diaz of Mexico that he dismissed arguments about the immorality of polygyny by stating that he placed far more value on the children who were making his empire rich than he did on such concerns.[71]

Reports from 'a Mormon Mecca', or Salt Lake City, helped Quilliam's Muslim followers to imagine a capital in the West where polygynous families flourished. Perhaps the rhetorical reference to their own place of pilgrimage even prompted some feelings of affinity or connection. Playing upon common class anxieties and fears of degeneration, one related how cultured and refined Mormon plural wives were among the upper classes of Salt Lake City and gave birth to children with superior endowments both physically and mentally.[72] Another described a recent golden anniversary celebration for one husband and his two wives, noting that he had been in love with both of them since the very beginning of their relationship. Over the years, the three produced seventeen children and over 100 grand- and great-grandchildren.[73]

By depicting polygyny in a positive light and as having benefits that served to strengthen the race, nation and empire, Quilliam sought to justify an aspect of his faith that was both controversial politically and important to him on a personal level. Yet these types of representations also provided a counter-narrative to the contemporary dominant imperialist ideologies that regarded the spread of Islam in Britain as a type of miscegenation that would lead to degeneration, thereby undermining the integrity of all three imagined collectivities. For during the late nineteenth and early twentieth centuries, race was defined not only by physical type but also by culture, including religion, as well as other factors such as political institutions, customs and language. In fact, ethnologists and others considered authorities in this area usually ranked cultural characteristics as more important than physical ones in determining the race of an individual.[74]

The close link between fears of degeneration and imperial gender politics[75] meant that, in order to maintain a strong nation capable of ruling an empire, British patriarchal structures had to preserve cultural and racial homogeneity at home.[76] In this context, the idea of British women converting to Islam and marrying 'non-white' Muslim men, from India and other colonial areas, would have been shocking. These unions were so controversial, in fact, that even G.W. Leitner, a contemporary of Quilliam who had been instrumental in establishing the Shah Jehan mosque in Woking, Surrey, refused to allow any such weddings in that place of worship.[77] Quilliam, however, rejected this way of thinking and challenged it by openly performing 'mixed marriage' ceremonies, even drawing attention to them. Articles covering the weddings appeared regularly in both the publications he edited and in local and national newspapers.

One wedding, originally reported in the Liverpool *Evening Express* and then republished in the *Crescent* for the benefit of the Muslim community, drew attention to racial differences, both physical and cultural, between bride and groom, and even romanticised them. It related how an accomplished 'Mohammadan' doctor from India had become 'enamored of a fair English damsel', a 'highly-born' heiress to a title. Yet, despite being of a 'different race and religion', the two were married: 'the English-woman plighted her troth to the doctor from "India's burning sand"'. This reference to 'burning sand' would have called to mind familiar images of the 'torrid zones' of empire and the supposed distinct traits of colonial peoples who hailed from those regions.[78] In addition, during a time when language was regarded as 'the most reliable indicator of racial affinity',[79] the author went on to explain the need for incorporating three different languages into the wedding ceremony: English was used for the benefit or the bride; Hindustani made the proceedings understandable to the groom; and finally Arabic, the language of God according to Muslims, helped to ensure religious authenticity.[80]

A wedding between an Indian prince and the daughter of a French count, who had been living in London, drew considerable attention from the public and the press. His Highness the Nawab Mahmood Ali Khan, next in line to the throne of the kingdom of Rampur in north-west India, and not surprisingly described by the *Crescent* as possessing the virtue of 'chivalry', married Miss Emily Florence Blanch Rouy in a 'full Muslim ceremonial' conducted in English and Arabic. Quilliam's followers decorated the Liverpool Institute for the occasion, hanging

Islamic and Ottoman flags, banners and bunting, and thousands gathered in hopes of getting a glimpse of the bride. The event and related festivities were covered by the press both in Liverpool and on the nearby Isle of Man, where the couple honeymooned and the wedding party stayed and celebrated for ten days.[81] Yet, attracting attention was not without risks. While most in the crowd may have been curious onlookers, some could be hostile. On that particular occasion, two of the Institute's windows were broken, a matter of no small concern in a city where religious differences could turn violent.[82]

Quilliam faced opposition in other areas as well. An issue of the *Daily Mail* ran a report of a wedding he officiated, expressing outrage that the event was allowed even to occur and advocating a 'clampdown' on anyone found encouraging or facilitating 'liaisons' between foreign men and English women.[83] Given the previously discussed gender politics involved in imagining the race, nation and empire, it is perhaps not surprising that the Home and Foreign Offices also took notice of the mosque marriages in Liverpool. Both contacted the Law Society with the intent of forcing Quilliam to stop performing wedding ceremonies, but were told that while the unions in question may be 'immoral', they were not illegal.[84] One letter to the editor of the *Manx Sun* used such inflammatory language to condemn Quilliam's activities, and the religion in general, that the author almost seems to conflate Muslim gender relationships with crimes against humanity, describing the Liverpool community as 'disciples of the great Assassin—apostles of polygamy and *harems*, of Bulgarian atrocities and Armenian massacres'.[85]

The reference to '*harems*' is significant. For, despite Quilliam's explanation of the *harem* as simply the private quarters for female members of the household as well as his efforts to show Muslim gender relationships as beneficial to women and society as a whole, negative representations of that institution continued to appear.[86] Often, as in the above-mentioned letter, the term was used to signify female enslavement and the violence that would have to accompany it. In other contexts, it became a place of licentiousness and vice, an imaginary space where fantasies of all types could be projected. Quilliam's neighbours on the Isle of Man amused themselves with scurrilous stories of what they fancied he might be doing during his frequent trips to Istanbul or behind closed doors on their own island.[87] As a result, rumours about him continued to circulate for decades after his death. In fact, a 1961 description of his former residence at Woodland Towers included tongue-in-cheek speculation that the ghosts of Quilliam's wives still haunted the house, presumably because their tormented souls could not find peace.[88]

Conclusion

While the counter-narratives regarding Muslim gender roles that Quilliam maintained through his life and work never replaced the dominant discourses in British society, they nevertheless testify to the creative possibilities available to the modern colonial, and later postcolonial, individual whose life is characterised by hybridity, or the experience of simultaneously having a foot in two worlds. Because of this position, Quilliam was able to discover harmony or points of intersection between the East and West in seemingly unlikely places. For example, he considered contemporary feminist and progressive concerns in British society, such as the liberalisation of divorce or the injustices caused by the sexual double standard, and found solutions to them in Islamic laws and practices. This process reflected and informed his actions from opening the Medina Home and providing legal help to women in need to choosing a polygynous lifestyle.

His position regarding polygyny is particularly interesting, and the issue appeared repeatedly in his life and discourses. He even presented it as a solution to prevent the possibility of degeneration and British imperial decline. Yet, his decision to argue for its merits presented, in many ways, as much of a counter-narrative among Muslim reformers as it did among British ones. For, during the late nineteenth and early twentieth centuries, the monogamous Western bourgeois home was replacing the polygamous Ottoman *harem* as a model for domestic social organisation in the Middle East, and leaders throughout the Islamic world were reconsidering the Quranic verses on polygamy and interpreting them, not as sanctioning, but rather as forbidding the practice. Equally unconventional among Muslims was Quilliam's celebration of medieval chivalry and courtly love poetry. For just as he proposed unexpected methods for addressing English social problems, he also presented a particular version of Islam that, while not unrecognisable, was not common among his co-religionists at that time.

By having a foot in two worlds, Quilliam could create a discourse and lifestyle that went against the grain of each, while simultaneously incorporating elements from both. Certainly, he occupied a place of privilege: as an educated man of means he had opportunities that female converts, or even the Muslim lascar sailors in his community, could never have. Yet he also possessed a certain talent and vision not common among his peers. His relevance to us today lies not so much in the specific version of Muslim gender roles that he advocated but rather in his willingness to cross established boundaries and engage with various ideas and influences. Quilliam's life and work point to the extensive repertoire of possibilities in creating a gendered self in the context of a vast, global, cultural, imperial system of the late nineteenth and early twentieth centuries. In that respect, he serves as an example to us in the early twenty-first century, Muslim and non-Muslim; white and non-white; male, female and all who do not fall neatly into the above categories.

5

ABDULLAH QUILLIAM, MARMADUKE PICKTHALL AND THE POLITICS OF CHRISTENDOM AND THE OTTOMAN EMPIRE

Geoffrey Nash

Introduction

This chapter situates the respective discourses of Abdullah Quilliam and his British Muslim convert contemporary, Marmaduke Pickthall, with regard to Christendom, Islam and Ottoman Turkey's positioning within the late Victorian and early twentieth-century world order. In a recent contribution to a collection of essays on Pickthall, Ron Geaves describes Pickthall and Quilliam as arguably the most significant British converts to Islam in the period of their lifetimes. He proceeds to set out the similarities between the pair as regards their Muslim activism and also probes their divergences, most notably over the issue of Abd al-Hamid II's Caliphate and pro-Turkish agitation during the Great War.[1] In asserting Ottoman singularity, they were almost of necessity drawn into a debate with the idea of Europe/European civilisation as the domain of

Christendom, and in Quilliam's case at least, to the combative assertion of the superiority of the *dar al-Islam* (lit. 'abode of Islam').

As scholars and thinkers turn increasingly again to the Ottoman polity and what the loss of it has meant for Islam in the modern world, Quilliam's and Pickthall's varied responses raise some stimulating perspectives on topics such as the meaning and importance of Caliphate, the progressive thought of the Young Ottoman / Young Turk type, the search for a unified Islamic authority, and what role, if any, race and nationalism should have in a confluence of Islamic peoples.

My discussion of their various statements on these topics probes the commonality of their defence of the Ottoman empire as leader of the Islamic world and their geopolitical awareness of its significance as the last enduring Islamic power in a world of crusading European states in part opposed to it out of long-standing religious animosity. Their promotion of the Ottoman empire as leader of the Muslim world is situated within a specifically late nineteenth-century imagining of Turkey. The personal and creative manipulations of these currents by both figures helped them articulate views of Islam that were both individual and of their time, and which progressed in tension alongside their troubled orientations towards the British empire. While much has been made of both men's attempts to balance allegiance to Islam with their membership of the British nation, the focus here is on the significance of how as international Muslims they imagined Turkey in relation to European Christendom.

A tempering of chauvinist attitudes to the East in general and Islam in particular developed along with the spread of Britain's imperial sway in the Victorian period before the First World War and 'shattered the self-confident belief of European civilization … and … shook European ethnocentrism'.[2] Maxime Rodinson's view was that sympathy for Islam began with colonial discovery of the exotic and favoured esoteric forms such as the traditionalist Islam embraced by René Guénon, while Richard King has argued that European conceptions of Eastern spirituality were inflected by colonial imperatives projected on to Indian religious culture as a way of controlling and manipulating the Orient.[3] Although travellers and orientalists like Wilfrid Scawen Blunt and Edward Granville Browne well exceeded such quietist positions in their adoption of anti-colonial stances in support of Muslim nations, the career of a figure like Quilliam changed the course altogether, setting it on entirely new tracks.

Shaykh Abdullah Quilliam, Henri de Léon, Sultan Abd al-Hamid II and Turkey

Ron Geaves' summary of Quilliam's creed as a Muslim identifies him as 'a traditionalist belonging to the Hanafi school' but influenced by the modernism of Muhammad Abduh and Sayyid Ahmad Khan insofar as they presented Islam as 'fully compatible with reason and able to draw upon the resources of modern knowledge and technical discoveries without any conflict between science and religion'. What marked out his position as a Muslim above all was Quilliam's 'conviction that all Sunni Muslims owed their allegiance to the caliph of Islam, who was also the sultan of the Ottoman empire. He was an Ottomanist by conviction because that is where he was convinced the authority of the caliph remained.'[4]

The details surrounding Quilliam's fulfilment of the role of Shaykh al-Islam of the British Isles (conferred by al-Hamid II in 1894) are set out in Chapter 6 of this book. Suffice to say that, during his period as Abdullah Quilliam (c.1887–1908), his identification with the Ottoman polity was an integral part of his public role as a Muslim figure in Britain. This was enhanced by his first visit to Constantinople in 1891, and thereafter caused him to lend it his support over such issues as the Armenian disturbances of 1894/6, and the Greco-Turkish war over Crete in 1897. In 1894, al-Hamid appointed Quilliam to be his emissary at the opening of a new mosque in Lagos, which helped cement West African donations to the Liverpool mosque.[5] The Shaykh also delivered a *fatwa* against fighting the sultan's rebellious vassal Khalifa in Sudan in 1896, and involvement in British naval manoeuvres against the Ottoman navy in 1906. Frequent visits to the territories of the Ottoman empire—for example his visit to Macedonia in 1903 at the sultan's behest—culminated in his sudden flight to the capital in the spring of 1908 followed by his return to Britain late in 1909 after the fall of al-Hamid II.

According to Jamie Gilham, between 1910 and 1913, Quilliam, henceforth known as Henri de Léon, is likely to have flitted between

Lancashire and the Middle East. Once settled in London, though he attended several Islamic centres, Léon, in contrast to his former self, 'was more anxious than he had ever been in Liverpool to demonstrate his loyalty to Crown and country and had, in fact, repudiated his earlier rhetoric about religion taking precedence over patriotism'.[6] There is therefore a decisive turn in the stance adopted by Henri de Léon to that of Abdullah Quilliam. 'In the high tide of Empire, Quilliam wrote his subversive pan-Islamist tracts in favour of defensive *jihad*, *ummatic* solidarity and the support and defence of the beleaguered caliphate.'[7] However, when al-Hamid II was deposed after the counter-revolutionary coup attempt of 1909, the centre of Quilliam's allegiance disappeared. As Geaves has emphasised, this was a personalised allegiance to al-Hamid as caliph; though the caliphate continued alongside the constitutional sultanate for nearly a decade and a half until its abolition in 1923, Léon does not appear to have had as intense a connection with it as he had with the Hamidian autocracy.

Quilliam, Pickthall and the leave-taking from Christendom

As Muslim converts, Quilliam and Pickthall adopted different stances as leave-takers from Christianity. Background and character conspired to create the former in the mould of an extrovert pathfinder and organiser who clearly derived satisfaction and élan from public disputations. Introverted, and more at home as a controversialist on paper, Pickthall spent a gestation period of three years (1914–17) before making a public declaration of his new faith. Their respective connections with late-Victorian Christianity were markedly dissimilar. Quilliam was from a Wesleyan Methodist family who devolved towards Unitarianism and developed Masonic connections; his politics were liberal and anti-establishment and these, together with his background in temperance agitation and profession as a criminal lawyer, account for his appetite for public crusades. Pickthall's religious and political orientations, on the other hand, were of an opposite cast. Through his father, rector of Chillesford, Suffolk, he could trace several generations of loyalty to Anglicanism; a high church, natural-born Tory, 'he had a nostalgic view of a fading rural Arcadia: squire, parson and peasants supporting each other against cultural and economic invasion from the towns'.[8] As Gilham's research has shown, the backgrounds of the later Victorian and early twentieth-century British Muslim converts were various. However, nothing in Quilliam's or Pickthall's cases suggested that either would follow the paths they did: the radical adopting a conservative loyalty to the Ottoman caliph, while the Tory allied himself with the Young Turk revolution and the party adopting the 'extreme liberal position'.[9]

In an earlier article, I have discussed Quilliam and Pickthall's contribution to British Muslim polemics and *da'wa* within the context of Islamic modernism and the background of religious disputation between Christian missionaries and Muslims—of a predominantly modernist frame of mind—in colonial India. The article also situated Quilliam's positioning in a key early publication, *The Faith of Islam: An Explanatory Sketch of the Principal Fundamental Tenets of the Moslem Religion* (1889), according to the epochal episteme of late Victorian doubt, scientism and esotericism.[10] Geaves also highlights Quilliam's debate with Christianity in his early writings in terms of:

> his impatience with the Christian lack of unity, the religion's difficulties with the discoveries of science and the problems caused by modern Biblical scholarship ... he used all three of these issues in the defence of Islam and as a means of attacking Christianity as a failed and flawed truth.[11]

What is lacking in such approaches, however, is the specificity of the conjunction of the categories 'British' and 'Muslim', which disrupts the configuration that would normatively pit European Christendom against Eastern (that is to say Asian, Middle Eastern or African) Islam. In his debates with the Anglican and Nonconformist Christians of Liverpool, Quilliam radically disturbs this norm by upholding Muslim peoples not as friend or admirer as those he cites in *The Faith of Islam* (Thomas Carlyle, David Urquhart, Reginald Bosworth-Smith, Canon Isaac Taylor), but as someone speaking from within the boundaries of the Islamic *umma*.[12] For example, in the report of his speech in 1903 in the debate with the bishop of Liverpool on the latter's motion condemning the actions of Turkey in Macedonia, it is stated that, though ranged against a hostile audience, it was agreed 'the Sheikh' defended his case bravely and eloquently.[13] Geaves notes that 'the campaign to defend the Ottomans would be viewed as treason by many in Britain', adding that 'Quilliam was becoming aware of the tensions between his dual loyalties to Islam and the nation of his birth.'[14] Much has been written about the stance of both Quilliam and Pickthall as 'loyal enemies' with regard to their allegiance to two political entities, the British and Ottoman empires respectively. My task is to articulate this dichotomy in terms of the religion-tinted politics of the period in which their stances constituted not only a reversal of Christian attempts at proselytising Muslims within the British empire but an intentional undermining of the adhesion of Britain to Christendom, the imagined but historically embedded entity that conjoined Christianity and European civilisation.

This project runs through Quilliam's early writings even though the approach is frequently that of comparative—or more properly contrastive—theology. The piece entitled *The Religion of the Sword* (1891), for Quilliam a relatively long polemic, signals a subversion of a charge routinely levelled at Islam by Christian adversaries. The effect, however, is to stage a wide-ranging attack on beliefs inscribed into standard Christian narratives. Taking as his point of departure the conflation of Old and New Testaments as the Word of God, Quilliam proceeds from a position of long-standing moral revulsion at the violence sanctioned in the Hebrew scriptures. Enacting enlightenment rationalist arguments, he goes so far as to criticise both Moses and Jesus. While as a Muslim he must 'revere both his name and his memory as one of the chosen messengers of God on this earth', he quotes Thomas Paine's epitome of Moses' character as 'the most horrid that can be imagined'. Moses' sentence on the defeated Midianites—to 'butcher the boys, to massacre the women, and debauch the daughters'—laid the groundwork for further atrocities of this kind perpetrated by his successor Joshua and later Israelite conquerors.[15] While Jesus's coming to the world was announced by the angels as bringing 'peace and goodwill to all men', this was contradicted by the remarks attributed to him: 'I come not to send peace but the sword.'[16] However, for Quilliam, the doctrine of turning the other cheek reduced man 'to a level lower than … the worm which tradition tells us will turn if trod upon'.[17]

Although a criticism widely levelled against the Christians by Muslim *'ulama* (religious scholars) was that they had tampered with their scriptures, Quilliam clearly goes further in linking the attack set out above with a wholesale condemnation of the history of the church, singling out such key figures as Constantine, Justinian and Charlemagne in a narrative which, Gibbon-like, argues that the history of Christendom is one of sustained 'prosecution and terrible persecution' that called into question 'the system which allows such things to be done in the name of what is sacred under the pretence of promulgating a faith claimed to be of divine origin'.[18] It should be stated that Quilliam's tactics can operate unfairly: he often measures against the failings of Christian believers and their institutions, verses of the Qur'an and the practice of the Prophet. In addition to a rationalist undermining of Christian doctrines such as the Trinity, the incarnation, salvation by faith and eternal punishment, he chooses Quranic texts that emphasise the 'more merciful doctrine of Islam',[19] eluding ones that deploy similar threats of punishment to those found in the Bible. Likewise, he is not averse to turning the tables on the species of Christian chauvinism that branded Islam a 'religion of the sword'. At the end of an article entitled 'The Moorish Conquest of Spain', he mobilises an Islamic triumphalism that is probably intentionally provocative: 'the standard of the Cross went down before the Crescent … The Christians fled at all points, and the Moor was everywhere triumphant.'[20]

Such statements coming from the pen of an English author at that time seem all the more remarkable if set against the background of the cross-versus-crescent polemic revived in the early twentieth century by ideologues of Christian missions in the Middle East. For example, in 1882, 'Egypt had come under British control … and from that time on Anglican work in that country was resumed.'[21] In 1912, a British and an American missionary, W.H.T. Gairdner and Dr Samuel M. Zwemer respectively, established the Cairo Study Centre 'for training missionaries in Arabic and Islamics'.[22] This project had been a direct result of the Edinburgh World Missionary Conference of 1910 (the fourth of a series of international assemblies on world missionary affairs, the first of which had been held in Quilliam's home city, Liverpool, in 1860). Gairdner and Zwemer both wrote books in the Edwardian decade that were published by the Student Volunteer Missionary Union, London and Student Volunteer Movement for Foreign Mission, New York, in 1909 and 1907 respectively. Gairdner's *The Reproach of Islam* went through several editions, in later ones the title changing to *The Rebuke of Islam*.[23] In his work, *Islam, a Challenge to Faith*, Zwemer called Islam 'a concoction; there is nothing novel about it except the genius of Mohammed in mixing old ingredients into a panacea for human ills, *and forcing it down by means of the sword.*'[24] Surveying the lands and peoples over which Islam then held sway, Gairdner's first chapter, 'The Extent of Islam', begins with an evocation of 'the garden city' Damascus where, en route from Jerusalem, 'a man with threatening mien' is struck down by 'a dazzling light from heaven':

> there arises in that great city … a glorious fane, where the one God is worshipped through the Lord Jesus Christ. And the Cross, the Symbol of suffering, has became [*sic*] the symbol of Triumph … Yet today, when the traveller stands in that city and contemplates that great fane, what does he see and hear? … that book which the Reader is now reciting is not the Gospel … And when [he] passes out of the building and raises his eyes aloft, *he sees no Cross crowning all but a Crescent moon—a Crescent that reminds him also of a Scimitar.*[25]

If Quilliam ever experienced pangs of separation from the religion of his forefathers, he left no record of it. In contrast to his unflinching abrogation of Christendom's civilisational primacy and appropriation of this on behalf of a narrative valorising the supremacy of Islam, Pickthall's disengagement from the faith that apparently sufficed him up to his fortieth year is, at least initially, considerably more muted. In the spring of 1913, during a sojourn in Istanbul, he continued to attend the Crimean Memorial Church.[26] Anne Fremantle's biography of Pickthall has him exit Christianity the following year on hearing a Church of England congregation sing an anti-Muslim hymn.[27] Pickthall's departure from Christianity is usually portrayed as the regretful culmination of a fruitless campaign to dissociate religion from the politics of the Balkan Wars in which the 'Christian' nations of Bulgaria, Serbia and Greece were set to triumph over their Muslim 'oppressors', the Ottoman Turks. His crisis, which grew over several years and climaxed at the point Turkey entered the First World War in November 1914, can be traced from its beginning in a handful of articles he wrote for *The New Age* between 7 November and 5 December 1912 entitled 'The Black Crusade'. They register a strong sense of injustice and rising anger at the treatment of Ottoman Turkey by the major European powers, pre-eminently Britain. The articles set up a clash of signs that their author wrings through a number of torturous permutations: Christian, Muslim, crusade, fanaticism, advanced, backward, lower and higher races, liberalism, progress, reform:

The Balkan States and Greece hate El Islam, and nothing less than a 'crusade' could have allied them, for Greeks regard Bulgarians as schismatics, and their co-religionists in Macedonia have suffered even more than have poor, wretched Moslems from Bulgarian 'hands' [i.e. Bulgarian irregulars]. They are resolved that Turkey shall not have reforms, at any rate until they have shorn her of two provinces. They thirst for vengeance for the memory of former wrongs—avenged already by no end of murders. The last thing they desire is to see the Christian subjects of the Porte contented. Theirs is the lowest tribal and sectarian standpoint. And why their savage, most un-Christian sentiments should waken sympathy in Western Europe one cannot conceive. [28]

For Pickthall, the Balkan Wars represented a recrudescence of the old crusading spirit Europe-wide, but the real objects of his ire were his fellow countrymen: government, press, and significantly the churches:

It is natural, too, that Serbs and Bulgars, Greeks and Montenegrins should deal in priestly benedictions and Te Deums when preparing for a slaughter of mere Unitarians. But when one hears (as I did lately) in an English church, the Turks compared to Satan, the Bulgarian advance to that of Christian souls in Paradise, one can only gasp. Are we really in the twentieth century?[29]

The liberals in particular wanted to expel the Turk from Europe. They denied Europe's 'progress' to the Ottoman empire because it was Muslim, and thus—Pickthall implies—European supremacy morally undermined itself: 'The wish to drive him out, expressed fanatically, at a turning point in his career, is neatly calculated to destroy all hope of Moslem progress.' The result could only be 'an outbreak of Mohammedan fanaticism', the fulfilment of a predetermined prophecy. [30]

Nestling within the argument about Europe's mobilisation of Christianity against Islam is the sentiment that would precipitate Pickthall's departure from Christendom. It appears at first as an Englishman's defence of the underdog. The author begs 'for charity for El-Islam whatever happens. Her proud and childish peoples have been offended.' He wrote as one who 'love[d] Mohammedans ... and rever[ed] their faith'. [31] This reverence had been a long time in the making and went back to Pickthall's travels in Syria as a young man. In the last article of the 'Black Crusade' series, in a passage that commentators often refer to but usually out of context, Pickthall reveals the intimate story of the shaykh al-ulema of the Umayyad mosque in

Damascus who had refused to accept his declaration of belief on account of his youth and vulnerability. This man had been 'another type of Moslem, whose equal would be far to seek among us'.[32] The memory crystallises the sense of a nurturing unfinished and points forward to the near future when the process would be accomplished. The catalyst was the struggle articulated by his series of articles for *The New Age*, which, though outwardly political, it would be a mistake to delimit solely in those terms. The author concedes that they were 'hurried' and 'disconnected', and that their composition 'had been hampered by strong feeling'.[33] In essence, they narrate the tipping point for his ancestral Christianity: the ganging up of Christendom against Ottoman Muslims who aspired to a similar level of civilisation. Shortly after, in a letter published in *The New Age* under the heading 'The Fate of the Mohammedans of Macedonia', Pickthall pronounced the motive for his impending leave-taking: 'Like the Consuls of Salonika, I am heartily ashamed of being a European and a Christian at this juncture.'[34] As Quilliam had been before him, he too was brought to the point of separation from his nation and its identity codes, imbricated as they were in the sign of a triumphalist religion he no longer espoused.

Imagining Muslim unity: Western Muslims and the Ottoman empire

Recent rehabilitation of indigenous British Muslims has brought into focus the individual profiles of native British converts to Islam in the later Victorian and early twentieth-century period. In addition to work locating these individuals within the context of a British Muslim community, further research has established a picture of a network of Islamic centres spread across Europe, from London to Tirana, before the outbreak of the Second World War.[35] In the rest of this chapter, Quilliam and Pickthall are addressed as significant international Muslim figures who, responding to the spirit of their age, imagined an *umma* with Ottoman Turkey at its head, dynamic and striving to take its place in the world of modernity. The discussion will draw upon recent developments in scholarship, mainly produced by Turkish academics, reassessing the significance of the Ottoman empire as part of the global order of the period under review. As a point of departure, I intend to evoke the cross-cultural contacts, cemented by espousal of a common religion, that distinguish Quilliam's and Pickthall's views of Ottoman leaders from the mostly Orientalist constructions of Ottoman Turks by their British non-Muslim contemporaries. Then I will attempt to situate the two men's writings on Ottoman Turkey within recent discussion of its status as a specifically Muslim empire and imagined leader of the Islamic world.

Quilliam's connection with Sultan Abd al-Hamid II, who was responsible for appointing him Shaykh al-Islam of Britain, appeared to validate his da'wa and consolidation work within the worldwide umma. In addition to sojourns spent in the Ottoman capital as the sultan's guest, the connection led him to make the acquaintance of high-ranking Ottoman visitors to England. For example, in 1892 he met with Hakki Bey, the imperial commissioner for the Ottoman government, en route to the Chicago Exhibition where he would be its official representative.[36] In July 1897, Quilliam encountered General Mohammed Fereydoun Bey of the Imperial Ministry of Foreign Affairs. Both were visitors at the Liverpool mosque, as was Ahmad Pasha, chief of the design department of the imperial navy arsenal in Constantinople, who visited in 1904.[37] Other Muslim nations and peoples with whom he was in contact, such as Morocco, which he visited a number of times and where his life as a Muslim began, Sierra Leone, where he had strong personal connections,[38] Afghanistan, whose amir was a contributor to the refurbishment of the Liverpool mosque and who endorsed his status as Shaykh al-Islam, and Persia, whose Standard hung on the walls of the dining hall,[39] as well as the other centres of the Muslim world that drew visitors from all ranks of society to the Liverpool mosque,[40] might be considered radial points in the umma, with the caliphate its centre point. Quilliam stated that 'Islam is not like Christianity. It is a fraternity ... The True-Believers are brethren, and the power which strikes at the Caliph of the Faithful at once places itself in antagonism with the whole Muslim world.'[41] Quilliam's role as Shaykh al-Islam facilitated his even-handed approach to the wide variety of Muslims who came to the Liverpool mosque, from the highest dignitaries to impoverished lascars. Geaves' biography of Quilliam projects a well-respected member of the urban elite of Liverpool skilfully balancing pro-Hamidian sympathies with patriotism for monarch and country until it began to break down in the Edwardian decade.

VICTORIAN MUSLIM

Like Quilliam, Pickthall's attraction to Islam compounded more than one focal point. It started from a period spent in a predominantly Muslim region, Greater Syria, which he travelled around as a young man between 1894 and 1896, visiting Constantinople on his journey home. His second, climactic stay in the capital of the Ottoman empire began in March 1913 and lasted for a few months. The centre of Pickthall's fascination with the Islamic Near East was therefore for well over a decade the Arabs of the Levant. He did not come to fully devote his sympathies to Ottoman Turkey and appreciate the Turkish contribution to Islam until the outbreak of the Young Turk revolution in 1908. In 1913, he was able to make contact with key supporters of the Young Turks such as Ali Haidar Bey, son of the reforming Ottoman grand vizier, Midhat Pasha, and members of the government, most notably the Committee of Union and Progress (CUP) leader Talaat Pasha. Pickthall's 'Black Crusade' articles discussed above make their case for Ottoman reform by resort to a discourse that I have elsewhere discussed in connection with Ottoman Orientalism.[42] They begin by positing a racial hierarchy in which the Turks are 'the most advanced of human races' and fulfil the role of a Muslim imperial ruling caste. The Turk is credited with having the 'brains ... of Europe ... He knows how to adapt his words to reach [the lower Muslim races'] minds. They are folk of his own household.'[43] Pickthall the Tory was therefore, at least at the outset, less egalitarian than Quilliam in his view of Muslims and was initially unable to cut loose from the racial discourse of imperialism. His imagining of a unified Muslim world under the Ottoman empire developed when that empire had all but lost its European provinces and was focused on the Turks as a race rather than on the Ottoman caliph as a spiritual leader.

Needless to say, both Quilliam's and Pickthall's attitudes towards Ottoman Turks were quite different from those of British contemporaries such as Mark Sykes, David Hogarth and T. E. Lawrence, of whom the first two especially decried the reforming, westernising Tanzimat Ottoman elite as 'corrupted by their superficial exposure to western civilization ... gradually turning into amoral and degenerate creatures who embodied the worst of both civilizations ... Restrained within his own cultural world the Turk was a barbarian.'[44] Pickthall reserved this type of discourse for Ottoman Christians, particularly the Greeks and

Armenians, 'who were gradually breaking away from empire, either because of a growing attachment to the West, or because of rising anti-Islamic feelings'.[45] In comparison, the veteran Christian campaigner and vehement critic of al-Hamid II, Edwin Pears, who lived forty years in Constantinople for the most part championing the cause of the Balkan nations, while not a disparager of Turks, clearly saw them as an inferior people to Europeans, although he believed there was 'no race in Europe so amenable to discipline and so easy to govern'.[46] Pears was joined in this belief by Sykes: both considered the Turkish masses hard-set upon, but stoic and brave when enlisted in the army.[47] Pickthall's assessment of the ordinary Turkish people was not greatly dissimilar. Where he differed was in his creed that the Turkish elite constituted the vanguard of Islamic civilisation. The question as to which group of Ottomans should lay claim to leadership of the Muslim world, as we shall see shortly, divided Quilliam and Pickthall. However, over the larger matter of Turkey's role as the leading Muslim power and focal point of the Islamic world they were as one.

In 2014, Cemil Aydın raised the following question: 'Why did the Ottoman empire begin to be seen as a "Muslim Empire", even as leader of an imagined "Muslim world" on the eve of World War 1, almost after a century of Ottoman diplomatic efforts to be a part of European International society?'[48] Since the fourteenth century, the empire had been integrated into the great power system of Europe in a relationship that 'could never be reduced to Islam versus Christianity dynamic'. However, 'the imagined border between the Ottoman Empire as pre-dominantly Muslim political domain and Europe as predominantly Christian space was a product of the second half of the nineteenth century'. In the last quarter of that century, the Ottomans came to be excluded from the European regional order.[49] Quilliam and Pickthall endorsed Aydın's assessment when they argued that Britain's stance towards the Ottomans had changed after the 1878 Congress of Berlin. Significant for our appraisal of both, their recognition of this shift confirms their stance as international Muslims who each in different ways championed the notion of Ottoman Turkey as the leader of an imagined Muslim world, and empirically tested the proposition that the Christian powers of Europe were singling it out for unfavourable treatment because it was a Muslim empire. Many of Quilliam's statements in his books, pamphlets and in the *Crescent*—in particular his pronouncement of *fatwas*—were intended to rally British Muslims round the caliphate. They exemplify Aydın's argument that 'as the Ottoman caliphate became the symbolic focus of Pan-Islamic imaginations of the world order, the conflict between the values of Christianity-white race based European imperial order and its Muslim, Asian and African alternatives led to a re-negotiation of the foundations of the world order'.[50]

That white-race Europeans should shift their allegiance from their birth identity to solidarity with Muslim non-Europeans is one of the key fascinations of the discovery of Britain's Anglo-Muslim heritage. However, juxtaposed alongside this assessment should be placed the complicating reality that, during the same period, Quilliam and Pickthall's birth nation was, as a much-quoted statement by Cheragh Ali of 1883 attested, the greatest Muslim power in the world.[51] Both men were cognisant of this fact, even as they faced up to the European Christendom/Ottoman Islamicate divide Aydın speaks of. Quilliam was, after all, actively involved in the dissemination of the *Crescent* across the British empire. For his part, Pickthall strove with a dual consciousness: on the one hand that of a European Christian, and on the other of a passionate sympathiser with the Ottoman empire who recognised Turkey as the main reforming agency within the Muslim world at the same time as he understood that Europe supported its Balkan opponents precisely because it was a Muslim power and would not allow its reforms to succeed. The triangulation: (1) Britain and Ottoman Turkey are great Muslim powers; (2) British Muslims owe loyalty to both; (3) Britain, once the mainstay of the Ottoman empire, is now seeking to undermine it—made for the, at times, almost unbearable aporia that hovers above much of Pickthall's writing on Islam.

Aydın's statements about the place of the late Ottoman empire in the global order of the late nineteenth and early twentieth century were prepared for by a substantial body of work that revised the European cliché about it being 'the sick man of Europe', and reevaluated al-Hamid II's pan-Islamic policies.[52] Others have emphasised the essentially defensive posture such policies underwrote. As Selim Deringil points out, the Ottoman state's legitimising policies (including pan-Islamism) were based on its perception of the need for the 'preservation of that state'.[53] In practice, the Porte was forced to accept that the millions of Muslim subjects of the Russian, British and French empires—to whatever degree they expressed loyalty to the Ottoman caliphate—had to be treated as foreigners.[54] The reality was that the power system of world politics in the early twentieth century excluded religious affiliations (except insofar as they were opportunistically invoked to further the war effort by both Germany and Turkey in late 1914). This fact dawned only slowly on Pickthall, who during the war continued in his bid to engineer a separate peace between the two nations he loved the most. Quilliam, operating as Henri de Léon, could see the hopelessness of such a position, though this may have been because al-Hamid II was no longer in power.

The split over the caliphate

Events in Turkey between 1909 and 1914 precipitated the key difference between Quilliam and Pickthall over the direction taken by that country. The former experienced at first hand the overthrow of Sultan al-Hamid II in April 1909 before returning to Britain. Pickthall went to Istanbul in the spring of 1913, where he developed his strong admiration for the Young Turks. Both worked together in the Anglo-Ottoman Society of which Henri de Léon was vice-president, but the ramifications of their divergence became apparent at the outbreak of the First World War. Léon resigned from the Anglo-Ottoman Society, blaming the Young Turk leaders for bringing Turkey into the war on the side of the Triple Alliance. However, after the war, both renewed their association in the Khilafat movement.[55]

Ron Geaves has stated that 'Abdullah Quilliam's loyalty to the Ottoman empire was first and foremost religious whereas Pickthall's, at least until his conversion, was cultural.'[56] Geaves sees Pickthall's adherence to the Young Turk cause as politically inflected, while Quilliam's support for al-Hamid II primarily concerned his role as caliph and was religiously inspired. We might consider that there is some elision in this view, though it appears basically accurate. However, it only partially explains why Léon withdrew his loyalty from the Ottoman empire once al-Hamid II fell. It might, for example, be queried as to why this could not have extended to al-Hamid II's successors of the 'constitutional caliphate', created in his stead. In the absence of any document that clearly spells out Quilliam's views at this point—and it is doubtful one will be found since it is precisely at this moment that his life as Henri de Léon, which was intentionally clouded by obfuscation, commences—his exact motives are open to speculation. Did his involvement with the deposed sultan's regime stretch further than formal religious commitment? What has perhaps still to be convincingly explained is why Quilliam maintained the line he did on al-Hamid II—especially given the criticism levelled against him and his regime by many Britons who knew Turkey, ranging through Turcophiles like Aubrey Herbert ('we all hated the old regime')[57] to converts like Pickthall. On the other hand, many pan-Islamists from the Indian subcontinent of course readily lent al-Hamid II loyalty as their caliph. Like Quilliam, Mushir Hussain Kidwai, for example, paid several visits to Turkey and received the decoration of the Osmania order personally conferred on him by al-Hamid II in 1905.[58]

Pickthall's case as an Ottoman enthusiast is also not without its peculiarities. He can be said to have embraced the modified progressive policies of Young Ottomanists like Namik Kemal who, notionally at least, reinstated Islamic dimensions to the Tanzimat modernisation project, but his support for the CUP developed in the face of what was at the time commonly understood to be the lukewarm attachment to Islam of their leaders and the practical implementation of Turkification measures in the Arab provinces. Admiration for the Turks as a race still comes through even in his post-Khilafat reviews in *Islamic Culture* on subjects connected to republican Turkey and Mustafa Kemal. Though he does not appear to have bought into the racial propaganda of Kemalism, were it not for his commitment to Islam there might be grounds for seeing in Pickthall a bourgeois nationalist manqué.[59]

Conclusion: Quilliam, Pickthall and Muslim futures

Other than in purely academic terms, the differences between Quilliam and Pickthall today seem less important than their commonalities. As European converts, they raised questions concerning the conditions of possibility for the future of Islam in the world, arguing strongly for the validity of Ottoman Turkey as the historical leader of the worldwide Sunni Muslim community, proclaiming the universality of the message of Islam, decoupling Europe from Christendom, and projecting a modernity in which Islam not only fitted but could lead. Their strong belief in a central authority to head the Muslim world, fixed as it had been on Ottoman Turkey, was the main casualty of the First World War. They did not specifically set out to make a case for Islam as an historical or future presence within Europe, and while the causes they advocated continue to have resonance, the deleterious forces which from a Muslim point of view they warned about and fought against have continued to deteriorate. As things stand at present, with ever-larger numbers of Muslims arriving on Europe's shores, Islam continues to be seen by many in that continent as an alien imposition, and articulated as a challenge to Europe's Christian values and civilisation.[60] The old chauvinistic spirit reappears, with some Europeans perceiving their continent to be under siege. For their part, Muslims in Britain of differing orientations have laid claim to the heritage of both Quilliam and Pickthall—either as pathfinders of a 'moderate British' form of Islam; or, alternatively, as figures who denounced accommodation to the Islamophobic prejudices of their own age.[61]

This chapter has endeavoured to situate Quilliam and Pickthall as international Muslim actors, who were both individual and of their time, and whose passion for Islam and Ottoman Turkey progressed in tension alongside 'attempts to define a Muslim world identity loyal to the British empire'.[62] Their respective messages concerning Muslim futures might seem optimistic today, performing their faith as they did before the authority of 'the Ottoman Sultan ... the sole religious reference point ... was lost [and] extremism, fundamentalism, radicalism and sectarian conflict were all invited to visit'.[63]

6

ABDULLAH QUILLIAM, FIRST AND LAST 'SHEIKH-UL-ISLAM OF THE BRITISH ISLES'

Jamie Gilham

Introduction

In 1894, the Ottoman sultan and caliph, Abd al-Hamid II, gave Abdullah Quilliam the honorific title Shaykh al-Islam of the British Isles (or, to use the typical contemporaneous—and Quilliam's—spelling, 'Sheikh-ul-Islam'), effectively making him the supreme authority on Islam in Britain and leader of British Muslims. This chapter examines Quilliam as the first and, to date, only Shaykh al-Islam of the British Isles. Focusing on the period up to Quilliam's emigration to Turkey in 1908, it begins by explaining how and why Quilliam became the Shaykh al-Islam. It then considers what it meant to be the Shaykh al-Islam in late nineteenth- and early twentieth-century Britain, and illustrates how Quilliam performed the role in practice. Taking stock of the years between 1894 and 1908, the chapter concludes by assessing how successfully Quilliam performed and delivered as the Shaykh al-Islam.

Quilliam and the sultan

The title 'Shaykh al-Islam' has its roots in tenth-century Khurasan (north-east Persia) but is more typically associated with the Ottomans, who applied it essentially to religious dignitaries—governors of the religious affairs of the state as well as lesser officials—between the fourteenth and early twentieth centuries.[1] To explain how and why Quilliam became an honorific Shaykh al-Islam, it is necessary to trace his earliest connections with the Ottoman sultan–caliph and the sultan's court in Constantinople. Quilliam was certainly in communication with the court of al-Hamid II by 1890, some three years after his public conversion to Islam. During the autumn of 1890, Muslims in Britain and India successfully campaigned against plans to stage the popular playwright Hall Caine's latest work, *Mahomet*, in London. These Muslims, outraged that the Prophet Muhammad was to be portrayed in the popular theatre, attracted the attention of Constantinople. In October 1890, the Turkish ambassador to Britain relayed the sultan's opposition to the proposed production directly to the prime minister, Lord Salisbury.[2] Writing as president of the 'Moslem Union' (an early name for what became the British Muslim Association), Quilliam sent a resolution to Constantinople thanking the sultan 'for the efforts successfully made by him to prevent the suggested stage play of *Mahomed* [*sic*] being performed'.[3] Henry Felix Woods, popularly known as Woods Pasha and vice-admiral and aide-de-camp general to the sultan, acknowledged the resolution from Constantinople. Quilliam proudly sent a transcript of Woods' letter to several newspapers, including the *Times* in London, which reprinted it under the headline 'The Sultan and Liverpool Moslems'.[4]

The *Mahomet* affair put Quilliam and the Liverpool Muslims on the sultan's radar: in the spring of the following year, the *Liverpool Echo* reported that Quilliam was the only Englishman to be invited to attend 'the forthcoming International Conference of Islam at Constantinople'.[5] Accompanied by his eldest son, Robert Ahmad, Quilliam stayed at the sultan's Yildiz Palace for over a month, during which time he met the sultan.[6] This appears to have been Quilliam's first of many trips to Turkey, which, in turn, prompted numerous Ottoman officials to visit Quilliam in Liverpool. In the autumn of 1892, for example, Quilliam met Ibrahim Hakki Bey, the imperial commissioner for the Ottoman government, who was passing through England *en route* to Chicago for the World's Columbian Exposition, or Chicago World's Fair, which officially opened the following year. The commissioner visited the Liverpool Muslim Institute (LMI), including its 'Moslem College', and joined Quilliam and other Muslims at *juma namaz* (Friday prayer). Hakki Bey told an audience at the LMI that, in Turkey, 'they regarded [Quilliam ...] as the Omar of England—the man who had dared to stand alone and to lead where others had feared to tread'.[7]

Quilliam's reputation in Turkey and the wider Muslim world had indeed grown steadily by the time Hakki Bey visited him. Early the following year, 1893, Quilliam returned to Morocco—the country that had triggered or at least encouraged his conversion to Islam in the early1880s.[8] During this return trip, the ancient Islamic University of al-Qarawiyyin (or Al Quaraouiyine) in Fes recognised Quilliam's authority in Islam by making him an honorary 'Doctor of Mussulman Law' and, quite remarkably for an Englishman and one who had publicly converted to Islam just six years earlier, an honorary *'alim*, or 'learned man'.[9] The *Manx Sun* reported some years later that Quilliam was also made Shaykh al-Islam of the British Isles in 1893,[10] but almost all other contemporary sources indicate that the title was conferred in the following year, 1894.[11]

Accepting 1894 as the correct year, it is striking that news of Quilliam's achievement was not immediately reported in the British press. Alas, issues of the weekly *Crescent*, which commenced publication in January 1893, have not survived for the year 1894. It is also uncertain whether or not the news was announced in Quilliam's *Islamic World*, which was issued monthly from May 1893 onwards, because issues for 1893 and early 1894 have also not survived. Quilliam does not appear to have publicly used the Shaykh al-Islam title in 1894: for example, in December 1894 he signed a letter to the London-based pan-Islamic society, the Anjuman-i Islam, as 'Sheikh of the United Societies of English-speaking Muslims of England and America', rather than the 'Sheikh-ul-Islam'.[12] However, the *Liverpool Mercury* reported two months later, in February 1895, that, when he presided at a LMI lecture, Quilliam 'appeared in his full robes as *Sheikh-ul-Islam* of the United English and American Muslim Societies'.[13] This appears to be the first public record, almost in passing, of Quilliam's elevated status in the Muslim world.

The conferment of the Shaykh al-Islam title was indeed much more significant than the lack of reportage on the matter might suggest. It was a personal triumph for Quilliam to be honoured with, as one provincial newspaper later put it, 'the highest Muslim ecclesiastical dignity he could receive' by al-Hamid II.[14] For an orthodox Sunni like Quilliam, al-Hamid II represented universal Islamic fraternity and the grandeur and continuity of a triumphant Islam dating back some thirteen centuries. Moreover, no Western Muslim had previously been honoured by the Ottomans in this way—which, again, begs the question: Why was Quilliam uniquely made Shaykh al-Islam?[15] For the Ottomans, the conferment had clear strategic benefits: it indicates that Quilliam was, quite rightly, considered to be a faithful ally of al-Hamid II, who was deeply unpopular in late Victorian Britain for his autocratic and absolutist leadership, which only encouraged the popular belief that the Ottoman Turks were the embodiment of unjust, despotic and incompetent Muslim rule.[16] It also showed that Quilliam, already a prominent Muslim activist in the West, could be trusted to work in the interests of the vast Ottoman empire at a time when the European powers were threatening its dismantlement.[17]

The Shaykh al-Islam in Britain

What did it mean to be Shaykh al-Islam in Britain in this period? If the office of a British Shaykh al-Islam was strategically important for the Ottomans, Quilliam generally downplayed it. Described almost ten years after he became the Shaykh al-Islam by the lord mayor of Liverpool as 'a representative of Turkey', Quilliam replied that 'I do not officially represent Turkey in Liverpool, but I do represent the Muslim Faith, and I am the Sheikh of Mussulmans in the British Isles.'[18]

If the role was to represent British Muslims, Quilliam's first official engagement as Shaykh al-Islam was geographically removed from them. In 1894, the sultan selected his new Shaykh al-Islam to officially open the Shitta Bey Mosque in Lagos, an important event for the consolidation of Islam in West Africa.[19] Quilliam claimed to have been 'summoned' to Constantinople by the sultan on other occasions thereafter, most notably in 1905 when he was sent on 'a special mission of enquiry' to obtain 'an independent and thoroughly reliable report as to the condition of affairs in Eastern Roumelia', but more specifically to determine the degree of Bulgarian involvement in the region's recent anti-Turk insurgencies.[20] Quilliam was awarded many additional honours by the sultan each time he returned to Constantinople; when he visited before his 'special mission' in 1905, for example, 'His Imperial Majesty the Sultan conferred [upon Quilliam] the double decoration of the Imtiaz in both gold and silver.' Notably, the medal was inscribed: 'This man has done his very best for God, his religion and his Caliph, and for Turkey.'[21] It followed that Muslims of all classes and across many continents recognised Quilliam as the British Shaykh al-Islam.[22]

Back in Britain, Quilliam was also increasingly known as the 'head of the Mohammedan community'.[23] In the 1890s and early twentieth century, it would be more accurate to talk of *communities*, for, as Quilliam himself observed, Britain contained several distinct but loosely linked Muslim populations. Writing in 1891, Quilliam recognised that there were:

> now in England virtually three centres of Moslem activity, namely a small mosque at Woking, connected to the Oriental Institute there, and principally used by the residents at that Institution; the *Anjuman-i-Islamia* [sic] of London, an association of Indian Mahomedan gentlemen temporarily residing in this country for the purposes of study; and the Liverpool Moslem Institute, the members of which are mainly English converts to Islam.[24]

To these must be added the oldest established Muslim communities comprising predominantly Levantine settlers in Manchester and Yemenis and Indians in South Shields, East London and, in Wales, Cardiff's 'Tiger Bay'.[25]

While Quilliam claimed that Queen Victoria had endorsed him as Shaykh al-Islam,[26] there is no evidence to support this. The British authorities did, however, gradually come to acknowledge the position, primarily through Turkish consulate offices, which, as we shall see below, called upon the Shaykh al-Islam to carry out the funerals of Muslims, including serving military personnel. But, perhaps more importantly, further legitimacy was given by the Muslim rulers of Afghanistan, Morocco and Persia, each of whom confirmed Quilliam as Shaykh al-Islam during the 1890s.[27] By 1896, Quilliam was using personal writing paper inscribed with 'Office of the Sheikh-ul-Islam of the British Isles'.[28] Later, a *carte de visite* was printed of Quilliam pictured in a turban and wearing his many Islamic medals and decorations, with the caption 'H[is]. E[xcellency]. Abdullah Quilliam Bey Effendi. Sheikh-ul-Islam of the British Isles.'[29] Although there is little doubt that Quilliam took the title and role seriously, neither he nor any of his associates directly offered an explanation of what being the Shaykh al-Islam entailed in practice. Quilliam did apparently inform a *Daily Express* reporter in 1904 that his 'position as Sheikh-ul-Islam renders him to register all births, marriages, and deaths among the Moslems in England'.[30] Meanwhile, the *Daily Mail* explained that 'he is the shepherd of all Mahommedans resident in the United Kingdom'.[31]

It is difficult to disentangle the role of Shaykh al-Islam from Quilliam's position as LMI president. It is well documented that Quilliam was a truly dedicated champion of Islam in Britain, and a quick glance at the pages of the *Crescent* for any given year shows that he tirelessly defended Islam and Muslims in the press and lecture hall, corresponded with Muslims and non-Muslims worldwide (as early as 1893, he claimed to receive between thirty and fifty letters every week 'bearing upon Islamic matters'),[32] and met and inducted new and potential converts. What is also clear is that, in practice, Quilliam used the title and office of the Shaykh al-Islam to underscore his authority at official Islamic and wider public-facing events, and to issue legal opinions. Islamic events involved officiating at prayer meetings and festivals, weddings and funerals, and delivering and chairing lectures at the LMI and farther afield. Initially, these were overwhelmingly local Liverpool affairs—hardly surprising given Quilliam's gruelling professional schedule with 'the biggest advocacy practice in the North of England',[33] and busy two-family life (writing in 1892, the Christian missionary John J. Pool, who had recently met Quilliam in Liverpool, described him as 'an enthusiast, and seems to me to be killing himself with work').[34]

As founder and president of the LMI, Quilliam had always led many of the prayers and festivities at the Institute, but reports of these published in the *Crescent* at the turn of the new century explicitly referred to him as the 'Sheikh-ul-Islam'. Quilliam offered guidance and advice to Muslims in relation to prayer and worship, proving himself a role model in the local Liverpool community regardless of his status as

Shaykh al-Islam. For example, he kept to fasting during Ramadan in Liverpool, and stressed to his fellow Muslims that it was also their duty to observe the fast and attend the special services at the LMI. In a Ramadan lecture in December 1901, Quilliam reminded the converts that it was 'obligatory to keep the *Ramazan* [*sic*] fast'; and he also hoped that they would:

> be able to stand fast and observe all [the] five pillars of Islam, and feel the pleasing rushing of the fragrant and invigorating breeze which blows from the leaves of the trees of Paradise on the first day of *Ramazan*, and reap the rich reward promised to those who are of the household of faith and who fear God, love His Prophet, and by their acts and deeds prove themselves to be not merely in name, but in reality, True-Believers.[35]

Quilliam's articles in the *Crescent* reached a more national (and international) Muslim audience. Writing as 'Abdullah Quilliam Effendi, Sheikh-ul-Islam of the British Isles' in 1902, he published 'Salat, or Islamic Prayer Explained in English'.[36] Emphasising that prayer was 'one of the duties enjoined by God', Quilliam argued that it was incumbent upon every Muslim to pray five times a day, ideally at least once in the company of one or more Muslims. He extended this obligation to children from the age of seven years old and advised that 'A child over the age of 10 years who neglects to perform the *salat* should be seriously reprimanded and suitably corrected for such a lack of duty.'[37]

Quilliam had officiated at Muslim weddings and funerals in Liverpool since 1891.[38] While the weddings continued to be local affairs, celebrated at the LMI, once he became the Shaykh al-Islam, Quilliam was called upon to conduct the funerals of Muslims outside of the city. Acting as 'Sheikh-ul-Islam', he prepared the bodies of dead Muslims and presided at funerals as far south as London and the Muslim burial ground at Brookwood Cemetery in nearby Surrey, where he himself would eventually be laid to rest. To give just two examples: in 1902, the Turkish embassy asked Quilliam to oversee the Muslim funeral at Woking of Sergeant-Major Mehmet Hassan of the Cyprus Regiment, who had died in London; the following year, at the request of the Persian government in London, Quilliam prepared the body of a Persian Muslim who had been travelling in Europe.[39]

From 1887 onwards, Quilliam gave scores of lectures to explain and defend Islam and Muslims, mostly at the LMI (in 1895–6, for example, he delivered thirty-one of the fifty-six LMI lectures, and thirty-six of the fifty-three in 1901–2).[40] It was not until circa 1905 that Quilliam lectured more nationally—at venues in, for example, Southport, Glasgow and London, typically in defence of the sultan–caliph and the Ottoman empire, and speaking out against 'a conspiracy [...] to drive Turkey out of the Balkans, and ultimately out of Europe'.[41] Besides lecturing, Quilliam was invited to numerous public events as both a respected professional man and as Shaykh al-Islam. It was in the latter capacity that he sought to represent Islam and the British Muslim community on the public stage, albeit largely within Liverpool for most of this period. For example, in 1901 Quilliam attended the official memorial service for Queen Victoria at Liverpool Town Hall and, accompanied by Robert Ahmad and the Ottoman consul at Liverpool, represented 'the Islamic community' at the formal proclamation in the city of King Edward VII.[42] The following year, Quilliam was invited by the lord mayor of Liverpool to take part in the coronation procession.[43] The *Daily Dispatch* commented that 'The most picturesque portion of the procession was undoubtedly Sheikh Abdullah Quilliam in his full robes as a Muslim Emir, and his eldest son in full Turkish uniform.'[44]

As has been documented elsewhere,[45] Quilliam juggled his sometimes conflicting loyalties to his native Britain, 'the country to which we owe loyal allegiance as British subjects', and Turkey and the Ottoman empire, 'to whom we are also bound with ties of love and affection and the deepest feelings of religious sympathies',[46] to the British monarch and the sultan–caliph. As Shaykh al-Islam of the British Isles, he proudly celebrated Queen Victoria's Diamond Jubilee in 1897 by having the LMI and its orphanage, the Medina Home, 'specially decorated' with Turkish flags.[47] A note in the *Islamic World* highlighted that, for the coronation of King Edward VII, 'SPECIAL DOA [*du'a*, free prayer, as opposed to the obligatory five daily ritual prayers] [was] offered at the Liverpool Mosque by the SHEIKH-UL-ISLAM OF THE BRITISH ISLES.'[48] Quilliam continued to 'represent the British Muslims' at civic engagements through to 1908, one of the last being his participation in the lord mayor of Liverpool's 'state procession' of 1907.[49]

As Shaykh al-Islam, Quilliam also continued to meet Muslims who were temporarily in Liverpool, and more often than not, like Hakki Bey, typically *en route* to various parts of the Muslim and non-Muslim world. There is no doubt that Quilliam was very well-connected inter-nationally, though his claim in 1893 that he was 'in regular correspon-dence with over 500 of the leaders of Moslem thought in all parts of the world' might have been an exaggeration.[50] When distinguished Muslims—leaders, learned men and officials—visited Liverpool, Quilliam dined with them, took them to local attractions and show-cased the LMI premises and local Muslim community. In June 1895, not long after Quilliam had become Shaykh al-Islam, Nasrullah Khan—the son, or Shahzada, of the *amir* of Afghanistan—travelled to Liverpool as part of a diplomatic trip to Britain. Suitably dressed with 'a purple robe and turban of brilliant hue', Quilliam joined the delegation to meet the Shahzada at Liverpool Lime Street railway station:

> [B]owing deferentially, [Quilliam] remarked in Persian, 'A thousand wel-comes to England, son of the great Ameer.' He then attempted to kiss the hand of the Prince, but the latter avoided his devotional salute, uttering in the same language the words, 'It is not for you to kiss my hand; it is for me to kiss the hand of the Sheikh. Religion is before all dignity.' Mr. Quilliam then retreated backwards with a series of low bows.[51]

Later that summer, Quilliam and the LMI's *imam*, Moulvie Mahomed Barakat-Ullah (see Chapter 7), were invited to London to see off the Shahzada from England. Quilliam presented the prince with a hat pin and a 'valuable keyless gold watch', which was inscribed thus: 'Presented to his Majesty Abdur Rahman Khan, Ameer of Afghanistan, by the Moslems of Liverpool, W. H. Quilliam, Sheikh-ul-Islam, Mahomed Barakat Ullah, Moulvie and Imaum.'[52] The Shahzada pre-sented Quilliam with the *koola-izzat* (hat of honour), which he wore with his 'official robes' at subsequent LMI and civic events.[53]

Quilliam met many other Muslim leaders in Liverpool, including the *sharif* ('nobleman', chief) of the Holy City of Medina (who had dinner with Quilliam, attended *juma namaz* at the LMI and visited Quilliam's 'country residence' on the Isle of Man)[54] and a Hyderabad nawab, or prince (who toured the LMI and dined at the Quilliam family home in Fairfield).[55] But, following Hakki Bey's arrival in 1892, many more visi-tors were Turkish officials, some of whom travelled to Liverpool specifi-cally to meet and converse with the Shaykh al-Islam. In the summer of 1898, for example, General Syed Mahomed Fridoun Bey, minister pleni-potentiary of the sultan's court, visited Liverpool to meet Quilliam. At a special meeting of the LMI, the minister reported that 'the Caliph watches every detail of your progress in Liverpool with the keenest interest. He knows that the interests of Islam will be ever efficiently guarded while your president is Sheikh al-Islam of these Isles.'[56]

Quilliam occasionally left Liverpool for important meetings and events: in 1900, for example, he met the shah of Persia in Paris, who asked about Islam in Britain and conferred 'a Persian decoration upon the Sheikh'.[57] Many of these engagements, both within and outside Liverpool, had a political angle, no doubt increasing Quilliam's confidence to speak on behalf of the British Muslim community and to the *umma*. It followed that, in the late 1890s, Quilliam issued a series of provocative *fatwas* generally relating to areas of British foreign policy that threatened the prosperity of the Ottoman empire and, by extension, the caliphate—primarily in the Balkans but also in Sudan and Egypt. Quilliam was an honorary *'alim*, and therefore not strictly qualified to issue *fatwas*, so he used the 'office' of the Shaykh al-Islam to legitimise them. In fact, Quilliam first wrote explicitly as the Shaykh al-Islam in the *Crescent* in March 1896 when he issued his inaugural *them*. He warned Muslims against aiding or joining the British suppression of the Mahdist 'revolt' in Sudan, which relied on the manpower of Egyptian Muslim soldiers:

> For any True-Believer to take up arms and fight against another Muslim is contrary to the Shariat [*Shari'a*], and against the law of God and His holy prophet.

> I warn every True-Believer that if he gives the slightest assistance in this projected expedition against the Muslims of the Soudan [*sic*], even to the extent of carrying a parcel, or giving a bite of bread or a drink of water to any person taking part in the expedition against these Muslims that he thereby helps the Giaour [non-Muslim[58]], and his name will be unworthy to be continued upon the roll of the faithful [at the LMI].[59]

The *fatwa* was signed 'Sheikh-ul-Islam of the British Isles'.[60] This first *fatwa* attracted worldwide attention and publicity for Quilliam, who was more regularly referred to in the press as 'the Sheikh' and 'Sheikh-ul-Islam' thereafter.[61] Notably, it was not until 1897, three years after becoming Shaykh al-Islam, and hot on the heels of his first *fatwa*, that the sultan sent Quilliam the official seal, cut in silver, of the office of the Shaykh al-Islam.[62] Quilliam issued several subsequent *fatwas*, all of which were signed in the name of the 'Sheikh-ul-Islam' and especially targeted Muslims in Britain.[63] When British warships joined other European powers in a naval demonstration against the Ottoman empire in early 1906, for example, the 'Sheikh-ul-Islam' reminded readers of the *Crescent* that a general election was imminent: 'Demand from every candidate who seeks your suffrages—whether or not he is opposed to the action—… and unless you receive an assurance from such candidate that he does not approve of such action then refuse to give him your vote and support.'[64]

Once he became Shaykh al-Islam, Quilliam also directly lobbied local MPs and the British parliament on Muslim affairs. For example, in 1899, the Liverpool MP Charles McArthur presented to the House of Commons a petition on behalf of the British Muslims protesting against the desecration of the Mahdi's tomb by British soldiers in the wake of the Battle of Omdurman (1898); the petition was signed by Quilliam as the Shaykh al-Islam, with the 'seal of the Sheikh-ul-Islam also affixed'.[65] In 1905, Quilliam again wrote as 'Sheikh-ul-Islam of the British Isles' to the secretary of state for foreign affairs, the marquis of Lansdowne, urging against British intervention in Macedonia and Armenia.[66] Conversely, and typically for Quilliam, who was, after all, an astute lawyer and seasoned public speaker, when the occasion suited he publicly disregarded his status as Shaykh al-Islam. For example, at a Liverpool Town Hall meeting organised by the lord mayor in 1903 to protest against the alleged atrocities against Macedonian Christians by the Turks, Quilliam stood up and proposed an amendment to the resolution against Turkey, not as the Shaykh al-Islam, but 'as a ratepayer and a citizen of Liverpool'.[67] He did exactly the same during a Town Hall meeting about the Balkans two years later.[68]

The Shaykh al-Islam assessed

It is not an easy task to assess how successful Quilliam was in performing his role as Shaykh al-Islam between 1894 and 1908. This is primarily because the voices of contemporaneous converts and other Muslims, especially their objective responses to and opinions about Quilliam, are difficult to locate. Their contributions to publications such as the *Crescent* and *Islamic World* are important but must be read in the context of Quilliam's editorial control. Reading between the lines, it does seem that Quilliam was genuinely well respected by most of his fellow converts and other Muslims in Liverpool; this is hardly surprising given Quilliam's absolute commitment to Islam, the LMI and Muslim welfare. As we have seen, Quilliam personally converted many British converts in this period; but he also visited them—and other Muslims—when they were ill, conducted their weddings, inducted their children and other family members to Islam, and carried out their funerals. To give just one example, Francess Cates (née Murray) was Quilliam's second convert, aged just nineteen, after she attended his second lecture on Islam, at the Birkenhead Workingmen's Temperance Association in 1887.[69] Quilliam lent her his copy of the Qur'an and 'wrote a short explanatory treatise for her with reference to the faith', which he expanded to become his celebrated *The Faith of Islam* (first published 1889). When she converted, Quilliam gave Francess the Muslim name Fatima, and she became the first LMI treasurer. Quilliam supported her through mental and physical abuse from both her family and members of the public who were aghast that she had converted to Islam. He also encouraged her marriage to Hubert Cates, and oversaw the conversions to Islam of Hubert as well as Fatima's sister, Clara Murray. Shortly after Hubert's sudden death in the late 1890s, Fatima's own health deteriorated and she seldom visited the LMI. Quilliam, however, kept in touch with her. When, in 1900, Fatima caught influenza, which led to acute pneumonia, Quilliam visited her: she was 'perfectly conscious, and expressed to him her wish to be buried as a Muslim, as she would die in the Faith she had embraced'.[70] Quilliam carried out Cates' last wishes: he conducted her Muslim funeral and became the legal guardian of her son, who was raised as a Muslim.[71]

While some converts did leave Quilliam, the LMI and Islam in this period,[72] the majority, like Cates, remained loyal to their Shaykh and the Institute. Writing in the period just after Quilliam's departure from Liverpool, John Yehya-en Nasr Parkinson, a vice-president of the LMI, referred to him warmly as 'my old friend', while the LMI's 'London Correspondent', Bertram Khalid Sheldrake, noted that 'He was a charming personality, full of wit and repartee, kind and patient.'[73] But we do not know how far these Muslims actually followed Quilliam's advice as a fellow Muslim or Shaykh al-Islam. We cannot gauge the impact of Quilliam's *fatwas* on Muslims in Britain because there is little if any commentary on these from them (we do know that his first *fatwa* of 1896 was criticised by some Muslims in India who felt that the English Shaykh should steer clear of politics).[74]

We can, however, reflect on other aspects of Quilliam's role as the representative and leader of Muslims in Britain. It is clear that, after becoming Shaykh al-Islam, Quilliam continued to offer leadership to and for Muslims in Britain, but that, on the whole, he still operated local to Liverpool until shortly before his emigration to Turkey in 1908. This was partly a reflection of the LMI community, which was overwhelmingly Liverpool-based, but also—as we have seen—pragmatic, because Quilliam had a gruelling professional schedule as well as commitments to local Masonic lodges (see Chapter 2), trades unions and other professional societies (see Chapter 1). The *Sheffield Telegraph* suggested as late as 1906 that 'The [Muslim] movement has not made much progress. It is mainly centred in Liverpool, and a few other Lancashire towns, with a young society in London.'[75] The *Pall Mall Gazette* also noted around this time that 'Quite a large proportion of the [LMI] membership is constituted of Liverpool folk, born and bred.'[76]

Quilliam had established the Institute against the odds—it had grown from an initial group of four converts in June 1887 to a total of around 250 to 300 by 1908, and its members continued to experience the discrimination that in the early days had forced them from their original premises at the Temperance Hall in Mount Vernon Street to, eventually, Brougham Terrace.[77] Unsurprisingly, then, the LMI Muslim community remained close-knit. As founder and president since its inception, Quilliam of course loomed large, and members of his family were also closely involved in its affairs. The *Crescent* reported Quilliam family news such as updates on the academic achievements of Quilliam's children (in 1901, for example, 'Misses Ethel Mariam and Lillian Ayesha Quilliam both successfully passed their exam in the London Institute for the Advancement of Plain and Fancy Needlework')[78] and their health and wellbeing. When Quilliam's mother, Harriet Khadijah Quilliam-Holehouse, died in 1901, for example, Quilliam published a long obituary in the *Crescent* entitled 'Death of the Mother of the Sheikh-ul-Islam of the British Isles',[79] and held a 'special meeting' at the LMI to mourn her death. In a sign of solidarity, the meeting was well attended by Muslim converts and presided over by one who was also a family friend, Professor H. Nasrullah Warren, who said that the congregation recognised Mrs Quilliam as 'Mother of the Faithful' in England.[80]

This is not to suggest that Quilliam, the LMI and Liverpool/British Muslim Association did not attract converts and other Muslims from across the country—certainly, a minority were, to quote Quilliam in 1906, 'scattered throughout the United Kingdom'.[81] Quilliam personally corresponded with Muslims and potential converts nationally, such as John Baker of Manchester, who received a letter from Quilliam in 1906: 'I cannot describe the pleasure it gives me to sign the enclosed declaration of acceptance of the Holy Faith of Islam'; Quilliam subsequently gave Baker the Muslim name 'Abdur-Rahman'.[82] We have already seen that, despite being tied to the Liverpool region, Quilliam travelled abroad as Shaykh al-Islam when possible, especially to Turkey. Alas, with the continued absence of Ottoman primary sources, we still know little about how the sultan and his court viewed Quilliam's role and performance as the Shaykh al-Islam. Quilliam also corresponded with Muslims internationally, as the letters pages of the *Crescent* testify, and his monthly journal, the *Islamic World*, had a particularly international reach and readership.[83]

We have also seen that, between around 1906 and mid-1908, when he left Liverpool, Quilliam made more official visits outside of the city—to Glasgow, Manchester, Sheffield, Cardiff and London—where he met Muslims and gave lectures. In nearby Manchester—easily commutable from Liverpool by railway—Quilliam had for some time maintained good relations with the Levantine Muslim community, which had been established in the 1820s and 1830s by merchants attracted to the city as the textile manufacturing capital of the world.[84] As Ottoman citizens, the interests of this merchant community were represented by the Turkish consulate in Manchester, with which Quilliam also had a strong relationship. In 1897, for example, Quilliam prepared the body of Selim Muhamad Ideilbe, a merchant of Beirut and Manchester (and also a member of the LMI), and buried him in Liverpool; and, in 1902, he travelled to Manchester at the invitation of the city's Ottoman consul to carry out the funeral rites of a Syrian merchant, Mahomed Hollarby.[85] Quilliam also met predominantly

Indian Muslims in London, including, in 1906, Abdullah Suhrawardy and other representatives of the Pan-Islamic Society (which Suhrawardy had created from the Anjuman-i Islam)—and 'received an Englishman into the Faith'.[86] He met Suhrawardy again, and also one of the latter's converts, the young Khalid Sheldrake, in London the following year.[87]

It is not clear, however, if Quilliam visited the well-established communities of Yemeni and Indian settlers in Glasgow, Sheffield or Cardiff; he certainly did not seek to represent them publicly and there is little if any mention of these communities in his publications. This seems odd, especially given that Quilliam's propaganda for Islam in Britain emphasised the 'fraternity' of Muslims, and he was quick to point out the multiculturalism evident at the LMI, with the British converts joined by Muslims from across the Ottoman empire, India and North and West Africa in particular. A reporter for the *Daily Express* noted in 1904 that the Institute 'perhaps enjoys the most cosmopolitan congregation in the country. Negroes, Hindus, Chinamen, Arabs, and Englishmen are to be seen praying to Allah side by side.'[88] Quilliam appears to have welcomed all Muslims to the Institute, regardless of their ethnicity and sectarian allegiances and, as Shaykh al-Islam, he sometimes visited and represented vulnerable immigrant Muslims in the Liverpool area.[89] Yet, almost in passing, Parkinson indicated in 1911 that the LMI might not have been as welcoming to the many non-white Muslims in Britain—though it is unclear if his criticism is of Quilliam (which seems unlikely) and/or other members of the LMI (Parkinson had been critical in the past of the lack of support from Muslims in India): 'The time was when there was a Mosque, at least a building which served as a Mosque, in Liverpool, it gave [Muslims in England] one place to go to, not perhaps as inviting as it might have been made by good management and hearty support, but yet a place.'[90] While Quilliam might have failed to fully represent the diverse communities of Muslims in Britain, he went to some lengths in his official capacity as Shaykh al-Islam to engage with representatives of the Jewish communities and championed them. Conscious of their marginalisation in British society, he had an affinity with the Liverpool Jewish community early on, visiting their places of worship and occasionally delivering lectures in which he would typically stress the commonalities between Judaism and Islam, highlighting the parallels between the Prophets

Moses and Muhammad and the similarities between Jewish and Muslim beliefs about animal slaughter.[91] In the early years of the twentieth century, Quilliam also visited Jewish communities and, wearing his 'official robes', addressed Zionist societies in a few other English towns and cities.[92]

Conclusion

What, then, can we conclude from this assessment? Quilliam was a very 'part-time', honorific Shaykh al-Islam, who nonetheless served his local Muslim community very well indeed; that he failed to do so for other contemporary Muslim communities across Britain is, to some extent, to be expected. Importantly, though, Quilliam was a, if not the, figurehead for Islam in Britain during these years and, as the public face and mouthpiece of British Islam, he both led and spoke on behalf of Muslims and for Islam at home and abroad. Recognised by Muslim leaders worldwide, the British Shaykh al-Islam provided a direct link to the umma, and especially the Ottoman empire and caliphate. It is hardly surprising that, when he suddenly left England in May 1908, Quilliam went to Constantinople.[93] Personal circumstances had forced his emigration, but the timing was terrible: in July 1908, the 'Young Turks' forced al-Hamid II to repudiate his constitutional monarchy and restore the Ottoman Constitution of 1876. Quilliam returned to England less than a year after his emigration. In Nottingham and then London, he adopted the pseudonym Henri de Léon, which explicitly indicated his self-imposed change of status—from prominent Shaykh al-Islam to obscure and eccentric scholar of philology and physiology, who, while active in the London-based Muslim community and Woking Muslim Mission until his death in 1932, never sought to regain the influence he had during his Liverpool years.[94] Quilliam lived to see the end of his beloved Ottoman sultanate, caliphate and empire. The sultanate was abolished in November 1922, prompting shortly afterwards the resignation of the last holder of the formal office of the Shaykh al-Islam, the 131st. The office of the Shaykh al-Islam formally ended following the abolition of the Ottoman caliphate in March 1924.[95]

7

ABDULLAH QUILLIAM'S
INTERNATIONAL INFLUENCE

AMERICA, WEST AFRICA AND BEYOND

Brent D. Singleton

Introduction

In the late nineteenth century, news concerning Abdullah Quilliam and the establishment of a community of British Muslim converts in Liverpool spread across the world, particularly among Muslims. As a well-placed Victorian convert to Islam in the heart of British empire, Quilliam symbolised many things to Muslim communities worldwide, each group perceiving him in whatever light they needed to see him. For some Muslim converts in America he was a model, a mentor and a mediator. For many Muslims in the British empire, particularly West Africa, Quilliam provided a morale boost, a legitimisation for holding on to their religion and culture in the face of colonialism as well as a supporter—materially, emotionally and spiritually. This chapter discusses the relationship between Quilliam and the American converts;

West African Muslims; and case studies of two Muslims from the wider British empire who joined the Liverpool band of converts.

The Americans

Quilliam's reputation and resulting status among his contemporary American Muslim colleagues was complex and ever shifting—a case in point being Mohammed Alexander Russell Webb. By design, Webb and his Indian backers wove the model of Quilliam and the Liverpool Muslim Institute (LMI) into the 'DNA' of the American Islamic Propaganda (AIP) movement. While US consul at Manila, Webb had been in correspondence for several years with Budruddin Abdullah Kur, a member of the Bombay Municipal Council, concerning Islam. In 1892, Kur introduced Webb to other Indian Muslims interested in starting an Islamic mission to the United States.[1] The Indians fervently wanted to leave British-ruled India and emigrate to America, but they were reluctant to make the move without the establishment of Islamic institutions in the United States. Immediately, Quilliam's name was invoked to gain support for a proposal to send Webb to America to begin the process. Kur wrote in *The Times of India* that:

> About two years ago Mr. Quilliam, of Liverpool, appealed to the Indian Mussulmans to assist him to place the Liverpool Moslem Institute on a substantial basis. As I understand, within this period not more than forty thousand rupees have been remitted to England from different Mahomedan centres in India, with the result that we have now more than two hundred converts in England, and branch societies have been opened in Manchester and London.[2]

Whether or not Kur's account is entirely accurate, the article illustrates how Muslims in Bombay were keenly aware of the Liverpudlian achievements when they set their eyes on America. Reflecting on this period, Webb wrote that 'Because of the success of the Liverpool movement[,] Hajee Abdullah Arab, a wealthy merchant of Jeddah, Arabia, suggested the idea of propagating the faith in America.'[3] From that point forward, for better or worse, Webb's AIP movement and its offshoots—and off-shoots of offshoots—would be inexorably linked to Quilliam.

After the agreement between Webb and the Indians had been reached, it was decided that Webb should travel across India as well as to Egypt, Turkey and Liverpool to gain further support for his mission among Muslims. Soon after Webb's arrival in India, Kur published a letter in *The Times of India*, stating 'I should like to say a few words about my enthusiasm for the promotion of this American scheme. In order to emphasize my reason in support of this scheme, I shall place before your readers the results of the Liverpool Mission.'[4] Quilliam was regarded as key to American prospects for success, the thought being that, if a group of Muslim converts could establish itself in the heart of the British empire, success in America was assured. As such, in India, Webb and Quilliam were often mentioned in the same breath. For instance, transcripts of Webb's speeches in India were published as *Lectures on Islam: Delivered at Different Places in India*, which was introduced by a quote from Quilliam.[5] During interviews, Webb also used the LMI to bolster his credentials in trying to explain the potential for success in the United States, a tactic he likely later regretted when he no longer wanted to be in the shadow of the LMI and its relative success, while his own group splintered and the propaganda scheme sank.[6]

In the absence of travel journals from the second half of Webb's journey, it is unclear how much time he spent at the other proposed destinations outside of India, but he certainly passed through the Suez Canal and stopped in Liverpool. Despite this and the intentions of the Indian Muslims, there are no accounts of Webb visiting the LMI. In fact, Quilliam specifically noted that he had never met Webb.[7] This is further substantiated by the lack of any mention of Webb in the *Crescent*, which published its first issue nearly simultaneous to Webb's arrival in Liverpool. One could hardly think of a better way to kick off the publication than with news of a mission modelled after the LMI spreading to another part of the world. However, it would be several more months before the *Crescent* first mentioned Webb, only in passing, in April 1893, followed up a few weeks later with a brief announcement of his arrival in America.[8] It seems illogical that Webb would travel the world, arrive in Liverpool, and not seek out the community largely responsible for his new-found position; that is, unless Webb had already tired of his forced entwinement with Quilliam. Commenting on the two men, Webb's biographer, Umar F. Abd-Allah, notes that 'Their relationship does not appear to have been especially warm. Indeed, there are indications of an element of rivalry between the two.'[9] If a rivalry existed, it would seem to have been a rather one-way affair with Webb under pressure to meet or exceed Quilliam's success, but perhaps no longer being the singular Western representative of Islam was a blow to Quilliam as well.

Rivalry or not, the AIP mirrored the LMI on several fronts. For instance, it planned to publish two newspapers similar in approach to the LMI's *Crescent* and *Islamic World*. The *Crescent* was a weekly paper mostly concerned with local affairs of the Liverpool Muslims and their disparate interests, while the *Islamic World* was a monthly focused on the global world of Islam.[10] Webb's papers were to be the *Moslem World* and *Voice of Islam*. Although the publication schedule and actual papers never met his expectations, Webb had intended the *Moslem World* to be a monthly with wide distribution nationally and internationally, and the *Voice of Islam* a weekly newsletter.[11] Abd-Allah also contends that Webb's initial publicised plans followed Quilliam's model rather closely, as did his event scheduling, both in the types of events and when they were held.[12] Unfortunately, Webb did not fully follow the LMI's example with regard to introducing Islamic rituals into his meetings, which, as we will see below, would later lead to a schism.

Neither Webb nor Quilliam devoted much space to the other's organisation in their respective papers, although Webb did advertise Quilliam's books *The Religion of the Sword* and *Faith of Islam* in various issues.[13] Webb was in correspondence with members and former members of the LMI, in particular Hajee Abdullah Browne who had been sub-editor of the *Crescent* just prior to Webb publishing the first issue of the *Moslem World* in May 1893. In fact, he became Webb's agent in London for the paper.[14] Both Quilliam and Browne were featured in the *Moslem World*'s premiere issue; specifically, there was Quilliam's poem 'Moslem Morning Hymn' and an article discussing a lecture by Hajee Browne in Liverpool.[15] Browne had broken ties with the LMI and left for London the month before Webb's paper was published, and had an excerpt of his book published in the *Moslem World* for November 1893. In that issue, there also appeared an announcement of the formation of the 'Anjuman Angrezi' (English Society) in London with Browne as the president, an organisation, 'To promote the study, and propagate the knowledge of Islam … as a religious social and political system.'[16] In the midst of the later American Muslim turmoil, Webb described

Browne as 'One of the most earnest and devout of English Moslems,' and 'One of the most intelligent and well-informed of English Moslems.'[17] Browne and Quilliam seem to have had a falling out, as the former was never again mentioned in LMI news sources after leaving the LMI, this despite Browne's continued work in promoting Islam in London with the Anjuman Angrezi and in Egypt with his *Egyptian Herald*. Thus, Webb's characterisation of Browne may have been a dig at Quilliam as he extolled Browne's virtues without ever mentioning the British standard bearer of Islam in his paper. Other LMI members also had items published in the *Moslem World*, including two poems by William Obeid-Ullah Cunliffe as well as advertisements for his book *The Disintegration of Christianity* (1893), and a lecture on India by Moulvie Mahomed Barakat-Ullah.[18]

In the *Crescent*, the most descriptive note published about Webb came in April 1893: 'Mr. Mohammed Webb has arrived in America, and is about to commence the propaganda of our Holy faith in that continent. We cordially wish him every success.'[19] A similarly terse notice appeared upon the publication of the first issue of the *Moslem World*.[20] There would be only a handful of other brief notices concerning Webb that year, but nothing substantive compared to the *Crescent*'s later coverage of the AIP's offshoots.

Besides a mounting financial crisis faced by the AIP, the determining factor in the group's split was the arrival in New York of former LMI member Emin Nabakoff, and his juxtaposition of the AIP's utter lack of basic Islamic practices and his more orthodox experience in Liverpool. Nabakoff's vision of Western Islam came directly from his tutelage under Quilliam. Nabakoff persuaded John A. Lant and other confederates to form an organisation more in the mould of the LMI.[21] Ironically, Jamie Gilham hypothesises that Quilliam may have had similar complaints that his own 'diluted, syncretic Islam' presented in public did not adequately prepare British converts for orthodox practices once they joined the fold.[22] Nevertheless, the LMI and Quilliam's indirect influence both gave rise to the AIP and eventually tore it apart, all without Quilliam ever directly intervening. Henceforth, every time a dispute arose among the American Muslims, one party or another used Quilliam as an example to bolster their cause, called upon him to settle the issue, or asked for his support.

In December 1893, Lant and Nabakoff formed the First Society for the Study of Islam in America in Union Square, New York City. They introduced the *adhan* (call to prayer) to their proceedings and openly challenged Christianity, both practices in which Webb refused to engage and panned as non-Islamic for the manner that Lant and Nabakoff carried them out. During the dispute, Webb said he took Nabakoff into his fold based upon the strength of his acquaintance with Quilliam, even though Webb later claimed to hold letters questioning Nabakoff's character.[23] Webb then became angry with Quilliam for corresponding with Lant's associate, Hamid Snow, a Muslim convert and missionary in India. Quilliam wrote to Lant about the situation:

> During the time that Bro. Nabakoff was a member of our institution, he earned the respect, friendship, and fraternal regard of every member of our institution … he was so far as I knew, [a] tradesman not in a very large way of business, but still conducted it honestly and fairly and that if he returned to Liverpool tomorrow he would be welcomed back with open arms by the members of our society, as we believe him to be a thorough Muslim in heart, action and thought … [Webb] seems to have taken great umbrage and consequently I understand, he has delivered himself of sundry diatribes against myself. This I regard not, as I only pity the person who has uttered them.[24]

Indeed, Quilliam's words contradicted Webb's public description of Nabakoff as an offensive street peddler of questionable character with little knowledge of Islam. In response, Webb excoriated Quilliam while defending his own mission, stating:

> I have positive proof that the man Quilliam, who has established a mosque in Liverpool, and who now defends the character of Nabakoff, is a charlatan of the worst possible character. He publishes an obscene paper called 'The Liver', and succeeds in obtaining large sums of money from India on the strength of absolutely false reports concerning the progress which the Mahometan religion is making in Liverpool under his missionary work.[25]

Webb later backtracked from these criticisms, going so far as to deny ever uttering them.[26] Earlier, Snow intimated that Quilliam had warned him about the untrustworthiness of Webb. Snow wrote to Lant that 'Quilliam writes me clearly that Webb is not to be trusted & gives good reasons.'[27] Snow went on to relate that Quilliam understood that, despite Webb being in America for six months, only Lant and Nabakoff took steps to give the call to prayer and offer congregational prayers. In the end, Quilliam was none too pleased to be dragged into the imbroglio, lamenting 'I have been brought into this American business without any desire on my part.'[28] It is interesting to note that the First Society published a newspaper, *The American Moslem*, in early 1894 and the issues never mentioned Quilliam or the Liverpool Muslims. Although they were not formerly associated with one another at that time, it seems a bit of a mystery why Quilliam and his community were overlooked.

In July 1894, Webb had another falling out with a key member of his organisation, Nafeesa Keep. The latter had made charges of financial improprieties against Webb and locked him out of the Moslem World Publishing Company's offices for several days. After much ballyhoo in the New York papers, Webb regained control of the premises and removed its contents, but Keep remained firm in her mission as the editor of *Voice of Islam*.[29] Throughout 1894, Lant and Nabakoff's group was under fire from Webb, the press, and anti-Islamic protests at their meetings. In August 1894, Lant wrote to Quilliam about the ongoing troubles and must have asked for advice. With all of the American Muslim movements in some state of disarray, Quilliam tried to straighten out the principal players with whom he was on friendly terms, obviously excluding Webb at this juncture. It is unclear exactly at what point Keep entered into correspondence with Quilliam, but she is mentioned in Quilliam's September 1894 letter to Lant. Quilliam wrote:

> I regret to hear of the unfortunate disputes and misunderstandings between those in America who have accepted the faith … Is there no possible way of your getting together with the assistance of Mrs. Keep and Mr. Nabakoff enough Muslims to form a society in America or in New York and then you could formally write and ask to be affiliated with our institutions.[30]

Quilliam had transitioned from symbol and model to active participant in the American venture. It was not a one-way street: Quilliam clearly felt enhanced by the interactions with the Americans, publishing many of their correspondences and republishing articles about them from American newspapers. The letters from America were often quite reverential towards Quilliam, once again helpful to his image as a world figure.

According to Hamid Snow, Quilliam had first actively inserted himself into the American mess as early as the spring of 1894 by beseeching the Indian Division of Religious Endowments to stop funding Webb.[31] The timing of the request seems to fall soon after Webb attacked Quilliam in the press. The Indians had already questioned the entire American mission and were in open disagreement about whether to continue funding any Americans. They had stopped the contracted funding to Webb long before, although individuals were still sending him money. In the September letter to Lant asking that the Americans affiliate with the LMI, Quilliam wrote:

> I could then lay the proposal before those in India who originally found the funds for the work in America and I feel sure they would consent to such a course and then you would be put on a proper recognized basis. You would then be greatly assisted in your work.[32]

This suggests that Snow was correct in his assertion that Quilliam had more than passing familiarity with the Indian backers of the American venture. Later, in a letter to Lant, Snow references an article in the *Crescent* concerning Webb: 'Who believes him? No one. Glad to see in "Crescent" of Liverpool of 24th Nov that Bro Q[uilliam] has now come to appreciate you & understand Webb.'[33]

On the same day that Snow wrote to Lant, New York newspapers noted the first meeting of the American Moslem Institute (AMI), 'the Western branch of the English society'. Lant was named AMI president and Keep its secretary. It was also mentioned that Quilliam followed through with the Indian backers, who agreed to support the group if they could prove unity and staying power.[34] During the proceedings, Quilliam was selected as an honorary president and another LMI member, H. Haschem Wilde, as honorary secretary.[35] However, the desired unity within the AMI did not survive the week. At the first Executive Committee meeting, Lant resigned as president because he was upset that Keep, without consulting him, had called the police to protect the earlier gathering from a feared disturbance by Webb's associates, which never occurred. After several other committee members also resigned, Nabakoff was elected president.[36] Lant moved on to form the International Moslem Union, which some contend was affiliated with Turkish interests.[37]

At about this time, Quilliam began identifying himself as 'Sheikh of the United Societies of English-speaking Muslims of England and America', or alternately 'Sheikh-ul-Islam of the United English and American Moslem Societies', and referred to the AMI as 'Our American branch'.[38] In January 1895, Nabakoff informed Quilliam that Webb was hinting at financial impropriety in Liverpool, as paraphrased by Nabakoff: 'Certain account books of the Institute were kept by you, my dear Brother [Quilliam], under lock and key.'[39] At this same time, a letter to Lant from C.L.M. Abdul Jebbar in Colombo expressed satisfaction with the Americans allying with the LMI.[40] The next month, after being absolutely displeased by the entire body of American Muslim converts, Nafeesa Keep moved to Liverpool and quickly integrated herself into the LMI.[41] Quilliam wrote to Lant regarding this and the latter's squabbles with his colleagues:

> I was sorry to hear of the little breeze [with] Bro N[abakoff], which I trust will soon pass over & peace again reign supreme … Sister Nafeesa lectured for us on Sunday evening last, & really spoke excellently, she made quite a good impression. She has been so be-fooled by Webb, that she became I feel convinced, suspicious of everyone in American Islamic circles … here she is a representative of American Islam. In the meanwhile you have an open sea before you, at first you will only get the 'cranks' of all phases of thought, & your rooms will be a regular Cave of Adullam, but as time rolls on, you will be able to sift the grain from chaff & form a permanent society of real Muslims.[42]

Once again, Quilliam was the person each party ran to for support and influence.

After March 1895, the AMI no longer appeared in the press. Meanwhile, Lant and Nabakoff rejoined forces under the International Moslem Union and First Society for the Study of Islam, which was frequently mentioned in the *Crescent*.[43] However, this was short lived: the organisation had run its course by the end of 1895 as far as Lant and Nabakoff were concerned. Patrick D. Bowen argues that the American branch continued until at least 1899 through Lant's associate Dr Charles F. Elsner from Chicago, who was named an honorary president of the LMI in 1898.[44] However, there is no evidence of meetings or other trappings of an organisation led by Elsner. Lant and Nabakoff remained in correspondence with Quilliam for a short while longer, but the letters were less frequent, ending altogether in 1897 and 1898 respectively.[45] In the end, the American converts separated, the organisations disappeared and only smatterings of news about them appeared in the *Crescent*. Webb had become intertwined with Turkish affairs in New York and thus somewhat rehabilitated his reputation with Quilliam. Webb's travels to Constantinople were mentioned in November 1900 under the name Mohamed Iskander Webb.[46] Lant was last mentioned in a letter from Hamid Snow to Quilliam in 1900 concerning his 'Church of Islam', noting that J. Muhammed Lant had opened up an American branch of the group.[47] That same year, Nafeesa Keep, who had moved on to the London Temporary Mosque, came out with plans to return to America and begin another movement along with colonies of Muslims.[48] Neither of these ventures seems to have gone beyond the planning stage.

In the end, there would not have been the American Islamic Propaganda mission, the First Society for the Study of Islam in America, the American Moslem Institute, or the International Moslem Union American branch without Quilliam. At every critical phase of development for these organisations, the spectre of Quilliam and LMI lingered over the proceedings. It is impossible to know if Webb's AIP, already on life support by the end of 1893, could have recovered and had some level of success if not for Nabakoff's juxtaposition of the American venture with the LMI and the resulting schism. What is clear is that Webb tried to keep Quilliam at arm's length and possibly vice versa: the two were culturally, philosophically and religiously incompatible despite circumstances that thrust them together. Nonetheless, if not for Quilliam, Webb may have been forgotten to history with his name cropping up only in obscure references to his time as the American consul to the Philippines.

Inside the British empire

Quilliam's influence on Muslims in the British empire, particularly West Africa, was without the contentiousness of the American endeavour and based on the organic development of relationships and mutual respect, the latter of which was uncommon during the era. Referring to the late Victorian and early Edwardian years, Gilham notes that

'Discrimination against Muslim immigrants in this period was indeed framed in terms of "race" and ethnicity and a belief in the moral and even biological superiority of the British as imperial rulers.'[49] Furthermore, writing specifically about Africa, Kenneth Dike Nworah breaks the majority of British society into two camps with regard to colonial subjects and lands, the first being the racist school whereby the people were to be subjugated and the land utilised to further enrich the empire; the second being those forces unleashed to 'civilise' the colonies through Christianity and Europeanisation.[50] The LMI and a few other fringe organisations formed a third front, seeking to meet the Africans in the middle through engagement and promoting the retention of their African identity.[51] In this milieu, Quilliam and the LMI's open mind about race, colonial subjects and of course Islam resonated with many Muslims in the British empire, especially West Africans who were subjected to the harshest racist attitudes and religious discrimination of the time.

Africans were aware of Quilliam and the Liverpool Muslims from at least 1891 when reports of his writings were published in African newspapers. Quilliam himself had long held a fascination with Africa and often wrote and spoke about that continent. The LMI's first substantive contact with Africans came in the person of Dr Edward Wilmot Blyden, the pan-Africanist Liberian government minister whose sympathy for Islam is well documented.[52] Hardly a better association could have presented itself for Quilliam's entre into African affairs, and so began one of the longest and deepest correspondences Quilliam published in the *Crescent*, lasting nearly the entirety of the paper's existence. The British converts offered genuine friendship when Blyden travelled to Liverpool. Taken aback by the gesture, he responded by getting to the heart of the matter, enlisting the LMI to enhance educational opportunities for West African Muslims. Many West African Muslims wanted their children to have a liberal Western education, but not be exposed to Christianity and other undesirable influences of Western culture. With the LMI, there was an opportunity for educational advancement in Britain as well as at home with materials supplied in English that were palatable to Muslims.[53]

The second major African contact with the LMI came when Alhajj Harun-ar-Rashid of Foulah Town, Freetown, Sierra Leone travelled to

Liverpool with the expressed desire to be among the British converts. Accounts of ar-Rashid's full integration into the LMI's community were widely covered in the *Crescent*. He was known to have been an Arabic interpreter, an examiner for the Arabic classes at the LMI 'Moslem College', an *imam* and a lecturer. The brotherhood offered by the British converts in counterpoint to the British colonial structure in Africa was striking and endeared Quilliam to the Africans even further. This emerging bond was strengthened by ar-Rashid hand-delivering a letter to West African Muslim leaders inviting them to send boys to the LMI Moslem College.[54] At about this time, Muslim leader Alimami Mohammed Gheirawani of Sierra Leone wrote in the *Islamic World* that 'We were often told ... that Islam was the religion only of inferior races—that it could be received only by the black man. Ah! What will they say now when great Englishmen are bowing down under the rays of the Crescent?'[55] A couple of months later, ar-Rashid's visit to England was mentioned in the *Sierra Leone Weekly News*, which noted that 'The existence of Islam in Liverpool seems to have inspired the West African Mohammedans with new life.'[56]

In June 1894, Quilliam travelled down the west coast of Africa on behalf of the Ottoman sultan, Abd al-Hamid II, to bestow the Ottoman Order of Medjidie third class, and title of bey, to Mohammed Shitta for funding the construction of a mosque in Lagos.[57] His stops in Senegal, Gambia, Sierra Leone, Liberia, Gold Coast and Lagos were critical in solidifying Quilliam's role as a Muslim leader. He could boast of being both a representative of loyal British Muslims and the sultan. Quilliam's relationship with the Africans had gained the attention of the sultan who sought a foothold in the historically overlooked but fast-growing Muslim population of Sub-Saharan Africa, especially as his influence was waning in his own dominions and neighbouring lands. Conversely, Quilliam's relationship with the sultan gave him more credibility among the Muslims of West Africa, who relished the sultan's attention. Case in point, a couple of years after Quilliam's visit, Mohammed Sanussi of Sierra Leone went so far as to call on all Muslims to unite and defend the caliphate.[58]

Quilliam's role as gatekeeper between the West African Muslims and the sultan raised his profile among the parties as he served as the go-between for all communications. Reports of African conversions were sent to Quilliam in order to inform the sultan, and the sultan had Quilliam deliver messages to the Africans, such as when Dr Blyden was to receive the Imperial Order of Medjidie.[59] Quilliam's position provided a vehicle to push his pan-Islamic philosophy and support for the sultan and the Ottoman empire while also promoting loyalty to the British Crown. Although often hostile to the British empire's military and colonial apparatuses, Quilliam took pains to spare the monarchy of any criticism and was outward in his reverence for the Queen. For instance, in 1899 Quilliam led special birthday prayers for Queen Victoria as he and visiting Muslims had done similarly a few years earlier for her Diamond Jubilee. The West African Muslims may have been keen to be seen as loyal with or without Quilliam's intervention; however, their reverence for him and his words of loyalty to the Crown certainly created a climate of goodwill towards the British sovereign. Over the years, Quilliam became so widely known in the region that, in 1903, Dr Blyden quipped that Quilliam and shipping magnate Sir Alfred Jones were the two best-known English names in West and Central Africa.[60]

Outside of West Africa, Quilliam and the Liverpool Muslims were a beacon to some educated, politically minded, English-speaking Muslims in the empire looking for better prospects than the colonies had to offer. Although life in Britain held many challenges for Muslims emigrating from the colonies, it seems there were educational, business and political opportunities unavailable outside of the British Isles. Two examples of Muslims associated with Quilliam who came to Liverpool looking for better opportunities were Hajji[61] Mohamed Dollie of South Africa and Moulvie Mahomed Barakat-Ullah of India. Dollie was an active member of the Cape Town Malay Muslim community when a wave of political activism spread through in the late 1880s. At the time, the local paper described him as 'A most intelligent irrepressible Hadje [sic].'[62] Earlier that decade, Dollie and a colleague were responsible for establishing the Cape Town Hanafee Mosque in Long Street after a dispute with the Shafee community led to a split among Muslims along doctrinal lines.[63] For Dollie, the education of his son, Omar, was the driving force for him to seek out Quilliam and the LMI. As with the West Africans, an opportunity to send his child to England for education was only possible with the assurance that there was a Muslim community to support him.

Dollie enrolled Omar in the LMI Moslem College in March of 1893 after inspecting the school and finding it suitably British and Islamic.[64] Dollie moved the rest of his family to Liverpool around October 1893.[65] Omar was an active member of the LMI's youth programmes and his father also quickly integrated himself into the British Muslim community in Liverpool and beyond. At about the time Dollie set up residence in Liverpool, it was publicised that he had planned with former LMI member Hajee Browne to establish the aforementioned Anjuman Angrezi of which Dollie was named one of three vice-presidents.[66] Dollie soon moved to London where he was active in the Muslim community, joining the leadership of the pan-Islamic Anjuman-i Islam, as well as remaining a frequent correspondent to the *Crescent*. In December 1895, Dollie offered a portion of his home at Albert Street, Regent's Park, as the London Temporary Mosque until a suitable and permanent structure could be found or built. In his opening remarks dedicating the prayer space, it appears his time with the LMI influenced him deeply, as he made it clear that he wanted proselytisation done in a way that would make sense to the British, including possibly employing prayer and hymnbooks in English and even providing pews in the mosque.[67] The mosque hosted members from many parts of the world including Arabia, Morocco, South Africa, Turkey, Egypt and India, and was able to attract converts.[68] Near its fourth anniversary, in October 1898, the London Temporary Mosque moved to a more central London location at 189 Euston Road, but was still not yet a permanent mosque.[69]

Beginning in 1895, Dollie wrote extensively in the *Crescent* supporting the sultan and Turkey. He openly criticised statements from British officials concerning the treatment of Armenians under Ottoman rule.[70] Furthermore, he accused the British government of the greatest hypocrisy in denying advancement of Muslims in their colonial governments while advocating for Christians to take local control in Armenia. Further, he found British outrage dubious in response to a Turkish crackdown after a police official's assassination in Armenia and subsequent street disturbances, noting that the British reacted similarly in India when disturbances broke out there. He stated:

> The People of England seem to fancy that the world would stop and the sun cease to shine if by any chance she should disappear suddenly by some sort of evolution. But the loss of England would not be felt, except with

feeling of mixed thankfulness and satisfaction that we had one landgrabber the less to reckon with.[71]

Dollie later criticised the British government, which claimed it could not intercede on behalf of Indian rights in the Transvaal, yet somehow felt compelled to involve itself in Turkish affairs.[72]

A year later, exasperated at the calls for an Armenian uprising and British covert support for such actions, Dollie stated that:

> One trembles to think what the result would be should the green flag be hoisted (*Jehad* [*jihad*] declared). Then the question would not be confined to Turkey, but would extend to England, and wherever Moslems exist ... It is high time for us all to rally round the Ottoman Empire and do our duty as Moslems.[73]

The following month, he wrote that:

> I have been abused right and left, but so long as this insane crusade continues ... I shall feel it my duty to condemn those guilty of such conduct ... it is high time for all Moslems throughout the world to take as an example England's treatment towards the caliph and the religion of Islam.[74]

After several years of Dollie writing to the *Crescent* and prodding a wider response from the Muslim world, Quilliam responded with a similarly worded call to the *umma* concerning Turkish military gains in Greece and calls from the European powers for the Turks to withdraw. He wrote a proclamation which in part read, '"All Muslims are brethren". The triumph of the Ottoman Muslim is your, is my, triumph, an undeserved insult to one Muslim is an insult to every Muslim in the World.'[75] Then he called for calm, loyalty and redress through petitioning the Queen and parliament. It seems that the rhetoric used by Dollie and other Muslims in the empire inspired Quilliam to strengthen his language, but also to reiterate his eternal message that Muslims were 'peaceful and lawful' loyal citizens of the empire.

Although Dollie had an activist streak long before emigrating to England, his brief time with the LMI community and the very fact of its existence seems to have emboldened his rhetoric in criticising British imperialism and interference in Turkish affairs. A colonial subject could hardly feel the need to indulge in the idea of British exceptionalism when his English Muslim brethren so clearly rejected the core imperial concept of Christianity as a 'civilising' force. On the other hand, Quilliam fed off the boldness of the outspoken Muslims unwilling to flinch in their support of the sultan. It seems that the increased defence of Turkey and the strong language employed was directly connected to Quilliam and the colonial Muslims feeding off one another's rhetoric, although Quilliam almost always explained his criticism in terms of justice and even-handedness for an old British ally, Turkey.

Unlike Dollie, Mahomed Barakat-Ullah did not initially come to Britain to be part of the budding Muslim community in Liverpool. Although Barakat-Ullah's timeline is a bit sketchy and open to debate, according to Mohammed Ayub Khan he arrived in London around 1887 and worked as a private language tutor.[76] His first reported association with the LMI was his attendance at the mosque for a wedding in April 1891.[77] In February 1893, Quilliam passed through London on his way to catch a steamer to Morocco and was met by Muslims including Barakat-Ullah.[78] One of his associates on that day was William Obeidullah Cunliffe, the stalwart LMI member in London. It is likely that Quilliam or other members of the Liverpool community were in correspondence with Barakat-Ullah because, by May 1893, he had moved to Liverpool and was appointed professor of Arabic, Persian and Urdu at the Moslem College.[79] Soon, he was one of the more prominent and active members of the Institute, delivering lectures about once per month, writing articles for the *Crescent* and *Islamic World*, officiating as *imam* at funerals, weddings and eids (Muslim religious festivals), chairing meetings, and eventually being appointed vice-principal of the Moslem College.[80]

Barakat-Ullah never wrote about it specifically, but being among a thriving community of Muslims from all over the world, including a preponderance of British converts, must have had an influence on his pan-Islamic, anti-imperialist activism in the early twentieth century. A few months after arriving at the LMI, Barakat-Ullah mentioned that the Muslim world was in crisis and argued that true Islam would emerge from the West:

> It is time now that the sun of Islam should rise from the West—as it was prophesied by Mohammed himself—and illuminate every corner of the globe. The Moslem Institute in Liverpool and the other one at New York promise to turn out the pioneers of civilization in future. The reason why we look at them as the fountain head of good is simply because the Moslems in the West are Moslems by reason, not by birth.[81]

Most research offers very little analysis of his time at the LMI, essentially viewing it as an extension of his earlier teaching work in London. There is no evidence that Barakat-Ullah was openly political before his time in Liverpool, although Humayun Ansari asserts that Barakat-Ullah was inspired to travel to England to learn 'Western verities' after meeting with noted pan-Islamist Sayyid Jamal al-Din Afghani in India.[82] Most of Barakat-Ullah's biographers ignore his Liverpool years in favour of his subsequent time in London and beyond.[83] Ansari is an exception, and he acknowledges that Barakat-Ullah's activism was greatly affected by his time in Liverpool, describing the LMI as a 'pan-Islamic network' and his increasing politicisation due to hostility towards Islam and the sultan in the press as well as witnessing mob attacks against the LMI facilities during his three-year stay.[84] The London encounters undoubtedly broadened his consciousness, shaped his budding philosophical outlook and bolstered his open political dialogue; however, to overlook his experiences in the increasingly political milieu in which he was operating in Liverpool misses the point entirely. Barakat-Ullah was living in a community of Muslims of all stripes, including white men who claimed allegiance to the sultan. This was undoubtedly the genesis of his pan-Islamic worldview, at least from a practical standpoint.

The circumstances for the departure of Barakat-Ullah from Liverpool back to London in late August 1896 are unclear, but he joined Dollie, the London Temporary Mosque and Anjuman-i-Islam where, on 22 August, he chaired a banquet celebrating the Prophet's birthday.[85] According to Shafqat Razvi, this event thrust Barakat-Ullah into his first open political discourse. Apparently, his call for loyalty to the caliph was later criticised by British politicians and set off a series of pro- and anti-Turkish events, the former led by Barakat-Ullah.[86] A few days after the birthday celebration, a London paper argued that:

> It might not be inopportune to warn the *Anjuman-i-Islam* that it will be wise to keep itself entirely distinct from associations which are in overt or surreptitious connection with political intrigues of a highly dangerous character ... The *Anjuman-i-Islam* in London must show, not only by formal professions of loyalty to the temporal power, but also by its actual conduct, that it has no traffic with conspirators and revolutionaries.[87]

If Razvi is correct, this proves that Barakat-Ullah had already been politicised in Liverpool, as he had left the LMI only a week or two before chairing the celebration in question. Therefore, one of the twentieth century's pre-eminent Indian revolutionaries and a proponent of pan-Islamic and pan-Asiatic unity was directly influenced and politicised during his time with Quilliam and the LMI.

A Scotland Yard report nearly three decades after his departure from the LMI suggested that Barakat-Ullah was under surveillance as an agent of Amir Abd al-Rahman Khan of Afghanistan between 1896 and 1898.[88] Barakat-Ullah had spent eleven weeks in London during the state visit of the *amir*'s eldest son, Prince Nasrullah Khan, in 1895, and was an indispensable member of the LMI during this time. Barakat-Ullah was the conduit for Quilliam's continued relationship with the Shazada of Afghanistan. Pragha Chopra and P.N. Chopra note that Barakat-Ullah wrote weekly newsletters to the Shazada's agent in Karachi from 1896 to 1898, confirming his role for which he was apparently placed under surveillance.[89] Despite all of Barakat-Ullah's continued activities in pan-Islamic circles for the remainder of the *Crescent*'s publication, his name was never mentioned again after September 1896. It stands to reason that, if Barakat-Ullah was increasingly at odds with the British government and under surveillance, Quilliam may have come to know this and been alarmed; even more so considering he took great pains to maintain a balancing act between support for the sultan and fierce loyalty to the Crown.

Conclusion

It must be noted that Quilliam had contacts and influence well beyond what has been covered in this chapter. His influence on the communities and individuals covered here could be categorised as 'hit and miss'. In West Africa, his influence was extensive, personal and stood the test of time. In America, his influence, albeit often indirect, was all-encompassing among the small group of Muslim converts and their associates. Elsewhere, his name cropped up in news reports, generating some level of curiosity, but only a few Muslims sought out his counsel and company of the LMI. Quilliam was a man of his time and the face of Western Islam during a critical period in history—the end of the Victorian era, the decline of the Ottoman empire and rumblings of anti-colonialism. Nonetheless, it is difficult to quantify his lasting influence, if any, on the Muslim communities covered here. If the argument holds that Barakat-Ullah was indeed politicised in Liverpool, it would seem that that was Quilliam's longest lasting and most historically significant legacy of his influence on the subjects covered.

8

PREACHERS, PATRIOTS AND ISLAMISTS

CONTEMPORARY BRITISH MUSLIMS
AND THE AFTERLIVES OF ABDULLAH QUILLIAM

Yahya Birt

Introduction

On 8 January 1901, the future Indian politician, Mian Fazl-i-Husain, arrived in Liverpool from Cambridge with a sense of anticipation.[1] He was going to meet a man about whom he had heard a great deal. However, as his diary records, he was apparently disappointed:

> After a lot of trials and waiting about, I saw Mr. Abdulla[h] Quilliam. He is an unassuming sort of man, one whose appearance is not that of an enthusiast or one who would carry out wholesale changes, or one born to change the state of affairs. There is no fire in him. His appearance is not imposing or majestic. And yet he is the Sheikh ul Islam [*sic*] of the British Isles—what is his secret? In this case it appears to be immense application, perseverance and untiring energy—work and work. … Besides this, he possesses one virtue—common sense. And it is this unique and rare virtue which has secured him his large [legal] practice and his prestige.[2]

133

Not only was Quilliam uncharismatic (if hardworking and sensible) in Husain's estimation but he also found his offices 'shabby' and the mosque 'exceedingly dirty', with nothing distinguishing it as such except for some framed calligraphy; the Medina Home orphanage, meanwhile, was run by a 'maid' who knew little of the principles of Islam, and the printing press was in 'an awful state of uncleanliness'. That afternoon, Husain shared his misgivings with Quilliam: '[F]oreigners expect a great deal from the Liverpool Muslims, in fact more than I have seen.' Quilliam admitted to Husain that 'the net gain did not appear to be much, but that he had been trying to remove prejudice, and thus pave the way for the advent of Islam'.[3]

What is the significance of this brief encounter? Why does it possess a startling quality? The reason perhaps is that it runs counter to the received picture that contemporary British Muslims have of Quilliam as a charismatic, outspoken leader who, through sheer dedication and service, brought a Muslim community to life in a hostile environment. But, to date, we still know relatively little about how Quilliam's contemporaries saw him, while his private papers were lost to posterity in a house fire after his death.[4] The main sources for his life that we do possess, the periodicals *The Crescent* and *The Islamic World* that Quilliam published from the Liverpool Muslim Institute, are rich in content, but they must be treated with caution. Quilliam self-consciously promoted his message, his work and his community, and, as the appointed religious leader of Muslims in Britain, projected a complicated image of himself to multiple audiences, often writing about himself and the senior figures in the Liverpool Muslim community through the use of a pen-name.[5]

So why is this projected image so important in understanding Quilliam's growing reputation among contemporary British Muslims? The contentions offered here are first that the various roles projected by Quilliam's pen (with few Mian Fazl-i-Husains to gainsay it) feed directly into the various afterlives that the Shaykh al-Islam enjoys among British Muslims now, and secondly that the complexity of this inherited portrait allows for quite different interpretations of his legacy and significance, whatever current intricacies drive multiple appropriations of him today.

Yet, before the cultural impact of Quilliam grew and became appropriated in various ways, he was almost forgotten after the Second

World War. The British Muslim 'rediscovery' of Abdullah Quilliam came through at least two main conduits in post-war Britain: first, through a 'folk knowledge' of overlapping generations of Muslim converts who bridged the interwar and post-war periods and, secondly, the recovery of local knowledge about him among Muslims in Liverpool in the 1970s.

Convert folk memories: recalling the Shaykh al-Islam

The first conduit was a 'folk knowledge' of Quilliam transmitted by an older generation of converts associated with the Woking Muslim Mission to younger Muslim converts between the 1960s and the 1980s. The British Muslim Society (BMS, established in 1914), which became the Muslim Society of Great Britain (MSGB), had gathered together some of the leading converts from the Woking Muslim Mission and the by-then defunct Liverpool Muslim Institute with Lord Headley as its first president, Yehya-en-Nasr Parkinson its first vice-president, and Khalid Sheldrake its first secretary, with Quilliam listed among its thirty founding members. Its mission was to present Islam in a way that was not antagonistic to British culture or Christianity. Parkinson also emphasised that the Society was a means to connect together and support a highly dispersed convert community ideally defined by a non-sectarian ethos. When its leading founding figures had passed away or left Britain by the end of the 1930s, the MSGB continued into the 1960s but struggled to retain the same profile or clout it had enjoyed in its first two decades.[6]

Daoud Rosser-Owen (b.1943), who converted to Islam in November 1964 and was the founding amir of the Association of British Muslims (ABM, established 1976), knew at least two surviving MSGB members—Lieutenant-Colonel F.B. Abdullah Baines-Hewitt (d.1981) and Dawud Cowan (1915–2003)—and had consulted with them among others when the idea of a new association was first mooted in the late 1960s and early 1970s.[7] He saw William Bashyr Pickard (d.1974)—who, having converted to Islam in 1922, knew Quilliam (as Léon) and many other prominent converts of the time—leading the eid prayers at the Woking mosque in the 1960s, but it is unclear whether they knew each other.[8]

Shaykh Muhammad Nazim Adil al-Qubrusi al-Haqqani (1922–2014) of the Naqshbandi Haqqani Sufi order, who first came to preach Islam in London in September 1974, took on Rosser-Owen and his wife Bashiera as his first British Sufi disciples (*murid*s) and subsequently directed them in March 1975 to establish the ABM. Both Shaykh Nazim and Rosser-Owen regarded Abdullah Quilliam as the leading progenitor of British Islam. As such, they thought it important that Quilliam's 'mantle' as the Shaykh al-Islam of the British Isles be 'devolved' to Rosser-Owen. This was done in 1975 by a nephew of the late Sultan Abd al-Hamid II, who lived in London as an exile, and was overseen by Shaykh Nazim, in his role as an authorised Naqshbandi shaykh. As the sultan–caliph had originally granted the title to Quilliam in 1894 (see Chapter 6), it was reasoned that the office (if not the use of the actual title) could be revived on the basis of 'residuary sovereignty'.[9] According to Shaykh Nazim, caliphal residuary sovereignty was thus transferred through the last caliph's Naqshbandi *tariqa* (Sufi order), which continued beyond the Caliphate's formal ending in 1924.[10] In Rosser-Owen's view, additional legitimacy for the amir's office came from what he saw as the sultan–caliph's tacit recognition that Queen Victoria held the right to rule over her millions of Muslim subjects.[11] It is not known what exact form this transition of Quilliam's 'mantle' took at the hands of the caliph's nephew, His Excellency Sami Osmanli, but generally speaking the Prophet's mantle has been associated with the institution of the Caliphate as a tangible symbol of legitimacy, linking the latter's authority back to the Prophet himself.[12] Rosser-Owen also saw the ABM as 'reviving the *barakah* [*baraka*, blessing] of Shaikhu-l [*sic*] Islam Abdullah Quilliam Bey's organisation and authority'.[13]

However, this revival was short lived, as in 1978 the ABM's membership found the arrangement of an appointed amir to be 'undemocratic', which led to the adoption of a constitution on democratic lines.[14] For the second ABM *amir*, Rasjid Skinner, the idea of reclaiming the office was an irrelevant notion: he saw the ABM as a revival of Quilliam's legacy in a different sense, that of revivifying the fundamental aims and objectives of his work.[15] Subsequently, however, Rosser-Owen resumed his position as *amir* in 1986, a position he continues to hold today.[16]

Although Quilliam was a progenitor of British Islam whose office, organisation and approach to Islam were direct sources of inspiration for the ABM, 'knowledge [of these] was very slight' within the ABM in the early 1980s.[17] This brief account on the ABM website, dating from 1998, is redolent of 'folk knowledge' inasmuch as while it gets the overall story right, namely the continuity and overlap between the Liverpool and Woking communities as well as Quilliam's identity as Léon, many of the details were incorrect:

> In 1889, the Shaykhu-l [sic] Islam of the British Isles, HE Shaykh Abdullah Quilliam Bey (born William Henry Quilliam in 1857 of Manx parents), a Liverpool solicitor, founded the English Islamic Association. After Quilliam and his community were forced to migrate to the Ottoman Empire in 1908, the Association fell into abeyance. In the early 1920s, Quilliam (disguised as 'Professor Henri Marcel Léon') returned to England, and revived the organisation as the Western Islamic Association. By 1927, it was located in London's Notting Hill and the Amir was HE Khalid Sheldrake, who was for a while the Emir of Kashgar in Eastern Turkestan. Since its gradual decline, there have been several attempts to revive it.[18]

Seeing itself as a continuation of Quilliam's original organisation, the ABM was the first post-war Muslim group in Britain to regard him as an important role model for the culturally sensitive preaching (or da'wa) of Islam in Britain. In 1976, its first statement of its aims were published in an open letter that confirmed this focus on contextualised preaching, but also on teaching, companionship and support of and advocacy on behalf of converts.[19] While it was no longer practicable in the face of the large post-war Commonwealth migrations to Britain for converts to hold the leadership positions that Quilliam, Headley or Marmaduke Pickthall did before the Second World War, the ABM insisted that it should retain authority over the question of da'wa. Its objections in the 1980s were twofold: the post-war Muslim migrants lacked the acculturation to present Islam sensitively enough to the British, and as a result their efforts at proselytisation were overly dominated by the political concerns of Islamic revivalist movements like the Jama'at-i-Islami and the Muslim Brotherhood.[20] The argument that employed Quilliam in the cause of cultural sensitivity in da'wa was later widely deployed, particularly among converts from a variety of theological perspectives, which I sketch out further below.

Rediscovery in Liverpool: the first Muslim Community builder

Another important conduit for Quilliam was the Liverpool Muslim community. So far as can be ascertained, there was a total break in local community knowledge about Quilliam in Liverpool, and he had to be rediscovered. Two community activists were important in this regard: the educationist M. Akram Khan-Cheema (b.1942) and the consultant electrical engineer M. Akbar Ali (1922–2014). Both were active mosque committee members in the campaign of the Liverpool Muslim Society (LMS, established 1953) to get Al-Rahma Masjid, Liverpool's first purpose-built mosque, completed, the first stage of which was finished with some difficulty in 1975, to cater for a community then estimated to number around 3,000.[21] In the early 1970s, while researching a master's thesis on the history of Liverpool's Muslims, Khan-Cheema came across several of Quilliam's pamphlets and five volumes of the *Islamic World* (1896–1906) in the Liverpool Central Library.[22] He shared these discoveries with Akbar Ali and other members of the LMS's Executive Committee. A plan to publish a pamphlet about Quilliam through the LMS to raise monies for the mosque did not come to fruition, but copies of Khan-Cheema's research were given to Akbar Ali and the Islamic Foundation.[23]

Despite this rediscovery in the 1970s, not much was done to further knowledge of Quilliam or build on his legacy locally until the late 1990s, although Akbar Ali harboured ambitions in this regard from the early 1980s onwards.[24] One Muslim convert couple, Somaia and Rashid McTeer, who ran 'The Olive Tree', an Islamic bookshop in Renshaw Street in the city centre, set up the Abdullah Quilliam Society (AQS) in 1997. This was the culmination of work they had begun in the early 1980s to research Quilliam's life using the archival materials available in Liverpool and farther afield.[25] They organised the installation of a commemorative plaque at Brougham Terrace in the same year.[26] Akbar Ali, Ghalib Khan and others joined Somaia McTeer in registering the Society as a charity the following year. In 2000, the Society acquired the original home of Quilliam's Liverpool Muslim Institute at Brougham Terrace for the notional sum of one pound from the city council on the condition that it be restored, respecting its original purpose and its architecturally protected status as a Grade II listed building.[27]

Over the next decade, the AQS made little progress until the appointment of Jahangir Mohammed by Akbar Ali as executive project director in 2011, which brought new impetus. The Society began a programme of public outreach about Quilliam's life and work in order to support the restoration project. The Society co-hosted the launch of Ron Geaves' 2010 biography of Quilliam, the writing of which partly aimed at promoting the Society's mosque restoration project by bringing the story of its founder to a wider audience.[28] In 2012, the first Abdullah Quilliam Memorial Lecture was held.[29] Ambitious £4.5 million plans for a mosque, a heritage centre, research and archive facilities, and a 'da'wah and community engagement project' were announced. The Society decided to prioritise the refurbishment of the ground floor and the original mosque to make 'the mosque usable and allow for visits and hence make further fundraising easier'.[30] A more pressing reason to partially reopen Brougham Terrace earlier than anticipated was the failing health of Ali, the Society's chair, who had expressed a dying wish to see the mosque reopened. His wish was granted and he was able to open the Abdullah Quilliam Mosque and Heritage Centre on 27 June 2014, a fortnight before his death.[31]

In the Society's obituary notice for Ali, it is notable how Quilliam's legacy is celebrated and claimed in a way that emphasises community organisation through building institutions over da'wa. Hailed as the most important Liverpudlian Muslim after Quilliam, the following comparison is drawn: 'Much like Abdullah Quilliam, Dr Ali was an institution builder. He believed good work required institutions to perpetuate benefit beyond the lifespan of individual people.'[32] The focus on institution and community-building has strong grounds as both men established mosques and other local Muslim community institutions, engaged in civic and interfaith activism in Liverpool, addressed economic issues, were politically active with the Liberals, and also founded and participated in national Muslim organisations.

Akbar Ali played an integral role in founding three mosques besides reopening Brougham Terrace: Manchester's first post-war mosque in Victoria Road in 1948, Al-Rahma Mosque, Liverpool's first purpose-built mosque in 1975, and Penny Lane Mosque in Liverpool in 1998. Other organisations he founded or co-founded included the Manchester Muslim Students Association (1940s), Union of Muslim Organisations

(1970), Liverpool Interfaith Group (1985), Muslim Council of Britain (1997), Merseyside Council of Faiths (2000) and the Liverpool Muslim Enterprise Service (2001). He ran for parliament in 1987 for the Social Democratic Party–Liberal Alliance and in 1992 for the Liberal Democrats, was constituency chair for the Liberal Democrats in Mossley Hill, and had an important role in several civic organisations in Liverpool, including as a non-executive director of the local health authority. Here the portrayal and affinity with Quilliam is primarily as a community-builder, seen as a precursor to all such institution-building that typified the work of post-war first-generation migrants like Ali.[33]

Widening awareness: word of the Shaykh al-Islam spreads

By the late 1970s and early 1980s, news of Quilliam was beginning to spread in academic and community circles beyond a select few in the ABM or the Liverpool Muslim community. Academic and community interest was really sparked by the pioneering work of British Muslim activists and scholars like Khan-Cheema, M. Mashuq Ally (b.1951) and Tim Winter (b.1960). Khurshid Ahmed (b.1932), the founding director-general of the Islamic Foundation (then in Leicester), encouraged and supported Khan-Cheema and Ally's research.[34] Neither had access to the wealth of social history in the *Crescent*; however, Ally culled more detail from the Liverpool press and the *Islamic World* than did Khan-Cheema.[35] Subsequent scholarship on the early convert community in Britain built on these same sources or relied on these pioneers until the late 1990s; it was not until the 2000s that the academic literature began to make use of the *Crescent*.[36] In community circles, Tim Winter recalls first hearing about Quilliam at the ABM-sponsored circles of Daud Relf at the London Central Mosque in the early 1980s. Mashuq Ally spoke on the historic British Muslim community to ABM members in 1982.[37] Both studies—but more so Ally's—were picked up by community activists and intellectuals such as Ibrahim Hewitt, Jamil Sherif, Yaqub Zaki, Batool Al-Toma and Atif Imtiaz.[38]

Among the first post-war British Muslims to make use of the *Crescent* in the British Library was the journalist and community activist Fuad Nahdi (b.1957) in 1989, who considered doing doctoral research on Quilliam and his community.[39] In the same year, in memory of Quilliam,

Tim Winter founded the publishing house the Quilliam Press, which has devoted itself to translations of short traditional Islamic texts as well as to republishing what might be dubbed 'convert classics'.[40] In the late 1990s, Dr Salih Al-Samarrai, director of the Islamic Centre in Tokyo, who had come across Quilliam while researching Islam's history in Japan, had copies made of the British Library's holdings of the *Crescent* and *Islamic World*.[41] On the recommendation of the International Institute of Islamic Thought's London office, Dr Al-Samarrai sent free sets to the Islamic Foundation (by then relocated to Markfield), the Muslim College in London, the Oxford Centre for Islamic Studies, and to Tim Winter, who by then was a lecturer in Islamic Studies at the University of Cambridge.[42]

Once near-complete sets of the two main sources on Quilliam were available at these institutions, the possibilities of disseminating his story in fuller detail greatly increased. Tim Winter curated these resources carefully to present online materials by and about Quilliam and other notable converts attached to the Liverpool Muslim Institute like the Scottish poet and essayist Yehya-en-Nasr Parkinson and Quilliam's second convert, Fatima Cates. These form part of what is currently one of the largest online resources about British converts—entitled 'British Muslim Heritage'—that features other notable converts such as John Ward, Pickthall, William Williamson and David Chale.[43] Winter has drawn these fragmentary biographies together into an ambitious historical narrative that sees Islam in the British context as a natural outgrowth of Socinianism, Unitarianism and Nonconformism (with Quilliam's Methodism and teetotalism being a case in point).[44]

The other notable outcome of this dissemination was the commissioning of Geaves' Quilliam biography, which drew heavily on the *Crescent* archives at the Islamic Foundation's Markfield campus. At the time of writing, Geaves' biography has gone through two impressions, and helped to generate wider interest in Quilliam. Between 2010 and 2014, Geaves gave thirty-five lectures on Quilliam to various British Muslim audiences from summer camps (audience of 5,000) to retreats (audience of twenty-five). Quilliam's story evidently held wide cross-ethnic appeal with invitations from 'Yemeni, Turkish, Pakistani, Indian and Bangladeshi societies in London, Birmingham, Manchester, Cambridge and Preston'. This upsurge in public awareness was also driven by radio and television coverage: two BBC radio documentaries (Radio 4 and BBC World Service) and a 2012 BBC One television documentary *Great British Islam* and an episode of ITV's *Britain's Secret Homes* in 2013 on Brougham Terrace as Britain's first mosque.[45] There was also an indirect boost to Quilliam's profile with the launching of a 'counter-extremism' think-tank in 2008, the Quilliam Foundation, named after the Liverpudlian. This heightened profile has led to an intensified adoption of Quilliam in service of the ongoing public discussion around British nationalism and Muslim belonging, which is drawn out in debates on race and effective cultural engagement, and about Islam, politics and patriotism.[46]

Owning Quilliam: white privilege and preaching Islam

To whom does Abdullah Quilliam belong today? Who may most authentically lay claim to his example and how best might his legacy be honoured today? These questions are most acute in the rediscovery and promotion of Quilliam in the debate about how best to preach Islam in Britain.

The Association of British Muslims came of age during a transitional moment that marked the end of the myth that convert leadership could survive after the great post-war Commonwealth migrations. The Association recognised the political leadership of the Union of Muslim Organisations by affiliating to it in August 1976, partly as a means to allay concerns that its formation signalled a desire for converts to 'break away' from the rest of the community.[47] Nonetheless, Rosser-Owen made it clear that no compromise could be made in the matter of presenting Islam to the British. More than cultural knowledge was required, he argued; what was needed was true belonging and cultural intimacy:

> Knowing a people cannot be a remote exercise. One cannot read history books, geography books, sociology books, and so on, and 'know' a people. Meeting them from time to time is inadequate. Living among them for several years is insufficient. One must rule a people to know them, or one must get right into their culture for a long time. In spite of what overseas Muslims may have read, the culture of the British is Celtic. According to an old law of Celtic Britain, a migrant had to acculturate for nine generations before they accepted into the tribe. Thus, if the Muslims from over-

seas wish to 'know' the British they have a long task ahead of them. Things would be much simpler if they involved the natives themselves, and took their advice.[48]

It is notable that the Association's leadership knew better than to make so stark a claim publicly, or to contrast 'natives' from 'foreigners' so sharply for fear of causing offence, so such ruminations were left for internal discussion. There was perhaps a note of futility in this private insistence to set the bar for cultural competence and sensitivity so high. In its public work, the Association was in fact already beginning to cater for the needs of second-generation British Muslims, who took advantage of the Islamic studies the ABM provided in London for converts, which was comparatively rare to find in the English medium in the late 1970s and early 1980s. Not only was serving the needs of a growing community, convert and non-convert, becoming more central but the question of cultural competence was to become increasingly moot.

To give two more recent exhortations on *da'wa* that cite Quilliam as an inspiration by a pair of contemporary British convert preachers: while cultural sensitivity is still an issue, the Sunni neo-traditionalist Adam Kelwick (b.1982) and the Salafi Yusuf Chambers (b.1964) are addressing audiences full of British-born Muslims, converts or otherwise, to whom the demarcation between 'foreigners' and 'natives' has become irrelevant. During a fundraiser for the Islamic Education and Research Academy (iERA, established 2008), held in Birmingham in 2011, a video was shown in which Chambers visits the then-dilapidated LMI in Liverpool. Bemoaning its neglect, Chambers claims to pray the first prayers in Quilliam's mosque since its closure a century earlier, simultaneously evoking both continuity and revival.[49] This certainly shows a softening in Salafi attitudes towards Quilliam: as Chamber's iERA co-founder Abdurraheem Green (b.1962) recalls, 'In my stauncher Saudi-Salafi days, I looked at his methods of integrating Islamic and Christian practices as potentially heretical, but years of practical experience have made me realise just how many possibly insurmountable difficulties he was facing at the time.'[50] By contrast, in his speech, Chambers portrays Quilliam as a pious predecessor whose work has become forgotten and is an exemplar in the revival of the *Sunna* (custom, practice of the Prophet Muhammad and the early Muslim community):

He opened the *masjid* [mosque] on Christmas Day and his gift to the pov-
erty-stricken children of Liverpool was that he invited them to a free meal
that day to enlighten them, to give them some *baraka*, to give them some
blessing. Can you imagine us today opening the *masjid* and inviting the
poorest people in the UK to attend the opening of that *masjid*? I don't
think it's going to happen. This is surely the difference between us and a
person like Abdullah Quilliam. His whole rhetoric, his whole thought
process, was how could I implement the *Sunna* of the Prophet (peace and
blessings be upon him) here in Liverpool in the year 1889. One hundred
and twenty years later, where are we brothers and sisters? Where is the
Medina House [*sic*]? Where are the debating circles? Where are all of these
things that I've mentioned? Where are we, *mu'min* [believers], Muslims?
Who loves the Prophet (peace and blessings be upon him) more than he
loves himself? Why don't we demonstrate that we have that love? Why?[51]

Quilliam's openness in service to the poor is also highlighted by
Kelwick in a similar manner, namely that service for all is essential in
presenting Islam:

What his focus was in terms of *da'wa* was his serving of people, and he
would not differentiate in his service for people. He would follow the
Prophetic example, the guidance of the Messenger of Allah (peace and
blessings be upon him), when, as we see the Prophet arriving in Medina,
from amongst the first things he does is to spread peace and to feed people
food. And this was the way of Sheikh Abdullah Quilliam. So we see more
than 120 years ago in such a short time, so many hundreds of people
became Muslim with this man in his community. And when they became
Muslim, it wasn't just because of an intellectual argument; it was the person who they saw, and the example which they saw. And this is very
important to understand: The person-to-person relationships in *da'wa*, and
bringing people into Islam.[52]

For both Chambers and Kelwick, Quilliam's example is explicitly
tied to that of the Prophet's. Yet, Chambers is careful in his speech to
omit mention of Quilliam's most important patron, Abd al-Hamid II,
while naming all the others, for fear of alienating his Salafi audience
with mention of the Ottoman sultan–caliph who saw the Wahhabi
movement as a mortal enemy. However, for the neo-traditionalist
Sunnis like Kelwick or Sufis like Rosser-Owen or Ahmad Thomson
(b.1950), Quilliam's relationship with the caliph and his status as
Shaykh al-Islam is central to establishing his importance and authority
as a progenitor.[53]

It is certainly noteworthy that Quilliam's appeal has grown to encompass one of the most significant sectarian divisions in early twenty-first-century British Islam, the Sufi–Salafi divide,[54] which is testament to the breadth of his allure. There is something in the afterlives of Quilliam, lauded as an English Salafi exemplar or as an Anglo-Ottoman shaykh with a living link to his successors in the present day, to fit the gamut of theological orientations. Intellectuals such as Winter recognise that there is always a danger to laying claim to Quilliam in a manner that simply mirrors any one person's 'outlook and preferences'.[55]

From the interviews and questionnaires I have conducted, the majority view was that Quilliam serves as a pioneering exemplar for contemporary British Muslims. The most prominent themes are his role as an early pioneer, establisher of what is perhaps England's first mosque, as a highly successful preacher of Islam, compassionate towards the poor, a defender of the weak, and an outspoken advocate, all of which is seen to be done with great courage and against daunting odds.

However, along with the hagiography, three cautionary caveats were expressed. First, despite the burgeoning interest in him in the middle of the second decade of the twenty-first century, Quilliam is still far from being well known among British Muslims—if Quilliam as a British Muslim exemplar is an 'invented tradition', then surely it is one in embryonic formation, in a state of becoming or potentiality, as it has not yet attained a solidified or established status.[56] Secondly, there is wide awareness that he serves as a source of general inspiration rather than as someone who can provide a detailed blueprint, as it is appreciated that his times were quite different and distant. There are no powerful patrons left like the Ottomans, so British Muslims are essentially alone; and there can be no focus on doctrine and community as there was in Quilliam's time, as today Muslim communities are forced to react to '*fatwa* controversies' due to the prevalence of narrow jurisprudential rulings.[57] Others are more optimistic that Quilliam's pastoral work does provide a working model for an engaged mosque community, but with a 'modern twist' such as setting up an adoption agency instead of Quilliam's Victorian-style orphanage. And some reflect critically on Quilliam's failure to sustain his community after his departure from Liverpool, leaving his community to disperse and to drift away from Islam in some cases.[58]

The third and final caveat is a dissenting minority view that there is an unhealthy element to what is seen as a 'white convert' obsession with Quilliam, which is manifested as an excluding possessiveness in laying sole claim to his legacy and story. Many important personal and political questions about him remain unanswered or unclear—such as his Freemasonry, the nature of his multiple marriages, his reasons for leaving Liverpool, his stand against the Young Turks during the First World War, his adoption of a pseudonym in the latter part of his life, and possibly even orthodox Sunni creedal objections—which are felt to count against his accomplishments in Liverpool.[59]

Nahdi recalls the alienating impact of being told by some converts in Liverpool not to undertake doctoral research on Quilliam in the late 1980s: it seemed 'racist' to him that 'only white people could do research on white people'. His interest in Quilliam had been sparked in the late 1980s for the primary purpose of articulating the historic roots of Islam in Britain, in service of building an inclusive British Muslim identity, a definition that was at odds with the more exclusive sense of 'native Muslims' advocated by Rosser-Owen. Some unanswered questions about Quilliam, alongside this manifestation of 'white privilege', eventually put Nahdi off seeing him as particularly special:

> He's just a social anthropological phenomenon, I don't think he's a spiritual [leader] or anything like that. He did what a normal person would have done. Create an environment in the mosque in Liverpool. Of course I could give you an example from back home. ... you speak the language of the people, you respect their cultures. ... There is nothing outstanding like this is Quilliam's *wahy* [revelation], so that is why I left it.[60]

Nahdi points to an additional insight in the potential reaction white converts manifest when their 'white privilege' is threatened upon conversion to Islam. Famously described as a package of unearned assets or invisible privileges, white privilege is normally invisible to whites but highly visible to people of colour.[61] Leon Moosavi's research suggests that conversion threatens this white privilege. While there is 'respect and admiration' for white converts, there is a process of 're-racialisation' in wider society (as part of the 'racing' of Western Muslims generally), while in Muslim communities white converts can become highly visible in communal spaces, be treated with suspicion, regarded as incompletely Muslim or denied access to marriageable partners and so on.[62] This could be described another way, namely that conversion places white converts in a position of double marginality, which can lead to reassertions of white privilege as a manifestation of white supremacy.[63]

Although white supremacy is multidimensional in nature, for my purposes here I focus upon what Charles W. Mills defines as its cultural aspect, namely a Eurocentric view of history, a sense of cultural superiority, and unacknowledged cultural appropriation. This is relevant to Quilliam as a white icon of British Islam, with the subtext that only white converts can normalise Islam in Britain by 'whitewashing' it, thereby reinstating white privilege. Only white people can speak to other white people about Islam; non-white peoples can only alienate them: being 'other', they render Islam irretrievably alien. Thus, in the ultimate act of cultural appropriation, Islam only becomes attractive and thereby authentic if it has a white face.

However, what can be observed here about all those non-convert British Muslims who appropriate Quilliam as a progenitor of British Islam too? Mahdi Tourage's insight into how convert religious leaders can embody orthodoxy on behalf of a racially stigmatised minority anxious to present itself as a model community is relevant here, although, in the case of Quilliam, this search for acceptance is projected into the past, with the Shaykh al-Islam as the white progenitor who exemplifies Islam's deeper British roots.[64] That said, it should be obvious to any student of Islam that this racialisation makes parochial what is widely seen by Muslims as the universal nature of Muhammad's message to the whole of humanity, regardless of race or nation. Most saliently, it seems very much at odds with Quilliam's own Muslim community, which was resolutely multi-ethnic and inclusive, even to modern eyes.

Adnan Siddiqui, director of the advocacy organisation CAGE (established 2003), argues that Quilliam 'enjoyed white privilege that initially protected him from the ill-treatment that eventually befalls those who are considered outsiders. Community cohesion requires confident and active citizens engaging in society rather than being marginalised by venal politicians and those who peddle fear in society.'[65] I read this as making a subtle point about Quilliam's outspokenness as an advocate for the Ottomans and as an opponent of British imperial invasions in the Muslim world. He could trade on his insider social and racial status in ways that are unavailable to non-white racialised Muslims who are marginalised by both mainstream and militant forms of Islamophobia. Siddiqui is advising that this white privilege should be taken into account by British Muslims who view Quilliam the advocate as a role model to emulate.

Patriots and Islamists: Quilliam in the 'War on Terror'

The enthusiasm for Quilliam came of age in Britain towards the end of the first decade of the so-called 'War on Terror'. As such, it was inevitable that he would be disinterred and caught up in its rhetorical maelstrom. In 2008, two former British members of Hizb ut-Tahrir, the group that works worldwide to re-establish the Caliphate, Ed Husain (b.1974) and Maajid Nawaz (b.1978), established what they dubbed a 'counter-extremism' think-tank, which was named the Quilliam Foundation after the Liverpudlian. The original article that gave the rationale for this brand association is no longer available from the Foundation's website, but some phrases are still extant from response pieces written at the time. Its rationale was Quilliam's status as a 'forbearer' of British Islam: British Muslims should follow Quilliam's example to 'help foster a genuine British Islam, native to these islands, free from the bitter politics of the Arab and Muslim world'. As Geaves and others have pointed out, this said much more about meeting political expectations for a simple, uncomplicated construction of British Muslim loyalty and belonging than it did about Quilliam himself, who was 'deeply enmeshed in the politics of the Muslim world', or about the complexities of the attachments Muslim diaspora communities have.[66] As such, it represents a very interesting appropriation of Quilliam, making him almost a metonym for Britishness and Islam, hollowing out his historical complexity almost completely.

Although my survey questions made no direct or indirect mention of the Quilliam Foundation, a majority of respondents remarked, unprompted, that the association had harmed the reputation and potential legacy of Quilliam. Fears were expressed that, as the Foundation was probably better known than Abdullah Quilliam himself, it would stop people from wanting to know more about his life. Winter's observation here is generally representative: 'The "legacy" [of Abdullah Quilliam] is considerably confused by the Quilliam Foundation, which has an ideology diametrically opposed to Quilliam's, and which has tarnished the brand somewhat.'[67] It has also hampered the fundraising efforts of the Abdullah Quilliam Society to raise monies for the refurbishment of Brougham Terrace, as people refused to donate to the Society on the grounds of confusing it with the Foundation.[68]

It is again instructive that Quilliam also appeals to CAGE, which advocates on behalf of prisoners and others caught up in the 'War on Terror', and is on the other side of the political argument to the Quilliam Foundation. Its current director, Siddiqui, emphasises Quilliam's legacy as a legal advocate and public spokesperson on the foreign policy issues of his day, which mirrors his organisation's own work:

> His practical attitude and local philanthropy were in keeping with other charitable Victorian movements but his unashamed advocacy for Islam and the plight of his fellow Muslims suffering in other parts of the world resonated with my role as director of CAGE. And clearly he was able to differentiate between a love of England and its people and the blind patriotism derided by Samuel Johnson. The fact that he also was a solicitor for Irish dynamitards[69] and defending unpopular causes would have made him a CAGE employee/advocate *par excellence*.

> This tension between a love for one's nation but simultaneously being a critical friend, rather than traitor, makes his significance much greater at a time when British Muslims are being described by sections of the media and politicians as 'fifth columnists'. He was able to continue to work and be an active member of his local community, without necessarily proselytising, but also to advocate for his co-religionists being oppressed in Europe and addressing the base propaganda coming out from Fleet Street and Westminster.[70]

Siddiqui's response feeds into the contested expectations that now surround Muslim patriotism under the 'War on Terror', which has made Quilliam an oddly resonant figure, and accounts for the contemporary fascination with him, as his life dramatises but does not resolve what Geaves has called 'the pitfalls of divided loyalties when allegiance to the state and the dictates of conscience' point in opposite directions. He never resolved his dual loyalties to Crown and Caliph either intellectually or emotionally.[71] Siddiqui also imbues his case for 'critical friendship' with pathos, given that, as in Quilliam's time, these tensions cannot be easily resolved but only borne with dignified resolution:

> His legacy nowadays is profound as we are now entering a phase with a generation of new Britons emerging who are trying to reconcile the British and Muslim parts of their identity; and to cultivate balanced and confident citizens we must treat these identities like the children from a marriage between different races and harmonise, rather than the path of conflict and divorce that damages all. However, this also requires both parties to sit and listen and have an honest discussion, and accommodation rather than eternal conflict. Unfortunately, Quilliam was unable to reconcile the competing parts of his identity because the political powers that be were not prepared to reach peaceful accommodation, which resulted in him having to leave these shores but eventually returning a changed and ultimately forgotten man. I would venture to say that Quilliam's life and its lessons are also important for British politicians to learn from as we now have a far larger Muslim population which is increasingly aware of its rights.[72]

Conclusion: Quilliam's protean afterlives

As we have seen, Quilliam's afterlives are in rude health, encompassing much of the variety to be found in British Islam in the early twenty-first century. Patriot or rebel, reformer or traditionalist, community-builder or preacher, Quilliam's many incarnations have, over the last forty years or so, marked the tensions and developments among British Muslims themselves. If Quilliam's afterlives teach us anything, it is that the life itself is open-ended and that Muslim lives in all their irreducible complexity cannot ultimately be reduced to simple binaries, even as they are expressed through the protean, multifaceted and even contradictory appropriations of the Shaykh al-Islam. For an invented tradition-in-the-making, these protean and multiplex appropriations would seem to auger well for Quilliam's chief afterlife—as a progenitor of British Islam.

NOTES

PREFACE

1. See Diane Robinson-Dunn in Chapter 4 of this volume.
2. Jamie Gilham, *Loyal Enemies: British Converts to Islam, 1850–1950*, London: Hurst, 2014, p. 81.
3. Quoted in ibid., p. 82.
4. Yahya Birt, 'Abdullah Quilliam: Britain's First Islamist?', www.yahyabirt.com/?p=136/ (last accessed 26 August 2016).

INTRODUCTION

1. *Daily Express*, 26 April 1932, p. 11.
2. See, for example, *Daily Sketch*, 27 April 1932, p. 3 and 29 April 1932, p. 2; *Daily Mail*, 27 April 1932, p. 2.
3. *Isle of Man Examiner*, 14 April 1978, p. 4. The biography was not completed.
4. See Chapter 8.
5. See Ron Geaves, *Islam in Victorian Britain: The Life and Times of Abdullah Quilliam*, Markfield: Kube Publishing, 2010, pp. 282–3.
6. 'The UK's Oldest Mosque, Which is in Kensington, Opened its Doors to the Public', *Liverpool Echo* website, 8 February 2016; http://www.liverpoolecho.co.uk/news/liverpool-news/uks-oldest-mosque-kensington-opened-10855133 (last accessed 24 February 2016).
7. John Guilford, 'Quilliam, William Henry', in H.C.G. Matthew, Brian Harrison and Lawrence Goldman (eds), *Oxford Dictionary of National Biography*, Oxford University Press Online; www.oxforddnb.com/view/article/73031 (last accessed 22 August 2015).
8. 'Ex-extremists Call for "Western Islam"', BBC News website, 22 April 2008; www.news.bbc.co.uk/1/hi/uk/7360652.stm (last accessed 24 February 2016).

9. Geaves, *Islam*, p. 22.
10. Ibid., p. 322, n. 48.
11. Amjad Muhsen S. Dajani (Al-Daoudi), '*The Islamic World*, 1893–1908', *Victorian Periodicals Review*, 47, 3 (2014), pp. 454–75; Jamie Gilham, '"Upholding the Banner of Islam": British Converts to Islam and the Liverpool Muslim Institute, *c.*1887–1908', *Immigrants & Minorities*, 33, 1 (2015), pp. 23–44.
12. See, for example, Geaves, *Islam*, p. 174; Jamie Gilham, *Loyal Enemies: British Converts to Islam, 1850–1950*, London: Hurst, 2014, p. 93.

1. ABDULLAH QUILLIAM: A MUSLIM REVOLUTIONARY SOCIALIST?

1. T.W. Arnold, *The Preaching of Islam: A History of the Propagation of the Muslim Faith*, 2nd edn, London: Constable, 1913, p. 456.
2. Ibid., p. 457.
3. Ron Geaves, *Islam in Victorian Britain: The Life and Times of Abdullah Quilliam*, Markfield: Kube Publishing, 2010, p. 4.
4. Ibid., p. 107.
5. Ibid., p. 22.
6. Ibid., p. 25.
7. Peter Clark, *Marmaduke Pickthall: British Muslim*, London: Quartet, 1986, p. 39.
8. Geaves, *Islam*, pp. 22–4.
9. Jamie Gilham, *Loyal Enemies: British Converts to Islam 1850–1950*, London: Hurst, 2014, p. 52.
10. Ibid.
11. W.H. Quilliam, *Fanatics and Fanaticism: A Lecture*, 2nd edn, Liverpool: Dodd, 1890, p. i.
12. Ali Köse, *Conversion to Islam: A Study of Native British Converts*, London: Kegan Paul International, 1995, p. 12.
13. Geaves, *Islam*, pp. 26–7.
14. Gilham, *Loyal*, p. 52.
15. Gertrude Himmelfarb, *The De-moralisation of Society: From Victorian Virtues to Modern Values*, London: IEA Health and Welfare Unit, 1995, p. 7.
16. T.B. Bottomore, *Classes in Modern Society*, London: George Allen & Unwin, 1965, p. 35.
17. Geaves, *Islam*, p. 13.
18. Ibid., p. 14.
19. Ibid., p. 28.
20. Ibid., p. 29.
21. Ibid.

22. Quoted in ibid., p. 270.
23. Ibid., p. 13.
24. Humayun Ansari, 'The Infidel Within': Muslims in Britain since 1800, London: Hurst, 2004, p. 93.
25. Ibid., p. 121.
26. The Crescent [hereafter TC], 24 October 1906, p. 678.
27. Ansari, 'The Infidel', p. 73.
28. Ibid., p. 75.
29. Köse, Conversion, p. 12.
30. Gilham, Loyal, p. 101.
31. Geaves, Islam, p. 126.
32. Gilham, Loyal, p. 101.
33. Quoted in ibid.
34. William Miller, The Ottoman Empire and its Successor 1801–1927, London: Cambridge University Press, 1927, pp. 203–4.
35. Ansari, 'The Infidel', p. 82.
36. Köse, Conversion, p. 12.
37. Ibid.
38. Ibid., p. 13.
39. The Islamic World, 4, 40 (August 1896), p. 99.
40. Muhammad Mashuq Ally, 'The History of Muslims in Britain, 1850–1980', Unpublished MA thesis, University of Birmingham, 1981, p. 58.
41. Ibid., pp. 86–7.
42. Ibid., p. 62.
43. Köse, Conversion, p. 14.
44. Gilham, Loyal, p. 228.
45. Ibid., p. 227.
46. Köse, Conversion, p. 15.
47. Ally, 'The History', p. 75.
48. Köse, Conversion, p. 16.
49. Ibid.; Gilham, Loyal, pp. 214–5.
50. TC, 9 July 1902, p. 495.
51. Ibid.
52. Gilham, Loyal, p. 72.
53. Ibid.
54. Ibid., p. 73.
55. Ibid.
56. Quoted in ibid., p. 75.
57. Himmelfarb, The De-moralisation, pp. 131–4.
58. Cited in ibid., p. 132.
59. Ibid., p. 131.

60. Ibid.
61. Ibid., p. 132.
62. Ibid., p. 133.
63. John Westergaard and Henrietta Resler, *Class in a Capitalist Society: A Study of Contemporary Britain*, Aldershot: Avebury, Ashgate, 1995 [1975], p. 338.
64. Ibid.
65. A.H. Halsey, *Change in British Society*, Oxford: Oxford University Press, 1986, p. 82.
66. Ansari, 'The Infidel', p. 85.
67. *TC*, 13 March 1895, p. 3
68. Himmelfarb, *The De-moralisation*, p. 143.
69. Ibid., pp. 144–5.
70. Ibid., p. 147.
71. Ibid.
72. See ibid., pp. 154–9.
73. Cited in ibid., p. 157.
74. Max Weber, *The Protestant Ethic and the Spirit of Capitalism*, trans. Talcott Parsons, London: Routledge, 2001, pp. 121–2.
75. Qur'an, 9:103.
76. Geaves, *Islam*, p. 6.
77. Ansari, 'The Infidel', p. 85.

2. ABDULLAH QUILLIAM AND THE RISE OF INTERNATIONAL ESOTERIC-MASONIC ISLAMOPHILIA

1. The topic is only briefly touched on in Ron Geaves, *Islam in Victorian Britain: The Life and Times of Abdullah Quilliam*, Markfield: Kube, 2010, pp. 108–9; Jamie Gilham, *Loyal Enemies: British Converts to Islam, 1850–1950*, New York: Oxford University Press, 2014, pp. 52, 76; and Eric Germain, 'Southern Hemisphere Diasporic Communities in the Building of an International Muslim Public Opinion at the Turn of the Twentieth Century', *Comparative Studies of South Asia, Africa and the Middle East*, 27, 1 (2007), p. 126. A recent book, Angel Millar's *The Crescent and the Compass: Islam, Freemasonry, Esotericism, and Revolution in The Modern Age*, n.p. [Australia]: Numen Books, 2015, contains a chapter on Quilliam's Masonic ties, but its discussion leaves out multiple important facts and analyses, as the author apparently did not have access to many of the primary and secondary sources used in the present chapter.
2. See especially David Stevenson, *The Origins of Freemasonry: Scotland's Century, 1590–1710*, New York: Cambridge University Press, 1984; Margaret C. Jacob, *Living the Enlightenment: Freemasonry and Politics in Eighteenth-Century Europe*, New York: Oxford University Press, 1991.

3. I lay out a detailed argument for this in my *A History of Conversion to Islam in the United States, Volume 1: White American Muslims before 1975*, Leiden: Brill, 2015, pp. 66–74. Here I am building on the work of previous researchers, especially Ellic Howe, 'Fringe Masonry in England 1870–85', *Ars Quatuor Coronatoru*, 85 (1972), pp. 242–95; Joscelyn Godwin, *The Theosophical Enlightenment*, Albany: SUNY Press, 1994; T.M. Greensill, *A History of Rosicrucian Thought and of the Societas Rosicruciana in Anglia*, 2nd rev. edn, n.p.: Societas Rosicruciana in Anglia, 2003.

4. Godwin, *Theosophical Enlightenment*, pp. 219, 302.

5. For biographical information on Yarker, see William L. Cummings, 'John Yarker: A Study', *Nocalore*, 8 (1938), pp. 76–85; J.M. Hamill, 'John Yarker: Masonic Charlatan?', *Ars Quatuor Coronatorum*, 109 (1996), pp. 192–214; Richard Kaczynski, *Forgotten Templars: The Untold Origins of Ordo Templi Orientis*, n.p.: Richard Kaczynski, 2012, pp. 163–84.

6. Tracing Quilliam's participation in Freemasonry is a somewhat difficult task because of the state of the relevant primary source documents: we do not have many and, of the ones we do have, many are incomplete. The primary source for Quilliam's involvement in Masonry is his *Crescent* journal, which ran from January 1893 to May 1908—therefore, the bulk of the information we have falls within this date range.

7. *Balustre* (May 1902), reprinted in *Collectanea*, 1 (1947), p. 21; R.A. Gilbert, 'Chaos Out of Order: The Rise and Fall of the Swedenborgian Rite', *Ars Quatuor Coronatorum*, 108 (1995), p. 131.

8. *The Crescent* [hereafter *TC*], 12 March 1902, p. 174.

9. However, in August 1904, an article reported that at that time Quilliam had been a Mason, 'for over a quarter of a century' [author's emphasis]: see *TC*, 10 August 1904, p. 90. Since the earliest date we have for Quilliam joining a regular Masonic lodge is 1879, exactly—but not 'over'—twenty-five years before 1904, this leaves open the possibility that he was indeed a member of the Swedenborgian Rite, or another Masonic rite, before 1879. Admittedly, in other articles from that year, Quilliam's length of time in Freemasonry was reportedly exactly twenty-five years, not 'over' that amount (see *TC*, 15 June 1904, p. 378; *TC*, 17 August 1904, p. 107).

10. Martin Cherry (Librarian of the Library and Museum of Freemasonry, London), email message to the author, 8 February 2013. I have deduced that the group was mainstream because of its very mainstream type of name and because it was one of the few lodges of which Quilliam was a member whose records are held in the Library and Museum of Freemasonry. On Quilliam's wedding date, see *TC*, 15 June 1904, p. 378.

11. *Freemason's Chronicle*, 2 November 1901, p. 8; *Freemason's Chronicle*, 25 September 1880, p. 9. Germain (in 'Southern Hemisphere', p. 126) asserts that Quilliam was initiated in the Sat B'hai upon his return from his first trip to Morocco, which was sometime between 1882 and 1884, but he provides no source and the claim is not consistent with the 1880 date given in *Freemason's Chronicle*, 2 November 1901, p. 8.
12. For a succinct history, see Ellic Howe, 'The Rite of Memphis in France and England 1838–70', *Ars Quatuor Coronatorum*, 92 (1979), pp. 1–14. The following summary is largely based on this work.
13. Howe, 'Rite of Memphis', p. 1.
14. Calvin C. Burt, *Egyptian Masonic History of the Original and Unabridged Ancient and Ninety-Six (96°) Degree Rite of Memphis*, Utica: White & Floyed, 1879, p. 206. For more on the American group, see ibid., and Kaczynski, *Forgotten Templars*, pp. 142–62.
15. See vol. 1 of the *Kneph* (1881).
16. On connections with Tunis, see *Kneph*, 1 (1881), pp. 24, 53, 55; *Kneph*, 3 (1883), p. 41. On Egypt's Rite of Memphis and its connections with Yarker's group, see the *Kneph*, *passim*, and Gérard Galtier, *Maçonnerie égyptienne, rose-croix et néo-chevalierie: les fils de Cagliostro*, n.p.: Éditions du Rocher, 1989, pp. 151–8; Serge Caillet, *La franc-maçonnerie égyptienne de Memphis-Misraïm*, 2nd edn, Paris: Éditions Dervy, 2003, pp. 128–33. On the existence of a Rite of Memphis branch in Turkey, see Kaczynski, *Forgotten Templars*, p. 155.
17. Galtier, *Maçonnerie*, pp. 154–8.
18. *Kneph*, 1 (1881), pp. 6, 45.
19. Ibid., p. 26.
20. Ibid., p. 47.
21. See the AOZ advertisements that were run in *TC* between 1903 and 1904.
22. In 1908, a brief description of the group in an American esotericist journal incorrectly cites for the AOZ's 'Zamzumims' degree series Deut. 2:26, which suggests that the editor was simply transcribing a (so far unknown) difficult-to-read document that contained the correct citation; see *Rosicrucian Brotherhood*, 2, 4 (1908), p. 150.
23. *Collectanea*, 3 (1947), pp. 138–49.
24. *Kneph*, 1 (1881), p. 47. It is likely that whoever originally invented this story had read either J. Nightingale's 1829 *The Religions and Religious Ceremonies of All Nations* or Henry Stebbing's 1834 *History of the Christian Church*, vol. 2, both of which indeed mention Murone establishing a group called the 'Celestines' in the thirteenth century (Nightingale, pp. 548–9; Stebbing, pp. 287–9).

25. *Kneph*, 1 (1881), p. 47.
26. *Rosicrucian Brotherhood*, 2, 4 (1908), p. 150.
27. Ibid.; *TC*, 30 July 1902, p. 74; *TC*, 5 August 1903, p. 93.
28. *TC*, 10 December 1902, p. 378.
29. *Kneph*, 1 (1881), p. 30.
30. Ibid.
31. On the Masonic membership of Quilliam's father and grandfather, see *TC*, 10 August 1904, p. 90.
32. However, in a 1903 article about the group, apparently written by Quilliam, it was remarked that one J.B. Jeffery of Liverpool, a Muslim convert, had held the position of grand junior custodian since 1874, which further suggests an 1874 creation: see *TC*, 5 August 1903, p. 94. In another account of Jeffery, it is noted that he joined the AOZ in 1876, and that in 1880 he received its highest degrees—all of which at least supports a pre-1881 origin of the group: see *TC*, 23 May 1900, p. 332.
33. Geaves, p. 60.
34. *Kneph*, 3 (1883), p. 31; Geaves, *Islam*, p. 60.
35. There were additional volumes of the *Kneph*, but I have been unable to obtain copies.
36. *TC*, 19 January 1898, p. 35.
37. *TC*, 13 April 1904, p. 234.
38. For the 1874 date, see *TC*, 5 August 1903, p. 94; *TC*, 14 December 1904, p. 378. For the 1876 date, see *TC*, 23 May 1900, p. 332. According to the latter article, Jeffery had first become a Mason in 1870. He began listening to his friend Quilliam preach Islam in 1887 at 'public meetings', and converted in 1889.
39. Peter Clark, *Marmaduke Pickthall: British Muslim*, London: Quartet Books, 1986, p. 39.
40. W.H. Quilliam, 'La loi d'Islam', *La lumière d'Orient: revue bi-mensuelle de L'Islam*, 1, 1 (1892), pp. 6–7; W.H. Quilliam, 'La religion du sabre', *La lumière d'Orient: revue bi-mensuelle de L'Islam*, 1, 2 (1892), p. 5.
41. For more on Papus and his journal, see Marie-Sophie André and Christophe Beaufils, *Papus, biographie: la belle epoque de l'occultisme*, Paris: Berg International Éditeurs, 1995, especially p. 102.
42. Ibid., pp. 103–4.
43. Ibid., p. 105.
44. Quilliam was first contacted by the sultan of Turkey in 1890 (see Chapter 6).
45. *TC*, 9 January 1895, p. 11.
46. Ibid.
47. *Freemason*, 24 April 1869, p. 9.

48. John Yarker, *The Secret High Degree Rituals of the Masonic Rite of Memphis*, n.p.: Kessinger Publishing, n.d., pp. 34, 54–5.
49. Bowen, *A History*, pp. 123–35.
50. Ibid.; Aleister Crowley, 'In Memoriam: John Yarker', *Equinox*, 1, 10 (1913), p. xxi.
51. *TC*, 30 July 1902, p. 74. Yarker was also rumoured to have been the head of the AOZ at one point: see William G. Peacher, 'John Yarker', *Collectanea*, 11, 2 (1980), p. 104.
52. Quilliam may have also studied Islam on his own in the 1870s and early 1880s. It is noteworthy that Nightingale's *The Religions*, from which he had probably taken the Di Murone story for the AOZ, has an entire chapter on Muslims and their rituals.
53. *The Islamic World*, 6, 68 (1901), pp. 208–18.
54. For this and related theories, see Bowen, *A History*, pp. 115–19; John Patrick Deveney, *Paschal Beverly Randolph: A Nineteenth-Century Black American Spiritualist*, Albany: SUNY Press, 1996, pp. 213–14.
55. *The Islamic World*, 6, 68 (1901), p. 214.
56. Geaves, *Islam*, pp. 71–2; *TC*, 25 May 1898, pp. 330–1; *TC*, 1 June 1898, p. 346.
57. On Rawson, see Bowen, *A History*, pp. 119–23, 135–6, 144–59; K. Paul Johnson, 'Albert Rawson', *Theosophical History*, 2, 7 (1988), pp. 229–51; Johnson, *The Masters Revealed: Madam Blavatsky and the Myth of the Great White Lodge*, Albany: SUNY Press, 1994, pp. 25–30; John Patrick Deveney, 'Nobles of the Secret Mosque: Albert L. Rawson, Abd al-Kader, George H. Felt and the Mystic Shrine', *Theosophical History*, 8, 9 (2002), pp. 250–61; Deveney, 'The Travels of H.P. Blavatsky and the Chronology of Albert Leighton Rawson: An Unsatisfying Investigation into H.P.B.'s Whereabouts in the Early 1850s', *Theosophical History*, 10, 4 (2004), pp. 8–30; Susan Nance, *How the Arabian Nights Inspired the American Dream, 1790–1935*, Chapel Hill: University of North Carolina Press, 2009, pp. 92–7; John Patrick Deveney, 'Albert Leighton Rawson, Initiate of the Brotherhood of Lebanon, Bigamist, Plagiarist and Felon, and D.M. Bennett, Agent of the Theosophical Masters, "Foul-Mouthed Libertine" and "Apostle of Nastiness"', *Theosophical History* (forthcoming).
58. This group's official name is the Ancient Arabic Order of the Nobles of the Mystic Shrine.
59. Ibid.
60. John Yarker, 'The Order of Ishmael or B'nai Ismael', *Rosicrucian Brotherhood*, 1, 4 (1907), pp. 1[5]8–60.
61. *TC*, 5 October 1898, p. 204; *TC*, 21 December 1898, p. 377; *Freemason*, 18 November 1899, p. 4; *Freemason's Chronicle*, 29 July 1899, p. 10;

Martin Cherry, email message to the author, 8 February 2013. That Quilliam was a member of no. 1547 in 1899 conflicts with the records of the Library and Museum of Freemasonry, which state that Quilliam joined this lodge in 1901 (Cherry, email message to the author, 8 February 2013).

62. *TC*, 25 September 1901, p. 203.
63. Ibid.
64. *TC*, 16 October 1901, p. 250; *TC*, 9 October 1901, p. 233.
65. *TC*, 10 January 1906, p. 29; Clark, *Marmaduke Pickthall*, p. 39.
66. See *TC*, 19 February, 23 July, 24 September and 17 December 1902.
67. *TC*, 17 December 1902, p. 394.
68. *TC*, 12 March 1902, p. 174.
69. See *TC*, 9 July, 30 July, 5 September and 10 December 1902.
70. *TC*, 30 July 1902, p. 74.
71. *TC*, 10 June 1903, p. 362; *TC*, 11 November 1903, p. 814.
72. See *TC*, 9 March 1904, p. 154; *TC*, 10 August 1904, p. 91; *TC*, 17 July 1905, p. 26.
73. *TC*, 23 November 1904, p. 330; *TC*, 31 July 1907, pp. 75–6.
74. *TC*, 9 December 1903, p. 878.
75. *TC*, 13 April 1904, p. 234.
76. *TC*, 28 June 1905, p. 410.
77. *TC*, 3 April 1907, pp. 1047–8; *TC*, 10 July 1907, pp. 27–8; *TC*, 4 December 1907, pp. 355–7.
78. For a discussion of the Order of Ishmael, see Bowen, *A History*, pp. 123–35.
79. We currently lack any clear evidence of Quilliam's involvement with Masonry between late 1908 and early 1913. The copy of the AOZ ritual that was published in the 1940s, despite being dated April 1929, was, according to the publishing editor, 'evidently written circa 1903': see *Collectanea*, 3 (1947), p. 175.
80. See the letters from Crowley to Quilliam and his son Robert Ahmed in The Warburg Institute, University of London, Gerald Yorke Collection, NS 12.
81. Crowley, 'In Memoriam', pp. xxiii–xxv; Kaczynski, *Forgotten Templars*, pp. 278–80.
82. Kaczynski, *Forgotten Templars*, pp. 280–1.
83. This is not to say that there are not other possible explanations for Quilliam ending his Masonic involvement; nor am I arguing that we know with absolute certainty that he stopped participating in Freemasonry. More research in England's Masonic archives is needed.
84. Patrick D. Bowen, 'Abdul Hamid Suleiman and the Origins of the Moorish Science Temple', *Journal of Race, Ethnicity, and Religion*, 2, 13

(2011), p. 6. Also see Patrick D. Bowen, 'Prince D. Solomon and the Birth of African-American Islam', *Journal of Theta Alpha Kappa*, 38, 1 (2014), pp. 1–19.

85. Suleiman claimed that, before establishing his Canaanite Temple, he had incorporated a Masonic group called the Mecca-Medina Temple. Such a group was indeed established in New York in 1910 by an Egyptian named Prince De Solomon, which was almost certainly an alias of Suleiman.

86. The two men were involved with several of the same organisations in London, at which time Quilliam was using the name Henri de Léon. See Ian Duffield, 'Dusé Mohamed Ali and the Development of pan-Africanism 1866–1945', Unpublished PhD thesis, Edinburgh University, 1971, pp. 453, 469–70, 523–5, 557–8; *African Times and Orient Review* (March 1917), p. 49; Gilham, *Loyal*, p. 217. It is worth noting that one of these groups, the Central Islamic Society, had a member named M.D. Suleiman who claimed to be from the Sudan, while Suleiman, who also claimed to be from the Sudan, sometimes went as *P*.D. Solomon: see Duffield, 'Dusé Mohamed Ali', p. 515.

87. Bowen, 'Prince D. Solomon', pp. 9–10.

88. Bowen, *A History*, pp. 103–5.

89. Ibid., pp. 172–5.

90. Ibid., pp. 99–100, 172–5, 218. On Quilliam's contact (as Henri de Léon) with Inayat Khan, see Inayat Khan, *Biography of Pir-O-Mushrid Inayat Khan*, London: East–West Publications, 1979, p. 147. Interestingly, Khan's first Western follower, Rabia Martin, had apparently been a Martinist and probably knew Gould: see Bowen, *A History*, pp. 215–17.

91. The AOZ was discussed in Gould's *Notes & Queries and Historic Magazine*, 18, 10 (1900), pp. 302–3 (this article was apparently taken from an early issue of the *Kneph*) and in Gould's *Rosicrucian Brotherhood*, 2, 4 (1908), p. 150. The January 1909 issue of *Rosicrucian Brotherhood* printed a notice on the *Crescent* and reprinted a poem by Quilliam that had originally appeared in the *Islamic World*. Interestingly, Gould may have had an international Muslim audience as early as 1896, when, on 29 February, the *Moslem Chronicle and the Muhammadan Observer* briefly mentioned his journal *Miscellaneous Notes & Queries*.

92. On Webb's Islamic movement, see Bowen, *A History*, pp. 139–59; Umar F. Abd-Allah, *A Muslim in Victorian America: The Life of Alexander Russell Webb*, New York: Oxford University Press, 2006; Brent D. Singleton, 'Introduction', in Brent D. Singleton (ed.), *Yankee Muslim: The Asian Travels of Mohammed Alexander Russell Webb*, n.p. [Maryland]: Borgo Press/Wildside Press, 2007, pp. 9–54; Brent D. Singleton,

'Brothers at Odds: Rival Islamic Movements in Late Nineteenth-Century New York City', *Journal of Muslim Minority Affairs*, 27, 2 (2007), pp. 473–86.

93. Nicholas Goodrick-Clarke, *The Occult Roots of Nazism: Secret Aryan Cults and Their Influence on Nazi Ideology*, New York: New York University Press, 1992, p. 138; Mark Sedgwick, *Against the Modern World: Traditionalism and the Secret Intellectual History of the Twentieth Century*, New York: Oxford University Press, 2004, pp. 65–6. The speculation of his Masonic lodge being the Rite of Memphis was made by Goodrick-Clarke. We do know that, by the late 1800s, the Rite of Memphis had indeed made it to Turkey, where von Sebottendorff was living at the time: see Kaczynski, *Forgotten Templars*, p. 155.

94. Sedgwick, *Against the Modern World*, pp. 59–63.

95. Ibid., pp. 80–3.

96. I would like to thank Brent Singleton and Martin Cherry for their assistance as I researched this topic.

3. THE SIGNIFICANCE OF ABDULLAH QUILLIAM'S LITERARY OUTPUT

1. *The Crescent* [hereafter *TC*], 23 August 1899, p. 123.

2. *The Review of Religions*, 11, 7 (July 1912), p. 287.

3. Sometime after his return from Constantinople, Abdullah Quilliam took the name of Henri Mustapha (Marcel) de Léon. He would remain partially concealed by this identity until his death in 1932, although it is apparent that family and friends were aware of the alternative identity. For an analysis of the Quilliam/de Léon identity conundrum, see Ron Geaves, *Islam in Victorian Britain: The Life and Times of Abdullah Quilliam*, 2nd edn, Markfield: Kube Publishing, 2014, pp. 260–2.

4. The first edition of Quilliam's *Studies in Islam* was actually published in 1895.

5. The Woking Muslim Mission and Literary Trust, *Islam: Our Choice*, www.aaiil.org/text/books/kk/islamourchoicemuslimconvertstories/islamourchoicemuslimconvertstories.pdf (second reprint, 1963), pp. 102–4 (last accessed 2 March 2016).

6. W.H. Quilliam, 'Preface' to the third edition of his *The Faith of Islam: An Explanatory Sketch of the Principal Fundamental Tenets of the Moslem Religion*, 3rd edn, Liverpool: Willmer Brothers, 1892. Some of Quilliam's writings are being placed online by the Abdullah Quilliam Society: see http://abdullahquilliam.com/abdullahquilliam-writings (last accessed 9 February 2016).

7. W.H. Quilliam, 'Preface' to the first edition of *The Faith of Islam* (1889), contained in the third edition.

8. Geaves, *Islam*, p. 63.
9. *TC*, 6 February 1901, p. 90.
10. Quilliam, 'Preface' to the third edition of *Faith*.
11. Quilliam, *Faith* (3rd edn), p. 9.
12. Ibid., p. 13.
13. Ibid., pp. 13–14.
14. Geaves, *Islam*, pp. 60–1, 64.
15. W.H. Quilliam, 'The Preface' to his *Fanatics and Fanaticism: A Lecture*, 2nd edn, Liverpool: T. Dodd & Co., 1890.
16. The Mount Vernon Temperance Society had been established by Quilliam himself in 1866. Quilliam had been an active supporter of the Temperance Movement since childhood. In Liverpool, he became known as the 'Temperance child', a phrase coined by the media. For a full account of his temperance activities, see Geaves, *Islam*, pp. 26–9. The temperance movement began in the early nineteenth century and was a social movement against the consumption of alcoholic beverages. It was particularly associated with Nonconformist churches in the Victorian period: see Brian Harrison, *Drink and the Victorians: The Temperance Question in England, 1815–1872*, 2nd edn, Keele: Keele University Press, 1994.
17. Quilliam, 'The Preface' to *Fanatics*.
18. Quilliam, *Fanatics*, p. 24.
19. Ibid., p. 29.
20. Quilliam placed an assortment of his lectures on geology and archaeology in Abdullah Quilliam, *Footsteps of the Past*, Liverpool: Crescent Publishing Company, 1907, appropriately subtitled 'a series of lectures demonstrating how the discoveries of geologists and archeologists are conformable with the Islamic faith'.
21. Some examples of essays on comparative religion can be found in Abdullah Quilliam, *The Religions of Japan*, Liverpool: Crescent Publishing Company, 1906. The collection contains essays on Buddhism, Shinto, Taoism, Confucianism, Christianity and Islam.
22. The only copy of this essay that I have discovered is in *TC*, 31 January 1906, pp. 67–71.
23. 'One burdened one shall not bear the burden of another, and nothing shall be imputed to a man for righteousness except his own labour; and verily his reward shall surely be made manifest hereafter, and the doer of good works shall be rewarded for the same with a most abundant reward.'
24. *TC*, 31 January 1906, p. 67.
25. Quilliam's motivation for converting to Islam was complex and included a number of factors. In the book *Islam: Our Choice*, produced

by the Woking Muslim Mission, and containing the conversion stories of prominent Western converts to Islam during the Victorian and Edwardian era, Quilliam/de Léon cites a famous *hadith* (report of the sayings/doings of the Prophet Muhammad) where the Prophet calls upon reason as one of the essential factors that make up Islam: see Woking Muslim Mission, *Islam*, pp. 102–4.

26. *TC*, 16 August 1905, p. 102.

27. W.H.A. Quilliam, *Studies in Islam: A Collection of Essays*, Liverpool: Crescent Printing and Publishing Co., 1895, pp. 194–7.

28. Hugh McLeod, *Religion and Society in England 1850–1914*, London: MacMillan, 1996, p. 184.

29. Quilliam, *Studies*, p. 51.

30. W.H. Quilliam, *The Religion of the Sword: An Enquiry into the Tenets and History of Judaism, Christianity and Islam*, Liverpool: Dodd, 1891.

31. *TC*, 8 April 1896, p. 646.

32. The *millet* system was adapted and organised by Ottoman Sultan Fatih Mehmed II following his conquest of Constantinople in 1453. It is based upon the concept of 'people of the Book' found in the Qur'an to describe Christians and Jews. There were commonly four *millets* or communities/administrative units based on religion: Muslim, Greek Orthodox, Armenian and Jewish. Their religious leaders were empowered to regulate the activities of their own communities including schools and courts, giving them partial autonomy. Only when a Muslim was involved in a dispute with a member of a *millet*, for example, did the Muslim courts come into play: see www.quora.com/What-is-a-millet-system (last accessed 2 March 2016) for a simple definition of the *millet* system.

33. See Geaves, *Islam*, pp. 141–3 for Quilliam's brand of Zionism.

34. *TC*, 28 October 1903, pp. 275–9.

35. *The Islamic Review and Muslim India*, 4, 2 (February 1916), pp. 80–90.

36. For example, W.H. Quilliam, 'The Moorish Conquest of Spain', in his *Studies in Islam*.

37. *TC*, 29 May 1907, pp. 1171–6, 1178–81, and 5 June 1907, pp. 1187–92, 1194–7.

38. See Geaves, *Islam*, pp. 57–8.

39. *TC*, 13 September 1905, p. 172.

40. Ibid., pp. 172–4.

41. O men, fear your Lord,
Who hath created you of one man,
And from they two hath multiplied many men and women;
And fear God by whom ye beseech one another;
And respect women, for God is watching over you (Quran, 4:1).

42. *TC*, 21 October 1903, p. 266.

43. See *TC*, 29 November 1905, pp. 339–42.

44. Ibid.

45. *TC*, 20 January 1904, p. 37.

46. Jamie Gilham, *Loyal Enemies: British Converts to Islam 1850–1950*, London: Hurst, 2014, p. 59.

47. Humayun Ansari, *'The Infidel Within': Muslims in Britain since 1800*, new edn, London: Hurst, 2009, p. 129.

4. 'FAIRER TO THE LADIES' AND OF BENEFIT TO THE NATION: ABDULLAH QUILLIAM ON REFORMING BRITISH SOCIETY BY ISLAMISING GENDER RELATIONSHIPS

1. Her involvement in resisting the extension of those acts into the British empire is mentioned in *The Islamic World* [hereafter *IW*], 6, 67 ([n.d., 1901]), pp. 189–91. For more on these acts and the movement to repeal them, see Judith Walkowitz, *Prostitution and Victorian Society: Women, Class and the State*, Cambridge: Cambridge University Press, 1980.

2. *The Crescent* [hereafter *TC*], 6 January 1897, p. 12.

3. *TC*, 4 January 1899, p. 8; *IW*, 5, 53 (September 1897), back cover.

4. The Qur'an allows a man to have four wives as long as he is able to treat them equally. Like seclusion and veiling, polygyny was practised both before and after the rise of Islam. One justification for it was the larger number of women than men due to warfare. However, 'marry such women as seem good to you, two, three, four; but if you fear you will not be equitable, then only one' is often interpreted by modern Muslim legal scholars as forbidding polygyny because complete equality among wives is impossible. Quotations from the Qur'an come from *The Koran Interpreted*, trans. A.J. Arberry, New York: Touchstone, 1996, vol. 1, p. 100.

5. As Quilliam related in a lecture presented in Alexandra Hall, Liverpool and then later reproduced in *TC* and in the form of a pamphlet: *TC*, 5 June 1907, p. 1195.

6. *TC*, 29 May 1907, p. 1171, and 5 June 1907, p. 1195.

7. Ibid.

8. *The Freethinker*, reproduced in *TC*, 20 October 1897, p. 667.

9. William Henry Quilliam, *The Faith of Islam: An Explanatory Sketch of the Principal Fundamental Tenets of the Moslem Religion*, 3rd edn, Liverpool: Willmer Brothers, 1892.

10. *TC*, 29 May 1907, p. 1180 and 5 June 1907, p. 1196.

11. *TC*, 29 May 1907, pp. 1180–1.

12. Ibid., p. 1180.
13. *TC*, 8 July 1896, p. 859.
14. There are a number of passages in the Qur'an forbidding the killing of children. The one referring specifically to female infanticide is 81:8–9: 'And the little girl buried alive is asked For what crime she was put to death.'
15. The poem 'Which of Them Was Neighbour unto Her?' was written by Quilliam in December 1894 and published in *TC*, 1 May 1895, p. 137.
16. *TC*, 22 July 1896, p. 886; *TC*, 10 November 1897, p. 714; *TC*, 7 October 1896, pp. 1062–3.
17. Here Quilliam refers to the Guardianship of Infants Act of 1886. He then goes on to discuss the terms of the later 1891 Act as well: see *TC*, 12 June 1907, pp. 1211–12.
18. *TC*, 5 June 1907, p. 1192. In the 1850s, English feminists began to publish the hardships caused by the laws and get signatures to petition Parliament: see Lee Holcombe, 'Victorian Wives and Property', in Martha Vicinus (ed.), *A Widening Sphere*, Bloomington: Indiana University Press, 1977, pp. 3–28. In addition, *TC*, 21 August 1907, p. 120 includes a discussion of the preceding law regarding married women's property rights in England passed in 1870.
19. *TC*, 29 November 1905, pp. 341–2. In 'The Sheikh on Islam and Polygamy', Quilliam details the changes in British divorce law from the Matrimonial Causes Act of 1857 to the Summary Jurisdiction (Married Woman) Act of 1895, including a number of changes and additions over the years: *TC*, 5 June 1907, pp. 1188–91.
20. *TC*, 5 June 1907, pp. 1179–80.
21. *TC*, 29 May 1907, p. 1180.
22. *IW*, 6, 83 ([n.d., *c*.1906–7]), pp. 377–8.
23. Ron Geaves, *Islam in Victorian Britain: The Life and Times of Abdullah Quilliam*, Markfield: Kube Publishing, 2010, pp. 254–5. The *Peel City Guardian* (28 November 1908, p. 5) suggested that Quilliam had an affair with Mrs Thompson, and that the two left the country together.
24. Geaves, *Islam*, pp. 3–4; B. Guinness Orchard, *Liverpool's Legion of Honour*, Birkenhead: Privately Published, 1893, p. 563.
25. John Minnion, *The Pool of Life: The Story of Liverpool in Caricatures*, Liverpool: Checkmate Books, 2008, p. 207.
26. *TC*, 17 July 1907, p. 60.
27. Discussion of Sufi mystical poetry, here and in the following paragraphs, comes from my study of classical or literary Arabic with William Chittick, author of *The Sufi Path of Love: The Spiritual Teachings of Rumi*, Albany: SUNY Press, 1983. Certainly, both the influences

leading to and the interpretation of any art form are always subject to debate. For an extensive analysis of the various scholarly theories, including but not limited to the Hispano-Arabic, that have been presented over the centuries, from 1500 to 1975, with regard to courtly love poetry, see Roger Boase, *The Origin and Meaning of Courtly Love: A Critical Essay of European Scholarship*, Manchester: Manchester University Press, 1977.

28. *TC*, 17 July 1907, p. 12.
29. Author's study with Chittick (see above).
30. *TC*, 18 January 1905, p. 39. Here Parkinson resembles his Muslim predecessors in that while the European troubadour almost always expressed his feelings for a woman of noble birth, the Arab poet frequently fell in love with a slave girl: see Boase, *The Origin*, p. 125.
31. *TC*, 23 October 1907, p. 12.
32. *TC*, 9 August 1905, p. 83.
33. Ibid.
34. *TC*, 20 March 1907, p. 1022.
35. *TC*, 3 July 1907, p. 120.
36. *TC*, 14 August 1907, p. 104.
37. Quilliam was nineteen years old when he and Hannah were engaged: Geaves, *Islam*, p. 52.
38. Ibid., p. 259.
39. *TC*, 29 May 1907, p. 1179 and 5 June 1907, p. 1196.
40. *IW*, 3, 3 (n.d.), p. 11.
41. *TC*, 21 August 1907, p. 12.
42. Ibid.
43. For example, *TC*, 6 March 1907, p. 990.
44. These references appear frequently, along with Adam and Eve.
45. Hannah's children were Robert (Ahmed), Elizabeth (Cadja), Harriet (Hanifa) and William Henry (Billal).
46. Geaves, *Islam*, pp. 52–3; *The Manxman*, 7 May 1898, p. 2.
47. Geaves, *Islam*, pp. 52–4, 57, 111–12, 280.
48. Ibid., p. 259. She had been using the Quilliam surname, even before this marriage: Dollin Kelly (ed.), *New Manx Worthies*, Douglas: Manx Heritage Foundation, 1996, p. 384.
49. Geaves, *Islam*, p. 259.
50. Ibid., pp. 281, 253. Dollin Kelly notes two other women in Quilliam's life: Louise or Comtess Ruoy de L'Abadesse, with whom he believes that Quilliam had a child Letitia; and Ethel Mary Burrows, to whom he speculates that Quilliam was possibly married in the Liverpool mosque: see Kelly, *New Manx Worthies*, p. 382. Geaves, however, who has done the most extensive research on Quilliam to date, considers the story of Louise to be fabricated: Geaves, *Islam*, pp. 257, 333. In

addition, while Geaves makes reference to a Muslim convert named Annie Burrows, who served as the president of the Liverpool Society for the Abolition of Capital Punishment, for which Quilliam was the advisor and legal solicitor, he makes no mention of a romantic relationship or of an Ethel: Geaves, *Islam*, p. 109.

51. Ibid., pp. 271, 281.
52. Kelly, *New Manx Worthies*, p. 384.
53. *TC*, 28 February 1906, p. 142.
54. *TC*, 16 May 1900, p. 12.
55. *IW*, 4, 40 (August 1896), p. 123.
56. *TC*, 2 September 1896, p. 989.
57. *TC*, 22 April 1908, p. 253.
58. *IW*, 6, 67 ([n.d., 1901]), pp. 189–91; Geaves, *Islam*, p. 23.
59. Geaves notes that they spoke alongside one another at a temperance event in Scarborough: Geaves, *Islam*, p. 27.
60. *TC*, 18 March 1903, p. 174.
61. For more about the institutionalisation of the role of Valide Sultan and women and power in the Ottoman dynasty, see Leslie Peirce, *The Imperial Harem: Women and Sovereignty in the Ottoman Empire*, New York: Oxford University Press, 1993.
62. The slave girls purchased for the imperial *harem* were often of non-Turkish origin: see Ehud Toledano, *Slavery and Abolition in the Ottoman Middle East*, Seattle: University of Washington Press, 1998.
63. *TC*, 3 March 1897, p. 131.
64. *IW*, 3, 35 (March 1896), p. 351.
65. *TC*, 9 October 1907, p. 237.
66. *TC*, 27 November 1907, pp. 348–9.
67. While Quilliam would go by this name later in life, the article was written by the real or original Henri de Léon: see Geaves, *Islam*, p. 260 and *Liverpool Daily Post*, 11 December 1926.
68. *TC*, 8 May 1904, p. 317.
69. *IW*, 8, 87 ([n.d., *c*.1907]), p. 74.
70. While the Mormon Church officially broke with that practice in the United States in 1890 and elsewhere in 1904, that did not prevent Quilliam from using them as an example of what polygyny could achieve.
71. *TC*, 29 June 1904, p. 29.
72. *TC*, 24 October 1906, p. 684.
73. *TC*, 21 August 1907, p. 125. Also see *TC*, 25 May 1904, p. 327.
74. As Robert J.C. Young has explained, during the nineteenth century, 'Culture and race developed together, imbricated within each other': Robert J.C. Young, *Colonial Desire: Hybridity in Theory, Culture and Race*, London: Routledge, 1995, pp. 27–8. For more on how Islam was seen

as racially as well as culturally 'Other' to Englishness during this period, and related fears of miscegenation, see Diane Robinson-Dunn, *The Harem, Slavery and British Imperial Culture: Anglo-Muslim Relations in the Late Nineteenth Century*, Manchester: Manchester University Press, 2014, especially pp. 16–18, 44, 94–6, 103, 134–5, 143, 158, 205.

75. For degeneracy was neither specific to the European nor to the colonial context, but can best be understood as a '"mobile" discourse of empire': Anne Laura Stoler, *Race and the Education of Desire: Foucault's History of Sexuality and the Colonial Order of Things*, Durham, NC: Duke University Press, 1995, p. 32.

76. Anne McClintock has examined the importance of gender with regard to this issue, noting how control of female sexuality served to preserve 'racial, economic, and political power': Anne McClintock, *Imperial Leather: Race, Gender, and Sexuality in the Colonial Contest*, New York: Routledge, 1995, p. 47, and Robinson-Dunn, *The Harem*, p. 135.

77. Geaves, *Islam*, p. 263.

78. See McClintock, *Imperial Leather* and Felicity Nussbaum, *Torrid Zones: Maternity, Sexuality, and Empire in Eighteenth-Century English Narratives*, Baltimore: Johns Hopkins University Press, 1995.

79. According to one influential nineteenth-century ethnologist quoted in George W. Stocking, *Victorian Anthropology*, New York: Free Press, 1987, p. 51.

80. *TC*, 14 January 1893, pp. 5–6.

81. *TC*, 27 July 1898, p. 12; *Isle of Man Examiner*, 30 July 1898, p. 8; Geaves, *Islam*, pp. 150–2.

82. Ibid., p. 151.

83. Ibid., p. 107.

84. Ibid., p. 149.

85. *Manx Sun*, 31 December 1900, p. 2.

86. He defined the *harem* in *TC*, 5 June 1907, pp. 1195.

87. Geaves, *Islam*, pp. 256, 275, 6; Kelly, *New Manx Worthies*, p. 383. A local genealogist implied that Quilliam's trips to 'consult the Sultan' were, in fact, to visit his Turkish *harem*: Edmund Goodwin, *Goodwin's Collection of Genealogical Scraps*, vol. 4, 1920, 45 in the manuscript archive, 334C, Manx National Library and Archives, Manx Museum, Douglas, Isle of Man.

88. *Isle of Man Daily Times*, 7 February 1961, p. 10.

5. ABDULLAH QUILLIAM, MARMADUKE PICKTHALL AND THE POLITICS OF CHRISTENDOM AND THE OTTOMAN EMPIRE

1. Ron Geaves, 'Abdullah Quilliam (Henri de Léon) and Marmaduke Pickthall: Agreements and Disagreements between Two Prominent

Muslims in the London and Woking Communities', in Geoffrey P. Nash (ed.), *Marmaduke Pickthall, Islam and the Modern World*, Leiden: Brill, 2016, pp. 72–88.

2. Maxime Rodinson, *Europe and the Mystique of Islam*, Seattle: University of Washington Press, 1987, pp. 71–3.
3. Ibid.; Richard King, *Orientalism and Religion: Postcolonial Theory, India and 'The Mystic East'*, London: Routledge, 1999, p. 6.
4. Ron Geaves, *Islam in Victorian Britain: The Life and Times of Abdullah Quilliam*, Markfield: Kube Publishing, 2010.
5. Ibid., pp. 73, 75; on Quilliam's broader defence of the *umma*, see Jamie Gilham, *Loyal Enemies: British Converts to Islam, 1850–1950*, London: Hurst, 2014, pp. 66–71.
6. Gilham, *Loyal*, pp. 76, 81.
7. Yahya Birt, 'Abdullah Quilliam: Britain's First Islamist?', www.yahyabirt1.wordpress.com/2008/01/25/abdullah-quilliam-britains-first-islamist (last accessed 14 November 2015).
8. Peter Clark, *Marmaduke Pickthall: British Muslim*, London: Quartet, 1986, p. 8.
9. Hasan Unal, 'Britain and Ottoman Domestic Politics: From the Young Turk Revolution to the Counter-revolution, 1908–9', *Middle Eastern Studies*, 37, 2 (2001), p. 10.
10. Geoffrey Nash, 'W.H. Quilliam, Marmaduke Pickthall and the Window of British Modernist Islam', in Geoffrey Nash, Kathleen Kerr-Koch and Sarah Hackett (eds), *Postcolonialism and Islam: Theory, Literature, Culture, Society and Film*, London: Routledge, 2014, p. 160; W.H. Quilliam, *The Faith of Islam: An Explanatory Sketch of the Principal Fundamental Tenets of the Moslem Religion*, 3rd edn, Liverpool: Willmer Brothers, 1892.
11. Geaves, *Islam*, pp. 37–8.
12. On Quilliam's conversion and preaching of Islam to Christian audiences, see Gilham, *Loyal*, pp. 53–7.
13. W.H. Quilliam, *The Troubles in the Balkans: The Turkish Side of the Question*, Liverpool: Crescent Printing and Publishing Company, n.d. [1904].
14. Geaves, *Islam*, p. 102.
15. W.H. Quilliam, *The Religion of the Sword: An Enquiry into the Tenets and History of Judaism, Christianity and Islam*, Liverpool: Dodd, 1891, pp. 11–12.
16. Luke 2:14; Matthew 10:34.
17. Quilliam, *The Religion*, p. 110.
18. Ibid., p. 105. Quilliam's ecclesiastical sources—J.L. Mosheim, *Ecclesiastical History: From the Birth of Christ to the Beginning of the Eighteenth Century*, trans. Archibald Maclaine, London: William Tyler, Bolt-Court,

1842 and Henry Hart Milman, *The History of Christianity: The Birth of Christ till the Abolition of Paganism in the Roman Empire*, 3 vols, London: John Murray, 1867—were orthodox clerics from the Dutch Reformed and Church of England respectively.

19. W.H.A. Quilliam, *Studies in Islam: A Collection of Essays*, Liverpool: Crescent Printing and Publishing Company, 1895, p. 118.

20. Ibid., p. 132.

21. Stephen Neill, *A History of Christian Missions*, 2nd revised edn, Harmondsworth: Penguin, 1986, p. 312.

22. C.E. Padwick, *Temple Gairdner of Cairo*, London: S.P.C.K., 1929, p. 223.

23. W.H.T. Gairdner, *The Reproach of Islam*, London: Student Volunteer Missionary Union, 1909.

24. Samuel M. Zwemer, *Islam: A Challenge to Faith; Studies on the Mohammedan Religion and the Needs and Opportunities of the Moslem World from the Standpoint of Christian Missions*, New York: Student Volunteer Movement for Foreign Mission, 1907, p. 24 (my italics).

25. Gairdner, *The Reproach*, pp. 3–4 (my italics).

26. Clark, *Pickthall*, p. 37.

27. Anne Fremantle, *Loyal Enemy*, London: Hutchinson, 1938, p. 227.

28. Marmaduke Pickthall, 'The Black Crusade' [part 1], *The New Age* [hereafter *NA*], 12 (7 November 1912), p. 8. Pickthall was partially correct in attributing to the Balkan states' motives to 'liberate our Christian brothers, liberate our historic lands'. However, 'simplicity was the key, and details were awkward. Nationalist romanticism, based on a dubious mixture of demographic and historical arguments, provided the justification for war. The real aim was cold, strategic and expansionist': Misha Glenny, *The Balkans 1804–1999: Nationalism, War and the Great Powers*, London: Granta, 1999, p. 232.

29. Pickthall, 'The Black Crusade' [part 1], p. 8.

30. Marmaduke Pickthall, 'The Black Crusade' [part 2], *NA*, 12 (14 November 1912), pp. 31–2.

31. Pickthall, 'The Black Crusade' [part 1], p. 8.

32. Marmaduke Pickthall, 'The Black Crusade' [part 5], *NA*, 12 (5 December 1912), p. 103.

33. Ibid.

34. Marmaduke Pickthall, 'The Fate of the Mohammedans of Macedonia', *NA*, 12 (20 February 1913), p. 389.

35. See Nathalie Clayer and Eric Germain (eds), *Islam in Inter-War Europe*, London: Hurst, 2008.

36. Geaves, *Islam*, p. 74; on Hakki Bey's role, see Selim Deringil, *The Well-Protected Domains: Ideology and the Limitation of Power in the Ottoman Empire, 1876–1909*, London: I.B. Tauris, 1999, pp. 158–60.

37. Geaves, *Islam*, pp. 87, 101.

38. Ibid., p. 103.

39. Ibid., p. 134.

40. Ibid., p. 100.

41. *The Crescent*, 9 May 1906, quoted in Geaves, *Islam*, p. 104. Emphasising his consciousness of the *umma* and the imagined Islamic spirit that united it, Quilliam published two poems in the *Crescent* in 1899 commemorating the death of General Ghazi Hafez Pasha in the Greco-Turkish War (1897) and of Khalifa Abdullahi in Sudan: see Brent D. Singleton (ed.), *The Convert's Passion: An Anthology of Islamic Poetry from Late Victorian and Edwardian Britain*, n.p.: Borgo Press, 2009, pp. 131, 137–8.

42. Geoffrey P. Nash, 'Pickthall, Ottomanism, and Modern Turkey', in Geoffrey P. Nash (ed.), *Marmaduke Pickthall, Islam and the Modern World*, Leiden: Brill, 2016, pp. 137–56; Selim Deringil, 'They Live in a State of Nomadism and Savagery: The Late Ottoman Empire and Postcolonial Debate', *Comparative Studies in Society and History*, 45, 2 (2003), pp. 311–42.

43. Marmaduke Pickthall, 'The Black Crusade' [part 3], *NA*, 12 (21 November 1912), p. 58.

44. Edhem Eldem, 'The Ottoman Empire and Orientalism: An Awkward Relationship', in François Pouillon and Jean-Claude Vatin (eds), *After Orientalism: Critical Perspectives on Western Agency and Eastern Re-appropriations*, Leiden: Brill, 2011, pp. 91–2; David G. Hogarth, *A Wandering Scholar in the Levant*, London: John Murray, 1896.

45. Eldem, 'The Ottoman', p. 93.

46. Edwin Pears, *Forty Years in Constantinople: The Recollections of Sir Edwin Pears*, London: Herbert Jenkins, 1916, p. 337.

47. See Mark Sykes, *Dar-ul-Islam: A Record of a Journey through Ten of the Asiatic Provinces of Turkey*, London: Bickers & Son, 1904.

48. Cemil Aydın, 'The Ottoman Empire and the Global Muslim Identity in the Formation of Eurocentric World Order, 1815–1919', in Fred Dallmayr, M. Akif Kayapınar and İsmail Yaylacı (eds), *Civilizations and World Order: Geopolitics and Cultural Difference*, Lanham, MD: Rowman and Littlefield, 2014, p. 117.

49. Ibid., p. 118.

50. Ibid., pp. 118–19.

51. John Slight, *The British Empire and the Hajj 1865–1956*, Cambridge, MA: Harvard University Press, 2015, p. 1. Ali's statement 'The British empire is the greatest Muslim power in the world' became almost a cliché repeated by British orientalists, imperial administrators and politicians: see ibid., pp. 325–6, n. 1.

52. Azmi Ozcan, *Pan-Islamism: Indian Muslims, the Ottomans and Britain*

(1877–1924), Leiden: Brill, 1990; Deringil, *Well-Protected*. As far as identification with a specific pan-Islamic message was concerned, this appears less clear for both Quilliam and Pickthall. Neither got on particularly well with Muslims from the Indian sub-continent, from where the pan-Islamic impetus chiefly came—although, after he went to live in India in 1920 and he engaged in Khilafatist agitation with the Ali brothers, Pickthall's attitude towards South Asian Muslims improved. In his later years in India, Pickthall validated the input into intellectual pan-Islamic ideas by the likes of Jamal al-Din al-Afghani and Muhammad Iqbal.

53. Selim Deringil, *The Ottomans, the Turks, and World Power Politics: Collected Studies*, Istanbul: Isis Press, 2000, p. 83.
54. Ibid., p. 75.
55. Gilham, *Loyal*, pp. 82–4. It is to be doubted that either entertained serious animosity towards the other. As editor of the Hyderabad journal *Islamic Culture*, Pickthall included a number of articles under the soubriquet 'H.M. Léon', on Islamic medicine, astronomy, philology and poetry. Léon's death was reported—'news has lately come to grieve his many friends throughout the Muslim world'—in a footnote to an entry responding to his article 'The Language of Afghanistan', *Islamic Culture*, 6 (1932), p. 397.
56. Geaves, 'Abdullah Quilliam', p. 80.
57. Aubrey Herbert, *Ben Kendim: A Record of Eastern Travel*, ed. D. MacCarthy, London: Hutchinson, 1924, p. 268.
58. S. Tanvir Wasti, 'Mushir Hosain Kidwai and the Ottoman Cause', *Middle Eastern Studies* 30, 2 (1994), p. 253.
59. On Pickthall's late comments on Kemalist Turkey, see Nash, 'Pickthall, Ottomanism'. It might be that, in emphasising the superiority of the Turks' progressive mindset in relation to Islam, Pickthall was engaging in what Deringil considers to have been a feature of the post-Tanzimat period in which the interchangeability of religious and secular discourse meant that 'the religious could express itself in secular terms, just as the secular could use religious motifs' (Deringil, *The Ottomans*, p. 196).
60. Pickthall would certainly have recognised the irony in Abdal Hakim Murad's cogent deconstruction of Euro-liberals' illiberal attitudes towards Islam today: see Abdal Hakim Murad, 'Can Liberalism Tolerate Islam?', www.masud.co.uk/can-liberalism-tolerate-islam (last accessed 14 December 2015).
61. See, for example, the following quote from the *Crescent* that appears on a dedicated Islamic website: 'O Muslims, do not be deceived by this hypocrisy. Unite yourselves as one man. Let us no longer be sep-

arated. The rendezvous of Islam is under the shadow of the Khalifate. The Khebla of the True-Believer who desires happiness for himself and prosperity to Islam is the holy seat of the Khalifate': Anon, 'Quilliam and the Caliphate', www.abdullahquilliam.wordpress.com/category/abdullah-quilliam/views (last accessed 24 December 2015); see also Birt, 'Abdullah Quilliam'.

62. Aydın, 'The Ottomans', p. 135.

63. Fadi Elhusseini, 'The Arab World between the Dilemma of Nationalism and Sectarian Conflicts', *Hemispheres*, 30, 2 (2015), p. 52.

6. ABDULLAH QUILLIAM, FIRST AND LAST 'SHEIKH-UL-ISLAM OF THE BRITISH ISLES'

1. J.H. Kramers, R. Bulliet and R.C. Repp, 'Shaykh al-Islām', in P. Bearman, Th. Bianquis, C.E. Bosworth, E. van Donzel and W.P. Heinrichs (eds), *Encyclopaedia of Islam*, 2nd edn, Brill Online 2015, http://referenceworks.brillonline.com/entries/encyclopaedia-of-islam-2/shaykh-al-islam-COM_1052 (last accessed 3 November 2015).

2. See Kristan Tetens, 'The Lyceum and the Lord Chamberlain: The Case of Hall Caine's *Mahomet*', in Richard Foulkes (ed.), *Henry Irving: A Re-evaluation of the Pre-eminent Victorian Actor-Manager*, Aldershot: Ashgate, 2008, pp. 49–63.

3. *The Times*, 20 December 1890, p. 12.

4. Ibid.

5. *Liverpool Echo*, 14 April 1891, p. 4.

6. Mohammed-ul-Mamoon, *An Account of the Rise of Islam in England*, Dacca: K.D. Basak/East Bengal Press, 1891, p. 6. See the quotation from Quilliam's interview with the sultan in W.H. Quilliam, *The Faith of Islam: An Explanatory Sketch of the Principal Fundamental Tenets of the Moslem Religion*, 3rd edn, Liverpool: Willmer Brothers, 1892, p. 20.

7. *Liverpool Mercury*, 14 November 1892, p. 6.

8. Jamie Gilham, *Loyal Enemies: British Converts to Islam, 1850–1950*, London: Hurst, 2014, p. 53.

9. Ibid., p. 63.

10. *The Manx Sun*, 19 October 1901, p. 7.

11. For example, *The Porcupine*, 21 November 1896, p. 10. See also Ron Geaves, *Islam in Victorian Britain: The Life and Times of Abdullah Quilliam*, Markfield: Kube Publishing, 2010, p. 223.

12. *The Crescent* [hereafter *TC*], 2 January 1895, pp. 4–5.

13. *Liverpool Mercury*, 18 February 1895, p. 7 (my italics). See Chapter 7 for a discussion of Quilliam's links with Muslims in the United States.

14. *Isle of Man Times and General Advertiser*, 5 January 1897, p. 2.

15. The sometime associate of Quilliam, American Muslim leader Mohammed Alexander Russell Webb, was awarded Ottoman medals and appointed honorary consul-general of the Turkish government in New York when he visited Constantinople in 1900. Webb also claimed that, during this period, he was named 'Sheikh-ul-Islam for America', though this has not been proven: see Patrick D. Bowen, *A History of Conversion to Islam in the United States, Volume 1: White American Muslims before 1975*, Leiden: Brill, 2015, pp. 166–7.

16. Gilham, *Loyal*, p. 34.

17. See A.L. Macfie, *The Eastern Question, 1774–1923*, revised edn, Harlow: Longman, 1996.

18. *TC*, 4 November 1903, p. 12.

19. On Quilliam in Lagos, see Chapter 7 and also Brent D. Singleton, '"That Ye May Know Each Other": Late Victorian Interactions between British and West African Muslims', *Journal of Muslim Minority Affairs*, 29, 3 (2009), pp. 369–85.

20. *TC*, 8 March 1905, p. 154. On Quilliam's missions for the sultan, see Geaves, *Islam*, Chapter 7.

21. *TC*, 15 February 1905, p. 108.

22. A rare surviving 1903 postcard to Quilliam from a subscriber to the *Crescent* in Lahore is simply addressed 'To Mr. Abdulla Quilliam, Shaikh al Islam, Liverpool, England': Author's Collection, Mohommed Ishaq to Quilliam, 24 June 1903.

23. *The Evening Post*, 1 April 1902, p. 6.

24. W.H. Quilliam, 'Islam in England', *Religious Review of Reviews*, 1, 3 (1891), pp. 159–60.

25. See Fred Halliday, 'The *Millet* of Manchester: Arab Merchants and Cotton Trade', *British Journal of Middle Eastern Studies*, 19, 2 (1992), pp. 159–76; Richard I. Lawless, *From Ta'izz to Tyneside: An Arab Community in the North-East of England during the Early Twentieth Century*, Exeter: Exeter University Press, 1995, Chapter 1; Fred Halliday, *Arabs in Exile: Yemeni Migrants in Urban Britain*, London: I.B. Tauris, 1992, Chapters 1 and 2; Mohammad Siddique Seddon, *The Last of the Lascars: Yemeni Muslims in Britain, 1836–2012*, Markfield: Kube Publishing, 2014, Chapter 2; Humayun Ansari, *'The Infidel Within': Muslims in Britain since 1800*, London: Hurst, 2004, Chapter 2.

26. Geaves, *Islam*, p. 147.

27. *Manx Sun*, 19 October 1901, p. 7.

28. Manx National Library and Archives, Manx Museum, Douglas, Isle of Man, Letters to Henry Hanby Hay, 1894–1911, MD 79–5: Abdullah Quilliam to Henry Hanby Hay, 26 December 1896.

29. See the Muslim Museum Initiative website, www.muslimmuseum.org.

uk/quilliams-125th-anniversary-project-bid-unsuccessful (last accessed 12 December 2015). In 1905, Quilliam was permitted by the sultan to use the honourable appellations 'His Excellency' before his name and 'Effendi Bey' after it. For the Ottomans, 'effendi' was a title equivalent to 'esquire', to signify high status; 'bey' was a title conferred on civil or military officers.

30. *Daily Express*, 1 July 1904, p. 7.
31. *Daily Mail*, 23 January 1903, p. 7.
32. *TC*, 9 December 1893, pp. 375–6.
33. *Liverpool Freeman*, reprinted in *TC*, 12 July 1905, p. 19.
34. John J. Pool, *Studies in Mohammedanism: Historical and Doctrinal with a Chapter on Islam in England*, Westminster: Archibald, Constable and Company, 1892, p. 401.
35. *TC*, 25 December 1901, pp. 403–7.
36. *TC*, 16 July 1902, pp. 35–9, 43–4.
37. Ibid., p. 35.
38. See *Liverpool Daily Post*, 20 April 1891, p. 7, and 3 April 1891, p. 7, respectively.
39. See *TC*, 20 August 1902, pp. 122–3, and 23 September 1903, p. 202, respectively.
40. *TC*, 5 August 1896, p. 923; *TC*, 23 April 1902, p. 260.
41. See, for example, articles in *TC*, 3 May 1905.
42. *TC*, 30 January 1901, p. 73.
43. *TC*, 4 June 1902, p. 362.
44. Reprinted in *TC*, 18 June 1902, p. 393. Following his first visit to Constantinople with his father in 1891, Robert Ahmed had been appointed a lieutenant-colonel in Ertuğrul Cavalry Regiment of the Imperial Guard.
45. Geaves, *Islam*, Chapter 7; Gilham, *Loyal*, Chapter 2.
46. *TC*, 9 May 1906, pp. 291–4.
47. *TC*, 23 June 1897, p. 392, and also see *TC*, 30 June 1897, pp. 409–10.
48. *The Islamic World*, 6, 71 ([n.d., c.1902/3]), pp. 311–12.
49. *TC*, 13 March 1907, p. 1006.
50. *TC*, 14 October 1893, pp. 308–9.
51. *Liverpool Mercury*, 12 June 1895, p. 5.
52. *Lloyd's Weekly Newspaper*, 18 August 1895, p. 11.
53. See, for example, *TC*, 19 May 1897, p. 314.
54. *TC*, 21 May 1902, pp. 330–1.
55. *Liverpool Mercury*, 1 April 1895, p. 6.
56. *TC*, 21 July 1898, p. 12.
57. *TC*, 15 August 1900, p. 105.

58. An offensive ethnic slur used by Muslims in Turkey and the Balkans to describe non-Muslims.
59. *TC*, 25 March 1896, p. 617.
60. Ibid.
61. See, for example, *TC*, 15 April 1896, p. 668.
62. *TC*, 14 August 1897, p. 12.
63. See, for example, *TC*, 14 July 1897, pp. 441–2; and, for more details about Quilliam's *fatwas*, Geaves, *Islam*, Chapter 6.
64. *TC*, 10 January 1906, p. 27.
65. *TC*, 12 April 1899, p. 230.
66. *TC*, 15 February 1905, p. 107.
67. *TC*, 28 October 1903, pp. 275–9.
68. See *TC*, 15 February 1905, pp. 99–102.
69. This and the following biography of Cates is from *TC*, 7 November 1900, pp. 298–9, and 21 November 1900, pp. 323–4.
70. *TC*, 7 November 1900, p. 299.
71. Ibid. On Cates's funeral, see *TC*, 7 November 1900, pp. 299–300.
72. See Gilham, *Loyal*, pp. 96, 111–12.
73. *The Islamic Review and Muslim India*, 3, 9 (September 1915), p. 464; *The Review of Religions*, 11, 7 (July 1912), p. 287.
74. *The Islamic World*, 4, 37 (May 1896), p. 89.
75. Reprinted in *TC*, 7 March 1906, pp. 149–50.
76. Reprinted in *TC*, 3 April 1907, p. 1048.
77. *TC*, 16 December 1893, p. 383.
78. *TC*, 3 July 1901, p. 9.
79. *TC*, 17 April 1901, pp. 243–5.
80. Ibid., p. 246.
81. *TC*, 18 July 1906, p. 459.
82. *TC*, 6 June 1906, p. 364.
83. See Amjad Muhsen S. Dajani (Al-Daoudi), 'The Islamic World, 1893–1908', *Victorian Periodicals Review*, 47, 3 (2014), pp. 454–75.
84. See Halliday, 'The *Millet*'.
85. For further details and a discussion of these funerals, see Geaves, *Islam*, pp. 158–62.
86. *TC*, 21 February 1906, p. 121.
87. *TC*, 24 July 1907, p. 62.
88. *Daily Express*, 1 July 1904, p. 7.
89. See Geaves, *Islam*, pp. 156–7.
90. *The Review of Religions*, 10, 7 (July 1911), p. 303.
91. See, for example, *TC*, 27 February 1895, p. 70. For more on Quilliam's relationships with Jewish communities, see Geaves, *Islam*, pp. 139–43.
92. For example, Manchester in 1903: see *TC*, 25 February 1903, p. 123.

93. On Quilliam's sudden departure from England, see *TC*, 13 May 1908, p. 313 and 20 May 1908, pp. 329, 334; Gilham, *Loyal*, pp. 71–5.
94. On Quilliam's 'London years' (1909–32), see Geaves, *Islam*, Chapter 8; Gilham, *Loyal*, pp. 75–86.
95. Kramers et al., 'Shaykh al-Islām'. See also A.L. Macfie, *The End of the Ottoman Empire, 1908–1923*, Harlow: Longman, 1998, Chapter 10; Eugene Rogan, *The Fall of the Ottomans: The Great War in the Middle East, 1914–1920*, London: Allen Lane, 2015, Chapter 1.

7. ABDULLAH QUILLIAM'S INTERNATIONAL INFLUENCE: AMER-
ICA, WEST AFRICA AND BEYOND

1. Howard MacQueary, 'American Mohammedanism', *Unitarian*, 8 (1893), p. 104.
2. *Times of India*, 25 November 1892, p. 7. Geaves also mentions donations for printing works from an Indian source in 1892: Ron Geaves, *Islam in Victorian Britain: The Life and Times of Abdullah Quilliam*, Markfield: Kube Publishing, 2010, p. 71.
3. Alexander Russell Webb, 'Preaching Islam in America', *Providence Journal*, 14 (1893), p. 469.
4. *Times of India*, 25 November 1892, p. 7.
5. Mohammed Alexander Russell Webb, *Lectures on Islam: Delivered at Different Places in India*, Lahore: Islamia Press, 1893, Preface.
6. Webb, 'Preaching Islam', p. 469.
7. Missouri Historical Society, St. Louis, John A. Lant Papers [hereafter Lant Papers]: Abdullah W.H. Quilliam to John A. Lant, 26 September 1894.
8. *The Crescent* [hereafter *TC*], 1 April 1893, p. 85; *TC*, 29 April 1893, p. 115.
9. Umar F. Abd-Allah, *A Muslim in Victorian America: The Life of Alexander Russell Webb*, New York: Oxford University Press, 2006, p. 72.
10. For a full analysis of *The Islamic World*, see Amjad Muhsen S. Dajani (Al-Daoudi), '*The Islamic World*, 1893–1908', *Victorian Periodicals Review*, 47 (2014), pp. 454–75.
11. For a full analysis of *The Moslem World* and *Voice of Islam*, see Brent D. Singleton, '*The Moslem World*: A History of America's Earliest Islamic Newspaper and Its Successors', *Journal of Muslim Minority Affairs*, 27 (2007), pp. 297–307.
12. Abd-Allah, *Muslim in Victorian America*, p. 164.
13. *The Moslem World* [hereafter *MW*], October 1893, p. 6.
14. *MW*, October 1893, p. 8.
15. *MW*, May 1893, p. 7.

16. *MW*, November 1893, p. 1 and front matter.
17. *Moslem World and Voice of Islam* [hereafter *MWVI*], May 1895, p. 3; *MWVI*, November 1895, p. 2.
18. *MW*, August 1893, p. 16; *MW*, November 1893, p. 11; *MW*, November 1893, front matter; *MW*, October 1893, p. 6.
19. *TC*, 29 April 1893, p. 115.
20. *TC*, 3 June 1893, p. 160.
21. For a full review of the schism among the American Muslims, see Brent D. Singleton, 'Brothers at Odds: Rival Islamic Movements in Late Nineteenth-Century New York City', *Journal of Muslim Minority Affairs*, 27 (2007), pp. 473–86.
22. Jamie Gilham, '"Upholding the Banner of Islam": British Converts to Islam and the Liverpool Muslim Institute, *c*.1887–1908', *Immigrants & Minorities*, 33, 1 (2013), pp. 31–2.
23. *Evening Sun*, 11 December 1893, p. 1.
24. Lant Papers, Quilliam to Lant, 26 September 1894.
25. *New York World* [hereafter *NYW*], 17 May 1894, p. 8.
26. Patrick D. Bowen, *A History of Conversion to Islam in the United States, Volume 1: White American Muslims before 1975*, Leiden: Brill, 2015, p. 156.
27. Lant Papers, Hamid Snow to Lant, 16 March 1894.
28. Lant Papers, Quilliam to Lant, 26 September 1894.
29. *NYW*, 2 August 1894, p. 9.
30. Lant Papers, Quilliam to Lant, 26 September 1894. Also, the *New York Herald* (9 December 1894, p. 12) confirms that Keep and Quilliam had entered into correspondence soon after she broke from Webb.
31. Lant Papers, Snow to Lant, 18 June 1894.
32. Lant Papers, Quilliam to Lant, 26 September 1894.
33. Lant Papers, Snow to Lant, 17 December 1894.
34. *NYW*, 17 December 1894, p. 8 and also 2 August 1894, p. 12.
35. *NYW*, 11 December 1894, p. 16.
36. *NYW*, 16 December 1894, p. 16.
37. Bowen, *History of Conversion*, p. 157.
38. *TC*, 2 January 1895, p. 5.
39. Ibid., p. 2.
40. Lant Papers, C.L.M. Abdul Jebbar to Lant, 17 January 1895.
41. *TC*, 13 February 1895, p. 49.
42. Lant Papers, Quilliam to Lant, 21 February 1895.
43. *TC*, 20 March 1895, p. 89 and 6 February 1895, p. 41.
44. Bowen, *History of Conversion*, p. 163.
45. Last note of Lant's correspondence: *TC*, 15 December 1897, p. 793; Nabakoff's last correspondence: *TC*, 26 January 1898, p. 57.
46. *TC*, 21 November 1900, p. 329.

47. *TC*, 16 December 1900, p. 407.
48. *Utica Sunday Journal*, 11 February 1900, p. 15.
49. Gilham, "'Upholding the Banner of Islam'", p. 29.
50. Kenneth Dike Nworah, 'The Liverpool "Sect" and British West African Policy 1895–1915', *African Affairs*, 70 (1971), p. 350.
51. Brent D. Singleton, "'That Ye May Know Each Other": Late Victorian Interactions between British and West African Muslims', *Journal of Muslim Minority Affairs*, 29, 3 (2009), p. 371.
52. For example, his 1887 treatise *Christianity, Islam and the Negro Race* extolled the virtues of Islam as a unifying African religion whereas he described Christianity as foreign, a mark of subjugation.
53. Singleton, "'That Ye May Know'", p. 372.
54. Ibid., p. 373.
55. *The Islamic World*, December 1893, p. 6.
56. *Sierra Leone Weekly News*, 3 February 1894, p. 5.
57. Singleton, "'That Ye May Know'", p. 374.
58. *TC*, 22 April 1896, pp. 681–2.
59. Singleton, "'That Ye May Know'", p. 381.
60. *TC*, 24 June 1903, p. 389.
61. One who has made the *hajj*, or pilgrimage to Mecca (the fifth 'pillar' of Islam).
62. Vivian Bickford-Smith, *Ethnic Pride and Racial Prejudice in Victorian Cape Town: Group Identity and Social Practice, 1875–1902*, Cambridge: Cambridge University Press, 1995, p. 195.
63. Achmat Davids, *The Mosques of Bo-Kaap: A Social History of Islam at the Cape*, Athlone: South African Institute of Arabic and Islamic Research, 1980, p. 183.
64. *TC*, 25 March 1893, p. 75.
65. *TC*, 4 November 1893, p. 331.
66. *MW*, November 1893, front matter.
67. *TC*, 18 December 1895, p. 387.
68. *TC*, 16 December 1896, p. 1128; *TC*, 13 January 1897, p. 25.
69. *TC*, 19 October 1898, pp. 233–4.
70. *TC*, 18 September 1895, pp. 181–2.
71. *TC*, 16 October 1895, p. 246; *TC*, 23 October 1895, p. 262.
72. *TC*, 27 November 1895, p. 347.
73. *TC*, 7 October 1896, p. 1070.
74. *TC*, 11 November 1896, pp. 1149–50.
75. *TC*, 14 July 1897, pp. 441–2.
76. Mohammed Ayub Khan, 'Universal Islam: The Faith and Political Ideologies of Maulana Barakatullah "Bhopali"', *Sikh Formations*, 10 (2014), p. 58. Several other sources note his arrival in London as between 1897 and 1890.

77. *The Times*, 21 April 1891, p. 4.
78. *TC*, 25 February 1893, p. 44.
79. *TC*, 20 May 1893, p. 139.
80. *TC*, 2 January 1895, back matter. The lectures, articles and other activities of Barakat-Ullah are drawn from articles in *The Crescent* and *The Islamic World*.
81. *MW*, November 1893, p. 13.
82. Humayun Ansari, 'Maulana Barkatullah Bhopali's Transnationalism: Pan-Islamism, Colonialism, and Radical Politics', in Götz Nordbruch and Umar Ryad (eds), *Transnational Islam in Interwar Europe: Muslim Activists and Thinkers*, New York: Palgrave Macmillan, 2014, pp. 182–3.
83. For example, Khan breezes over Barakat-Ullah's time in Liverpool, providing only a brief mention that Barakat-Ullah came under surveillance while with Quilliam, supplying no further explanation: Khan, 'Universal Islam', p. 58.
84. Ansari, 'Maulana Barkatullah', pp. 184–5.
85. *TC*, 9 September 1896, p. 1004. Barakat-Ullah presided over a banquet with Dollie.
86. Shafqat Razvi, 'Mawli Barkatullah Bhopali: A Revolutionary Freedom Fighter of the Early 20th Century', *Journal of the Pakistan Historical Society*, 37 (1989), pp. 141–2.
87. *TC*, 26 August 1896, p. 967.
88. Max Everest-Phillips, 'Colin Davidson's British Indian Intelligence Operations in Japan 1915–23 and the Demise of the Anglo-Japanese Alliance', *Intelligence and National Security*, 24 (2009), p. 677.
89. Pragha Chopra and P.N. Chopra, *Indian Freedom Fighters Abroad: Secret British Intelligence Report*, New Delhi: Criterion, 1988, p. 15.

8. PREACHERS, PATRIOTS AND ISLAMISTS: CONTEMPORARY BRITISH MUSLIMS AND THE AFTERLIVES OF ABDULLAH QUILLIAM

1. Tahir Kamran, 'Husain, Sir Mian Fazl-i-', in H.C.G. Matthew, Brian Harrison and Lawrence Goldman (eds), *Oxford Dictionary of National Biography*, Oxford University Press online, www.oxforddnb.com/view/article/95339 (last accessed 9 November 2015).
2. Azim Husain (ed.), *Mian Fazl-i-Husain: Glimpses of Life and Works, 1898–1936*, Lahore: Sang-e-Meel Publications, 1995, pp. 85–6; *The Crescent* [hereafter *TC*], 16 January 1901, p. 41.
3. Husain, *Mian Fazl-i-Husain*, p. 87.
4. Ron Geaves, *Islam in Victorian Britain: The Life and Times of Abdullah Quilliam*, Markfield: Kube Publishing, 2010, p. 253.

5. See Jamie Gilham, *Loyal Enemies: British Converts to Islam, 1850–1950*, London: Hurst, 2014, p. 77 on Quilliam's pen-name, and Geaves, *Islam*, for Quilliam's various roles as a religious leader, especially Chapters 5–7.
6. Gilham, *Loyal*, pp. 137–8, 200–6.
7. Daoud Rosser-Owen, 'The History and Organisation of the ABM', p. 1, Draft confidential memorandum to ABM Council, 21 July 1987, Typescript, 12pp., Rasjid Skinner Private Papers.
8. Daoud Rosser-Owen [writing as Shaykh Sharafuddin Murghanil], 'Islamists and the British', p. 1, Undated lecture to ABM (*c.* mid-1980s), Typescript, 7pp., Rasjid Skinner Private Papers. Rosser-Owen recounts seeing how Pickard, then an old man, was challenged by a young Indian student about how he had led the Eid prayer at the Woking mosque in the 1960s. Neither Baines-Hewitt, MSGB president in the 1950s and 1960s, nor Cowan, active in the BMS/MSGB since the 1930s, who served as *imam* at the Woking mosque in the 1940s and was a distinguished Arabist and lecturer at the School of Oriental and African Studies, London, met Quilliam, but his new identity as Léon was an open secret in the convert community. Another source for Rosser-Owen on Quilliam's life was the academic Dr Safa Khulusi (1917–95), who had edited the first edition of *Islam: Our Choice*, Woking, Surrey: Woking Muslim Mission & Literary Trust, 1961, which mostly featured profiles of converts culled from the pages of the *Islamic Review*, and who was active like Rosser-Owen in the Union of Muslim Organisations in the 1970s and 1980s: Author's interview with Daoud Rosser-Owen, January 2008; Sam Khulusi, 'Obituary: Professor Safa Khulusi', *The Independent*, 5 October 1995, p. 18.
9. Rosser-Owen, 'History and Organisation', p. 2; Daoud Rosser-Owen, 'A History of Islam in the British Isles: An Overview', Association of British Muslims website, 1998, www.members.tripod.com/~british_muslims_assn/history_of_islam_in_the_bi.html (last accessed 9 November 2015).
10. The nineteenth century saw significant incorporation of the Sufi orders into an increasingly bureaucratic and centralised Ottoman state—see Brian Silverstein, 'Sufism and Governmentality in the Late Ottoman Empire', *Comparative Studies of South Asia, Africa and the Middle East*, 29, 2 (2009), pp. 171–85.
11. Author's interview with former ABM *amir*, Rasjid Skinner, West Yorkshire, 21 October 2015. As a precedent of sorts to Quilliam's office, the settlement with the Hapsburgs after Ottoman withdrawal from Bosnia Herzegovina in 1878 left Islamic institutions and offices intact while recognising the new political authority. In the settlement,

NOTES

the sultan–caliph's authority became an unexecuted right, symbolic in nature but ultimately guaranteed by the Austro-Hungarian empire. It was in this sense that Quilliam understood his dual loyalty to the King–Emperor George VI and the Sultan–Caliph Abd al-Hamid II, a dual loyalty to both spiritual authority and temporal power in the execution of the office of Shaykh al-Islam of the British Isles. See Xavier Bougarel, 'From Young Muslims to Party of Democratic Action: The Emergence of a Pan-Islamist Trend in Bosnia–Herzegovina', *Islamic Studies*, 36, 2–3 (1997), pp. 533–49; Fikret Karčić, *The Bosniaks and the Challenges of Modernity: Late Ottoman and Hapsburg Times*, Sarajevo: El-Kalem, 1991; Karčić, 'The Office of Ra'is al-'Ulama' among the Bosniaks (Bosnian Muslims)', *Intellectual Discourse*, 5, 2 (1997), pp. 109–20; *TC*, 13 August 1902, pp. 102–3, which sets out his views on dual sovereignty in a reproduced text of supplication at the mosque offered on the occasion of George VI's coronation.

12. Suzanne Pinckney Stetkevych, *The Mantle Odes: Arabic Praise Poems to the Prophet Muhammad*, Bloomington: Indiana University Press, 2010, p. 64. Among the most prized relics kept at the Topkapi Palace in Istanbul, the historic seat of the Ottoman Caliphate, is what is claimed to be the Prophet's mantle.

13. Rosser-Owen, 'History and Organisation', p. 8.

14. Ibid., pp. 4–5.

15. Author's interview with Rasjid Skinner, 21 October 2015.

16. Rosser-Owen, 'History and Organisation', p. 6; Association of British Muslims, 'Our Team', Association of British Muslims website, www. aobm.org/our-team/ (last accessed 4 December 2015).

17. Tim Winter, email communication to author, 7 October 2015.

18. Association of British Muslims, 'A Brief History of the ABM', Association of British Muslims website, 1998–9, www.members.tripod.com/~british_muslims_assn/briefhistory.html (last accessed 9 November 2015). Quilliam was born in 1856; he was made Shaykh al-Islam by the sultan–caliph in 1894; the national organisation he established in 1888 was called the British Muslim Association (*TC*, 23 April 1902, pp. 259–62); Quilliam left Britain voluntarily in 1908 and did not take his community with him to Constantinople, and he returned under the name of Henri de Léon in 1909. Sheldrake founded the Western Islamic Association in 1926, but Quilliam acted as its patron along with the Aga Khan (Gilham, *Loyal*, p. 201). Elsewhere, the claim is made that Lord Headley founded the Woking mosque in 1887 (Rosser-Owen, 'History and Organisation', p. 1), when in fact its founder was G.W. Leitner who built the mosque in 1889, and the Woking Muslim Mission was established by Khwaja

Kamal-ud-Din in 1913, with Headley converting to Islam in the same year, who then went on to found the BMS in 1914: see K. Humayun Ansari, 'The Woking Mosque: A Case Study of Muslim Engagement with British Society since 1889', *Immigrants & Minorities*, 21, 3 (2002), pp. 1–24; Gilham, *Loyal*, Chapters 4–6; Jeremy Shearmur, 'The Woking Mosque Muslims: British Islam in the Early Twentieth Century', *Journal of Muslim Minority Affairs*, 34, 2 (2014), pp. 165–73.

19. Rosser-Owen, 'History and Organisation', pp. 3–4.
20. Rosser-Owen, 'Islamists and the British', pp. 2–3.
21. M.A. Khan-Cheema, 'Islam and the Muslims in Liverpool', Unpublished MA thesis, University of Liverpool, 1979, pp. 44–53; Liverpool Muslim Society, 'Liverpool Muslim Society and Masjid History', Liverpool Muslim Society website, www.liverpoolmuslimsociety.org.uk/1/liverpool-muslim-society-and-masjid-history (last accessed 13 November 2015), details the emergence of Al-Rahma Mosque from an informal prayer room in a British Yemeni's home, Al-Hajj Ali Hizzan, in 1948, to a purpose-built mosque in January 1975, overseen by the LMS.
22. Khan-Cheema, 'Islam', pp. 8–17.
23. Email communication from M.A. Khan-Cheema to author, 7 October 2015.
24. Facebook communication from M.A. Khan-Cheema to author, 14 November 2015.
25. Email communication from Batool Al-Toma, co-director, New Muslims Project, to author, 14 November 2010.
26. New Muslims Project, 'The Olive Tree', *Meeting Point: The Newsletter of the New Muslims Project*, 13 (July 1999), p. 11; Suhail Malik, 'The Mersey Terrace That Kops Them All', *Q-News*, 279–80 (20 November 1997), pp. 12–13.
27. Adam Kelwick, 'Shaykh Abdullah William Henry Quilliam', YouTube, 1 September 2014, www.youtube.com/watch?v=z0yhNDpo3h8 (last accessed 5 November 2015).
28. Islamic Foundation, 'Abdullah Quilliam Biography Launched', *Islamic Foundation Newsletter*, 37 (May 2010), p. 1. The Society regularly ordered copies of Geaves' work from Kube Publishing to promote its work (author's recollection).
29. A video recording of the AQS's first Abdullah Quilliam Memorial Lecture is available online: Ahmad Thomson, 'The Life of Shaykh-ul-Islam of the British Isles, W.H. Abdullah Quilliam', YouTube, 15 June 2012, www.youtube.com/watch?v=Z-ANc3XaM30 (last accessed 2 December 2015).
30. Abdullah Quilliam Society, 'Abdullah Quilliam Mosque and Heritage

Centre Progress Report' (13 August 2012), 3pp. [typescript], www.
abdullahquilliam.com/wp/pdfs/ABDULLAH-QUILLIAM-MOSQUE-
AND-HERITAGE-CENTRE-PROGRESS-REPORT-August–2012.pdf
(last accessed 13 November 2015); Abdullah Quilliam Society, 'The
Sheikh Abdullah Quilliam Mosque and Heritage Centre', project brochure (January 2012), 21pp. [typescript], www.abdullahquilliam.com/
wp/pdfs/Abdullah-Quilliam-Heritage-Centre-Brochure-JAN2012.pdf
(last accessed 13 November 2015).

31. Abdullah Quilliam Society, 'Obituary for Dr Mohammad Akbar Ali
    L.LD, MBE', Abdullah Quilliam Society website, July 2014, www.
    abdullahquilliam.com/wp/pdfs/Obituary-Akbar-Ali.pdf (last accessed
    10 November 2015); Neil Docking, 'Tributes to Man Who Led the
    Restoration of Britain's First Mosque in Liverpool Dies', *Liverpool Echo*,
    10 July 2014, www.liverpoolecho.co.uk/news/liverpool-news/man-
    who-led-restoration-britains-7387549 (last accessed 10 November
    2015).

32. Abdullah Quilliam Society, 'Obituary'.

33. Ibid., pp. 1–2; David Alton, 'The Death of Akbar Ali', David Alton
    website, 8 July 2014, www.davidalton.net/2014/07/08/the-death-of-
    akbar-ali/ (last accessed 23 November 2015); Muslim Council of
    Britain, 'Muslim Council of Britain Mourns the Passing of
    Dr Mohammad Akbar Ali', Muslim Council of Britain website, 2014,
    www.mcb.org.uk/dr-mohammad-akbar-ali-tribute/ (last accessed
    11 November 2015). Quilliam's multiple civic roles and institution-
    building are discussed in Geaves, *Islam* and Gilham, *Loyal*.

34. See the acknowledgements in Khan-Cheema, 'Islam and Muslims in
    Liverpool', p. iii, and Muhammad Mashuq Ally, 'History of Muslims
    in Britain, 1850–1980', Unpublished MA thesis, University of
    Birmingham, 1981, p. iii. At the time, Ally was employed as a
    researcher at the Islamic Foundation where the focus of his work was
    the history of Islam in Britain.

35. Ally, 'History', pp. 46–64.

36. Peter Clark, *Marmaduke Pickthall: British Muslim*, London: Quartet
    Books, 1986, pp. ix, 39, 127 n. 9, relies on a chapter from an unpub-
    lished manuscript on British Islam by Mashuq Ally and on Tim Winter;
    Ali Köse, *Conversion to Islam: A Study of Native British Converts*, London:
    Kegan Paul International, 1997, pp. 12–14, relies on Ally; John Wolffe
    (ed.), *Religion in Victorian Britain, Volume V: Culture and Empire*,
    Manchester: Manchester University Press, 1997, pp. 339–49, uses the
    same main sources as Ally and Khan-Cheema. For early academic use
    of the *Crescent*, see Humayun Ansari, *The Infidel Within: Muslims in Britain
    since 1800*, London: Hurst, 2004, pp. 83, 121–4; and Diane Robinson-

Dunn, 'Lascar Sailors and English Converts: The Imperial Port and Islam in late 19th-Century England', *Seascapes, Littoral Cultures, and Trans-oceanic Exchanges*, 12–15 February 2003, Library of Congress, Washington D.C., History Cooperative website, www.historycooperative.org/proceedings/seascapes/dunn.html (last accessed 29 January 2008), p. 11, n. 43.

37. *Association for British Muslims Bulletin* (January 1982), p. 4.
38. Email communications to author from Ibrahim Hewitt, 7 October 2015, Yaqub Zaki, 7 October 2015, Batool Al-Toma, 14 October 2015, Jamil Sherif, 9 October 2015, and Atif Imtiaz, 8 October 2015.
39. Author's interview with Fuad Nahdi, London, 7 November 2015; Mohammad Akram Khan-Cheema, 'Shaykh-ul-Islam of the British Isles', *Q-News*, 279–80 (1 November 1997), pp. 14–16, reproduced from the December 1989 issue of *MuslimWise*, a precursor to *Q-News*, also edited by Fuad Nahdi. In the same issue of *Q-News*, an article from *TC* (18 June 1892) is reproduced on p. 17.
40. Anon, 'About the Quilliam Press', www.quilliampress.com/about/ (last accessed 23 November 2015). Among its publications is Abdal Hakim Murad [Tim Winter], *Muslim Songs of the British Isles*, London: Quilliam Press, 2005, which brings together the poetry of Quilliam, Amhurst Tyssen and other converts of the period and sets it to British, Irish and Manx folk tunes as well as some Arabic and Turkish ones. Winter is also the musical director of the Cambridge-based Harmonia Alcorani choral group. Some of the group's singing of Quilliam's poems can be heard via the British Muslim Song website, www.britishmuslimsong.co.uk/?page_id=143 (last accessed 23 November 2015).
41. The stamp 'Present from Islamic Center Japan' with address and contact details is evident on the first page of every volume in each reproduced set of the *Crescent* and *Islamic World*. See also Salih Mahdi S. Al-Samarrai, 'Islam in Japan: History, Spread and Institutions in the Country', Islamic Center Japan website, 2009, www.islamcenter.or. jp/en/history-and-publications/history-of-islam-in-japan/ (last accessed 23 November 2015). It is claimed in this piece that 'Abdullah Guillaume' (Quilliam) preached Islam to Shotaro Noda, whom he met in Constantinople where Shotaro was teaching Japanese to Ottoman officers at the behest of Abd al-Hamid II. Shotaro embraced Islam, changed his name to Abdul Haleem Noda and is said to have been the first Japanese Muslim convert.
42. Email communication from Shiraz Khan, IIIT London Office, to author, 4 November 2015.
43. For a list of extensive resources in the project, see 'British Muslim

Heritage', Masud website, www.masud.co.uk/ISLAM/bmh/bmh.htm (last accessed 23 November 2015). There is also a spin-off project to promote Quilliam's poetic legacy through song—see n. 40 above.

44. T.J. Winter, *British Muslim Identity: Past, Problems, Prospects*, Cambridge: MAT Press, 2003, pp. 17–24; Abdal Hakim Murad [T.J. Winter], 'British Muslims and the Rhetoric of Indigenisation', Masud website, 15 July 2014, www.masud.co.uk/british-muslims-and-the-rhetoric-of-indigenisation/ (last accessed 1 December 2015).

45. Ron Geaves, 'Islam in Victorian Britain: The Life and Times of Abdullah Quilliam and His Contemporary Cultural Significance', REF2014 Impact Case Study, www.impact.ref.ac.uk/CaseStudies/CaseStudy.aspx?Id=42066 (last accessed 23 November 2015).

46. The following two sections are based on a short questionnaire circulated by the author through social media in October 2015 and through solicited email communications with activists known to have a track-record in interacting with Quilliam and his legacy in some way, through two face-to-face interviews, as well as looking at published online resources, particularly videos. The questions asked were: (i) How did you first come to know of Quilliam?; (ii) What impact has Quilliam's life and example had on you and/or your community work?; (iii) What significance in your view does Quilliam have today for British Muslims?; (iv) How can we explain Quilliam's new-found popularity and broad appeal in recent years?; (v) What do you think Quilliam's legacy actually is nowadays?; and (vi) What do you think Quilliam's legacy ought ideally to be?

47. Rosser-Owen, 'History and Organisation', p. 4.

48. Rosser-Owen, 'Islamists and the British', p. 2.

49. Yusuf Chambers, 'Great British Islam: The Lost Treasure', YouTube, 20 July 2012, www.youtube.com/watch?v=jrfjXLzlt1s (last accessed 6 November 2015).

50. Abdurraheem Green, email communication to author, 8 October 2015.

51. Yusuf Chambers, 'Dawah: The Activism of the 21st Century', YouTube, 19 January 2012, www.youtube.com/watch?v=R5dfpHBp2Qc (last accessed 2 December 2015).

52. Adam Kelwick, 'One Man and his Da'wah (Abdullah Quilliam)' [Message to Dawah Conference by the Myriad Foundation], YouTube, 29 March 2015, www.youtube.com/watch?v=jQp5JSVCIJA (last accessed 5 November 2015).

53. Thomson, 'The Life'; Kelwick, 'Shaykh Abdullah', noting the subtle distinction that Kelwick prefers 'Sheikh' over the more formal Ottoman styling of Thomson and Rosser-Owen's of 'Sheikh-ul-Islam'.

54. Sadek Hamid, *Sufis, Salafis and Islamists: The Contested Ground of British Islamic Activism*, London: I.B. Tauris, 2016.

55. Winter, email communication to author.

56. Eric Hobsbawm, 'Introduction: Inventing Traditions', in Eric Hobsbawm and Terence Ranger (eds), *The Invention of Tradition*, Cambridge: Cambridge University Press, 1983, pp. 1–14.

57. Winter, email communication to author.

58. Kelwick, 'Shaykh Abdullah'; Batool Al-Toma, email communication to author, 14 October 2015.

59. Items in this list of reservations are drawn from email communications to the author from Yaqub Zaki, 7 October 2015 and Jamil Sherif, 9 October 2015; Ahmad Thomson, 'The Life'; Author's interview with Nahdi.

60. Author's interview with Nahdi.

61. Peggy McIntosh, 'White Privilege and Male Privilege: A Personal Account of Coming to See Correspondences through Work in Women's Studies', Working Paper no. 189, Wellesley, MA: Wellesley College, Center for Research on Women, 1988, p. 1; Richard Dyer, *White*, London: Routledge, 1997, p. 9.

62. Leon Moosavi, 'White Privilege in the Lives of Muslim Converts in Britain', *Ethnic and Racial Studies*, 38, 11 (2015), pp. 1–15.

63. Philosopher Charles W. Mills defines white supremacy as white domination in political, judicial, 'economic, cultural, cognitive-evaluative, somatic, and in a sense even "metaphysical" spheres. There is a pervasive racialization of the social world that means that one's race, in effect, puts one into a certain relationship with social reality, tendentially determining one's being and consciousness.' See Charles W. Mills, 'White Supremacy as Sociopolitical System: A Philosophical Perspective', in A.W. Doane and E. Bonilla-Silva (eds), *White Out: The Continuing Significance of Racism*, New York: Routledge, 2003, pp. 35–48 (quotation on p. 42).

64. Mahdi Tourage, 'Performing Belief and Reviving Islam: Prominent (White Male) Converts in Muslim Revival Conventions', *Performing Islam*, 1, 2 (2013), pp. 207–26.

65. Adnan Siddiqui, email communication with author, 16 October 2015.

66. Geaves, *Islam*, pp. 306–7; see also Yahya Birt, 'Abdullah Quilliam: Britain's First Islamist?', Yahya Birt website, 25 January 2008, www.yahyabirt1.wordpress.com/2008/01/25/abdullah-quilliam-britains-first-islamist/ (last accessed 12 April 2016).

67. Winter, email communication with author.

68. 'Abdullah Quilliam Society Has Nothing to Do with Quilliam Foundation', Asian Image website, 4 February 2014, www.asianimage.

co.uk/news/north_of_england/10985951._Abdullah_Quilliam_ Society_has_nothing_to_do_with_Quilliam_Foundation_/ (last accessed 12 April 2016).

69. See Geaves, *Islam*, p. 31.
70. Siddiqui, email communication with author.
71. See n. 11 above and Geaves, *Islam*, Chapters 5–6.
72. Siddiqui, email communication with author.

BIBLIOGRAPHY

Chapter 1

Primary sources

Newspapers and journals

The Crescent
The Islamic World

Books and articles

Arnold, T.W., *The Preaching of Islam: A History of the Propagation of the Muslim Faith*, 2nd edn, London: Constable, 1913.
Corbet, R.G., *Mohammedanism in the British Empire*, London: Kegan Paul, Trench, 1902.
Miller, William, *The Ottoman Empire and Its Successor, 1801–1927*, London: Cambridge University Press, 1927.
Pool, John J., *Studies in Mohammedanism: Historical and Doctrinal, with a Chapter on Islam in England*, Westminster: Archibald, Constable and Company, 1892.
Quilliam, W.H., *Fanatics and Fanaticism: A Lecture*, 2nd edn, Liverpool: Dodd, 1890.

Secondary sources

Ally, Muhammad Mashuq, 'The History of Muslims in Britain, 1850–1980', Unpublished MA thesis, University of Birmingham, 1981.
Ansari, Humayun, *'The Infidel Within': Muslims in Britain since 1800*, London: Hurst, 2004.
Bottomore, T.B., *Classes in Modern Society*, London: George Allen & Unwin, 1965.
Clark, Peter, *Marmaduke Pickthall: British Muslim*, London: Quartet, 1986.
Geaves, Ron, *Islam in Victorian Britain: The Life and Times of Abdullah Quilliam*, Markfield: Kube Publishing, 2010.

BIBLIOGRAPHY

Gilham, Jamie, *Loyal Enemies: British Converts to Islam 1850–1950*, London: Hurst, 2014.

Halsey, A.H., *Change in British Society*, Oxford and New York: Oxford University Press, 1986.

Himmelfarb, Gertrude, *The De-moralisation of Society: From Victorian Virtues to Modern Values*, London: IEA Health and Welfare Unit, 1995.

Köse, Ali, *Conversion to Islam: A Study of Native British Converts*, London and New York: Kegan Paul International, 1995.

Weber, Max, *The Protestant Ethic and the Spirit of Capitalism*, trans. Talcott Parsons, London: Routledge, 2001.

Westergaard, John and Henrietta Resler, *Class in a Capitalist Society: A Study of Contemporary Britain*, Aldershot: Avebury, Ashgate, 1995 [1975].

Chapter 2

Primary sources

Archives

The Warburg Institute, University of London, The Gerald Yorke Collection, NS 12.

Newspapers and journals

African Times and Orient Review
Collectanea
The Crescent
Freemason
Freemason's Chronicle
The Islamic World
The Kneph
La lumière d'Orient
Moslem Chronicle and the Muhammadan Observer
Notes & Queries and Historic Magazine
The Rosicrucian Brotherhood

Books and articles

Burt, Calvin C., *Egyptian Masonic History of the Original and Unabridged Ancient and Ninety-Six (96°) Degree Rite of Memphis*, Utica: White & Floyed, 1879.

Crowley, Aleister, 'In Memoriam: John Yarker', *Equinox*, 1, 10 (1913), pp. xix–xxxix.

Khan, Inayat, *Biography of Pir-O-Mushrid Inayat Khan*, London: East–West Publications, 1979.

Nightingale, J., *The Religions and Religious Ceremonies of All Nations*, London: Printed for Sir Richa'rd Phillips and Co., 1829.

Stebbing, Henry, *History of the Christian Church*, vol. 2, London: Printed for Longman, Rees, Orme, Brown, Green, & Longman; and John Taylor, 1834.

Yarker, John, *The Secret High Degree Rituals of the Masonic Rite of Memphis*, n.p.: Kessinger Publishing, n.d.

Secondary sources

Abd-Allah, Umar F., *A Muslim in Victorian America: The Life of Alexander Russell Webb*, New York: Oxford University Press, 2006.

André, Marie-Sophie and Christophe Beaufils, *Papus, biographie: la belle epoque de l'occultisme*, Paris: Berg International Éditeurs, 1995.

Bowen, Patrick D., 'Abdul Hamid Suleiman and the Origins of the Moorish Science Temple', *Journal of Race, Ethnicity, and Religion*, 2, 13 (2011), pp. 1–54.

———— 'Prince D. Solomon and the Birth of African-American Islam', *Journal of Theta Alpha Kappa*, 38, 1 (2014), pp. 1–19.

———— *A History of Conversion to Islam in the United States, Volume 1: White American Muslims before 1975*, Leiden: Brill, 2015.

Caillet, Serge, *La franc-maçonnerie égyptienne de Memphis-Misraïm*, 2nd edn, Paris: Éditions Dervy, 2003.

Clark, Peter, *Marmaduke Pickthall: British Muslim*, London: Quartet Books, 1986.

Cummings, William L, 'John Yarker: A Study', *Nocalore*, 8 (1938), pp. 76–85.

Deveney, John Patrick, *Paschal Beverly Randolph: A Nineteenth-Century Black American Spiritualist*, Albany: SUNY Press, 1996.

———— 'Nobles of the Secret Mosque: Albert L. Rawson, Abd al-Kader, George H. Felt and the Mystic Shrine', *Theosophical History*, 8, 9 (2002), pp. 250–61.

———— 'The Travels of H.P. Blavatsky and the Chronology of Albert Leighton Rawson: An Unsatisfying Investigation into H.P.B.'s Whereabouts in the Early 1850s', *Theosophical History*, 10, 4 (2004), pp. 8–30.

———— 'Albert Leighton Rawson, Initiate of the Brotherhood of Lebanon, Bigamist, Plagiarist and Felon, and D.M. Bennett, Agent of the Theosophical Masters, "Foul-Mouthed Libertine" and "Apostle of Nastiness"', *Theosophical History* (forthcoming).

Duffield, Ian, 'Dusé Mohamed Ali and the Development of pan-Africanism 1866–1945', Unpublished PhD thesis, Edinburgh University, 1971.

Galtier, Gérard, *Maçonnerie égyptienne, rose-croix et néo-chevalierie: les fils de Cagliostro*, n.p.: Éditions du Rocher, 1989.

Geaves, Ron, *Islam in Victorian Britain: The Life and Times of Abdullah Quilliam*, Markfield: Kube, 2010.

Germain, Eric, 'Southern Hemisphere Diasporic Communities in the Building of an International Muslim Public Opinion at the Turn of the

BIBLIOGRAPHY

Twentieth Century', *Comparative Studies of South Asia, Africa and the Middle East*, 27, 1 (2007), pp. 126–38.

Gilbert, R.A., 'Chaos Out of Order: The Rise and Fall of the Swedenborgian Rite', *Ars Quatuor Coronatorum*, 108 (1995), pp. 122–49.

Gilham, Jamie, *Loyal Enemies: British Converts to Islam, 1850–1950*, New York: Oxford University Press, 2014.

Godwin, Joscelyn, *The Theosophical Enlightenment*, Albany: SUNY Press, 1994.

Goodrick-Clarke, Nicholas, *The Occult Roots of Nazism: Secret Aryan Cults and Their Influence on Nazi Ideology*, New York: New York University Press, 1992.

Greensill, T.M., *A History of Rosicrucian Thought and of the Societas Rosicruciana in Anglia*, 2nd rev. edn, n.p.: Societas Rosicruciana in Anglia, 2003.

Hamill, J.M., 'John Yarker: Masonic Charlatan?', *Ars Quatuor Coronatorum*, 109 (1996), pp. 192–214.

Howe, Ellic, 'Fringe Masonry in England 1870–85', *Ars Quatuor Coronatorum*, 85 (1972), pp. 242–95.

——— 'The Rite of Memphis in France and England 1838–70', *Ars Quatuor Coronatorum*, 92 (1979), pp. 1–14.

Jacob, Margaret C., *Living the Enlightenment: Freemasonry and Politics in Eighteenth-Century Europe*, New York: Oxford University Press, 1991.

Johnson, K. Paul, 'Albert Rawson', *Theosophical History*, 2, 7 (1988), pp. 229–51.

——— *The Masters Revealed: Madam Blavatsky and the Myth of the Great White Lodge*, Albany: SUNY Press, 1994.

Kaczynski, Richard, *Forgotten Templars: The Untold Origins of Ordo Templi Orientis*, n.p.: Richard Kaczynski, 2012.

Millar, Angel, *The Crescent and the Compass: Islam, Freemasonry, Esotericism, and Revolution in the Modern Age*, n.p. [Australia]: Numen Books, 2015.

Nance, Susan, *How the Arabian Nights Inspired the American Dream, 1790–1935*, Chapel Hill: University of North Carolina Press, 2009.

Peacher, William G., 'John Yarker', *Collectanea*, 11, 2 (1980), pp. 100–11.

Sedgwick, Mark, *Against the Modern World: Traditionalism and the Secret Intellectual History of the Twentieth Century*, New York: Oxford University Press, 2004.

Singleton, Brent D., 'Brothers at Odds: Rival Islamic Movements in Late Nineteenth-Century New York City', *Journal of Muslim Minority Affairs*, 27, 2 (2007), pp. 473–86.

——— 'Introduction', in Brent D. Singleton (ed.), *Yankee Muslim: The Asian Travels of Mohammed Alexander Russell Webb*, n.p. [Maryland]: Borgo Press/ Wildside Press, 2007, pp. 9–54.

Stevenson, David, *The Origins of Freemasonry: Scotland's Century, 1590–1710*, New York: Cambridge University Press, 1998.

BIBLIOGRAPHY

Chapter 3

Primary sources

Newspapers and journals

The Crescent
The Islamic Review and Muslim India
The Review of Religions

Books and articles

Quilliam, Abdullah, *The Religions of Japan*, Liverpool: Crescent Publishing Company, 1906.

——— *Footsteps of the Past*, Liverpool: Crescent Publishing Company, 1907.

Quilliam, W.H., *Fanatics and Fanaticism: A Lecture*, 2nd edn, Liverpool: T. Dodd & Co., 1890.

——— *The Religion of the Sword: An Enquiry into the Tenets and History of Judaism, Christianity and Islam*, Liverpool: Dodd, 1891.

——— *The Faith of Islam: An Explanatory Sketch of the Principal Fundamental Tenets of the Moslem Religion*, 3rd edn, Liverpool: Willmer Brothers, 1892.

Quilliam, W.H.A., *Studies in Islam: A Collection of Essays*, Liverpool: Crescent Printing and Publishing Co., 1895.

The Woking Muslim Mission and Literary Trust, *Islam: Our Choice*, www.aaiil. org/text/books/kk/islamourchoicemuslimconvertstories/islamour-choicemuslimconvertstories.pdf (second reprint, 1963) (last accessed 2 March 2016).

Secondary sources

Ansari, Humayun, *'The Infidel Within': Muslims in Britain since 1800*, new edn, London: Hurst, 2009.

Geaves, Ron, *Islam in Victorian Britain: The Life and Times of Abdullah Quilliam*, 2nd edn, Markfield: Kube Publishing, 2014.

Gilham, Jamie, *Loyal Enemies: British Converts to Islam 1850–1950*, London: Hurst, 2014.

Harrison, Brian, *Drink and the Victorians: The Temperance Question in England, 1815–1872*, 2nd edn, Keele: Keele University Press, 1994.

McLeod, Hugh, *Religion and Society in England 1850–1914*, London: MacMillan, 1996.

Chapter 4

Primary sources

Archives

Manx National Library and Archives, Manx Museum, Douglas, Isle of Man,

BIBLIOGRAPHY

Manuscript Archive, 334C: Edmund Goodwin, *Goodwin's Collection of Genealogical Scraps*, vol. 4, 1920.

Newspapers and journals

The Crescent
The Islamic World
Isle of Man Daily Times
Isle of Man Examiner
Liverpool Daily Post
Manx Sun
The Manxman
Peel City Guardian

Books and articles

Orchard, B. Guinness, *Liverpool's Legion of Honour*, Birkenhead: Privately Published, 1893.

Quilliam, W.H., *The Faith of Islam: An Explanatory Sketch of the Principal Fundamental Tenets of the Moslem Religion*, 3rd edn, Liverpool: Willmer Brothers, 1892.

Secondary sources

Boase, Roger, *The Origin and Meaning of Courtly Love: A Critical Essay of European Scholarship*, Manchester: Manchester University Press, 1977.

Chittick, William, *The Sufi Path of Love: The Spiritual Teachings of Rumi*, Albany: SUNY Press, 1983.

Geaves, Ron, *Islam in Victorian Britain: The Life and Times of Abdullah Quilliam*, Markfield: Kube Publishing, 2010.

Gilham, Jamie, *Loyal Enemies: British Converts to Islam, 1850–1950*, New York: Oxford University Press, 2014.

Holcombe, Lee, 'Victorian Wives and Property', in Martha Vicinus (ed.), *A Widening Sphere*, pp. 3–28, Bloomington: Indiana University Press, 1977.

Kelly, Dollin (ed.), *New Manx Worthies*, Douglas: Manx Heritage Foundation, 1996.

McClintock, Anne, *Imperial Leather: Race, Gender, and Sexuality in the Colonial Contest*, New York: Routledge, 1995.

Minnion, John, *The Pool of Life: The Story of Liverpool in Caricatures*, Liverpool: Checkmate Books, 2008.

Nash, Geoffrey. 'W.H. Quilliam, Marmaduke Pickthall, and the Window of British Modernist Islam', proof copy, 2013.

Nussbaum, Felicity, *Torrid Zones: Maternity, Sexuality, and Empire in Eighteenth-Century English Narratives*, Baltimore: Johns Hopkins University Press, 1995.

Peirce, Leslie, *The Imperial Harem: Women and Sovereignty in the Ottoman Empire*, New York and Oxford: Oxford University Press, 1993.

Robinson-Dunn, Diane, *The Harem, Slavery and British Imperial Culture: Anglo-Muslim Relations in the Late Nineteenth Century*, Manchester and New York: Manchester University Press and Palgrave, 2014.

Stocking, George W., *Victorian Anthropology*, New York: Free Press, 1987.

Stoler, Anne Laura, *Race and the Education of Desire: Foucault's History of Sexuality and the Colonial Order of Things*, Durham, NC and London: Duke University Press, 1995.

Toledano, Ehud, *Slavery and Abolition in the Ottoman Middle East*, Seattle and London: University of Washington Press, 1998.

Walkowitz, Judith, *Prostitution and Victorian Society: Women, Class and the State*, Cambridge: Cambridge University Press, 1980.

Young, Robert J.C., *Colonial Desire: Hybridity in Theory, Culture and Race*, London and New York: Routledge, 1995.

Chapter 5

Primary sources

Books and articles

Gairdner, W.H.T., *The Reproach of Islam*, London: Student Volunteer Missionary Union, 1909.

Herbert, Aubrey, *Ben Kendim: A Record of Eastern Travel*, ed. D. MacCarthy, London: Hutchinson, 1924.

Hogarth, David G., *A Wandering Scholar in the Levant*, London: John Murray, 1896.

Lawrence, T.E., *Seven Pillars of Wisdom*, new edn, London: Wordsworth, 1997.

Milman, Henry Hart, *The History of Christianity: The Birth of Christ till the Abolition of Paganism in the Roman Empire*, 3 vols, London: John Murray, 1867.

Mosheim, J.L., *Ecclesiastical History, from the Birth of Christ to the Beginning of the Eighteenth Century*, trans. Archibald Maclaine, London: William Tyler, Bolt-Court, 1842.

Pears, Edwin, *Forty Years in Constantinople: The Recollections of Sir Edwin Pears*, London: Herbert Jenkins, 1916.

Pickthall, Marmaduke, 'The Black Crusade' [part 1], *The New Age*, 12 (7 November 1912), p. 8; [part 2] 12 (14 November 1912), pp. 31–2; [part 3] 12 (21 November 1912), p. 58; [part 4] 12 (28 November 1913), p. 79; [part 5] 12 (5 December 1912), p. 103.

——— 'The Fate of the Mohammedans of Macedonia', *The New Age*, 12 (20 February 1913), pp. 388–9.

Quilliam, W.H., *The Religion of the Sword: An Enquiry into the Tenets and History of Judaism, Christianity and Islam*, Liverpool: Dodd, 1891.

BIBLIOGRAPHY

———— *The Faith of Islam: An Explanatory Sketch of the Principal Fundamental Tenets of the Moslem Religion*, 3rd edn, Liverpool: Willmer Brothers, 1892.

———— *The Troubles in the Balkans: The Turkish Side of the Question*, Liverpool: Crescent Printing and Publishing Company, n.d. [1904].

Quilliam, W.H.A., *Studies in Islam: A Collection of Essays*, Liverpool: Crescent Printing and Publishing Company, 1895.

Sykes, Mark, *Dar-ul-Islam: A Record of a Journey through Ten of the Asiatic Provinces of Turkey*, London: Bickers & Son, 1904.

Zwemer, Samuel M., *Islam: A Challenge to Faith; Studies on the Mohammedan Religion and the Needs and Opportunities of the Moslem World from the Standpoint of Christian Missions*, New York: Student Volunteer Movement for Foreign Mission, 1907.

Secondary sources

Anon, 'Quilliam and the Caliphate', www.abdullahquilliam.wordpress.com/category/abdullah-quilliam/views (last accessed 24 December 2015).

Aydın, Cemil, 'The Ottoman Empire and the Global Muslim Identity in the Formation of Eurocentric World Order, 1815–1919', in Fred Dallmayr, M. Akif Kayapınar and İsmail Yaylacı (eds), *Civilizations and World Order: Geopolitics and Cultural Difference*, pp. 117–44, Lanham, MD: Rowman and Littlefield, 2014.

Birt, Yahya, 'Abdullah Quilliam: Britain's First Islamist?', www.yahyabirt1. wordpress.com/2008/01/25/abdullah-quilliam-britains-first-islamist (last accessed 14 November 2015).

Clark, Peter, *Marmaduke Pickthall: British Muslim*, London: Quartet, 1986.

Clayer, Nathalie and Eric Germain (eds), *Islam in Inter-War Europe*, London: Hurst, 2008.

Deringil, Selim, *The Well-Protected Domains: Ideology and the Limitation of Power in the Ottoman Empire, 1876–1909*, London: I.B. Tauris, 1999.

———— *The Ottomans, the Turks, and World Power Politics: Collected Studies*, Istanbul: Isis Press, 2000.

———— 'They Live in a State of Nomadism and Savagery: The Late Ottoman Empire and Post-colonial Debate', *Comparative Studies in Society and History*, 45, 2 (2003), pp. 311–42.

Eldem, Edhem, 'The Ottoman Empire and Orientalism: An Awkward Relationship', in François Pouillon and Jean-Claude Vatin (eds), *After Orientalism: Critical Perspectives on Western Agency and Eastern Re-appropriations*, pp. 89–102, Leiden: Brill, 2011.

Elhusseini, Fadi, 'The Arab World between the Dilemma of Nationalism and Sectarian Conflicts', *Hemispheres*, 30, 2 (2015), pp. 39–56.

Fremantle, Anne, *Loyal Enemy*, London: Hutchinson, 1938.

Geaves, Ron, *Islam in Victorian Britain: The Life and Times of Abdullah Quilliam*, Markfield: Kube Publishing, 2010.

———— 'Abdullah Quilliam (Henri de Léon) and Marmaduke Pickthall: Agreements and Disagreements between Two Prominent Muslims in the London and Woking Communities', in Geoffrey P. Nash (ed.), *Marmaduke Pickthall, Islam and the Modern World*, pp 72–88, Leiden: Brill, 2016.

Gilham, Jamie, *Loyal Enemies: British Converts to Islam, 1850–1950*, London: Hurst, 2014.

Glenny, Misha, *The Balkans 1804–1999: Nationalism, War and the Great Powers*, London: Granta, 1999.

King, Richard, *Orientalism and Religion: Postcolonial Theory, India and 'The Mystic East'*, London: Routledge, 1999.

Murad, Abdal Hakim, 'British and Muslim?', www.masud.co.uk/ISLAM/ahm/british.htm (last accessed 14 December 2015).

———— 'Can Liberalism Tolerate Islam?', www.masud.co.uk/can-liberalism-tolerate-islam (last accessed 14 December 2015).

Nash, Geoffrey P., 'W.H. Quilliam, Marmaduke Pickthall and the Window of British Modernist Islam', in Geoffrey Nash, Kathleen Kerr-Koch and Sarah Hackett (eds), *Postcolonialism and Islam: Theory, Literature, Culture, Society and Film*, pp. 157–68, London: Routledge, 2014.

———— 'Pickthall, Ottomanism, and Modern Turkey', in Geoffrey P. Nash (ed.), *Marmaduke Pickthall, Islam and the Modern World*, pp. 137–56, Leiden: Brill, 2016.

Neill, Stephen, *A History of Christian Missions*, 2nd revised edn, Harmondsworth: Penguin, 1986.

Ozcan, Azmi, *Pan-Islamism: Indian Muslims, the Ottomans and Britain (1877–1924)*, Leiden: Brill, 1990.

Padwick, C.E., *Temple Gairdner of Cairo*, London: S.P.C.K., 1929.

Rodinson, Maxime, *Europe and the Mystique of Islam*, Seattle: University of Washington Press, 1987.

Singleton, Brent D. (ed.), *The Convert's Passion: An Anthology of Islamic Poetry from Late Victorian and Edwardian Britain*, n.p.: Borgo Press, 2009.

Slight, John, *The British Empire and the Hajj 1865–1956*, Cambridge, MA: Harvard University Press, 2015.

Unal, Hasan, 'Britain and Ottoman Domestic Politics: From the Young Turk Revolution to the Counter-revolution, 1908–9', *Middle Eastern Studies*, 37, 2 (2001), pp. 1–22.

Wasti, S. Tanvir, 'Mushir Hosain Kidwai and the Ottoman Cause', *Middle Eastern Studies*, 30, 2 (1994), pp. 252–61.

Chapter 6

Primary sources

Archives

Author's Collection, Postcard from Mohommed Ishaq to Mr. Abdulla Quilliam, 24 June 1903.

BIBLIOGRAPHY

Manx National Library and Archives, Manx Museum, Douglas, Isle of Man, Letters to Henry Hanby Hay, 1894–1911, MD 79–5: Abdullah Quilliam to Henry Hanby Hay, 26 December 1896.

Newspapers and journals

The Crescent
Daily Express
Daily Mail
The Evening Post
The Islamic Review and Muslim India
The Islamic World
Isle of Man Times and General Advertiser
Liverpool Daily Post
Liverpool Echo
Liverpool Mercury
Lloyd's Weekly Newspaper
The Manx Sun
The Porcupine
The Review of Religions
The Times

Books and articles

Mohammed-ul-Mamoon, *An Account of the Rise of Islam in England*, Dacca: K.D. Basak/East Bengal Press, 1891.

Pool, John J., *Studies in Mohammedanism: Historical and Doctrinal, with a Chapter on Islam in England*, Westminster: Archibald, Constable and Company, 1892.

Quilliam, W.H., 'Islam in England', *Religious Review of Reviews*, 1, 3 (1891), pp. 159–60.

————, *The Faith of Islam: An Explanatory Sketch of the Principal Fundamental Tenets of the Moslem Religion*, 3rd edn, Liverpool: Willmer Brothers, 1892.

Secondary sources

Ansari, Humayun, *'The Infidel Within': Muslims in Britain since 1800*, London: Hurst, 2004.

Geaves, Ron, *Islam in Victorian Britain: The Life and Times of Abdullah Quilliam*, Markfield: Kube Publishing, 2010.

Gilham, Jamie, *Loyal Enemies: British Converts to Islam, 1850–1950*, London: Hurst, 2014.

Kramers, J.H., R. Bulliet and R.C. Repp, 'Shaykh al-Islām', in P. Bearman, Th. Bianquis, C. E. Bosworth, E. van Donzel and W.P. Heinrichs (eds), *Encyclopaedia of Islam*, 2nd edn, Brill Online 2015, http://referenceworks.

brillonline.com/entries/encyclopaedia-of-islam-2/shaykh-al-islam-COM_1052 (last accessed 3 November 2015).

Bowen, Patrick D., *A History of Conversion to Islam in the United States, Volume 1: White American Muslims before 1975*, Leiden: Brill, 2015.

Dajani (Al-Daoudi), Amjad Muhsen S., '*The Islamic World*, 1893–1908', *Victorian Periodicals Review*, 47, 3 (2014), pp. 454–75.

Halliday, Fred, *Arabs in Exile: Yemeni Migrants in Urban Britain*, London: I.B. Tauris, 1992.

————— 'The *Millet* of Manchester: Arab Merchants and Cotton Trade', *British Journal of Middle Eastern Studies*, 19, 2 (1992), pp. 159–76.

Lawless, Richard I., *From Ta'izz to Tyneside: An Arab Community in the North-East of England during the Early Twentieth Century*, Exeter: Exeter University Press, 1995.

Macfie, A.L., *The Eastern Question, 1774–1923*, revised edn, Harlow: Longman, 1996.

————— *The End of the Ottoman Empire, 1908–1923*, Harlow: Longman, 1998.

Muslim Museum Initiative, www.muslimmuseum.org.uk/quilliams-125th-anniversary-project-bid-unsuccessful (last accessed 12 December 2015).

Rogan, Eugene, *The Fall of the Ottomans: The Great War in the Middle East, 1914–1920*, London: Allen Lane, 2015.

Seddon, Mohammad Siddique, *The Last of the Lascars: Yemeni Muslims in Britain, 1836–2012*, Markfield: Kube Publishing, 2014.

Singleton, Brent D., '"That Ye May Know Each Other": Late Victorian Interactions between British and West African Muslims', *Journal of Muslim Minority Affairs*, 29, 3 (2009), pp. 369–85.

Tetens, Kristan, 'The Lyceum and the Lord Chamberlain: The Case of Hall Caine's *Mahomet*', in Richard Foulkes (ed.), *Henry Irving: A Re-evaluation of the Pre-eminent Victorian Actor-Manager*, pp. 49–63, Aldershot: Ashgate, 2008.

Chapter 7

Primary sources

Archives

Missouri Historical Society, St. Louis, John A. Lant Papers: Correspondence between John A. Lant and C.L.M. Abdul Jebbar, Abdullah W.H. Quilliam and Hamid Snow.

Newspapers and journals

The Crescent
Evening Sun
The Islamic World
The Moslem World

BIBLIOGRAPHY

Moslem World and Voice of Islam
New York Herald
New York World
Sierra Leone Weekly News
The Times
Times of India
Utica Sunday Journal

Books and articles

MacQueary, Howard, 'American Mohammedanism', *Unitarian*, 8 (1893), pp. 104–8.
Webb, Alexander Russell, 'Preaching Islam in America', *Providence Journal*, 14 (1893), pp. 468–70.
Webb, Mohammed Alexander Russell, *Lectures on Islam: Delivered at Different Places in India*, Lahore: Islamia Press, 1893.

Secondary sources

Abd-Allah, Umar F., *A Muslim in Victorian America: The Life of Alexander Russell Webb*, New York: Oxford University Press, 2006.
Ansari, Humayun, 'Maulana Barkatullah Bhopali's Transnationalism: Pan-Islamism, Colonialism, and Radical Politics', in Götz Nordbruch and Umar Ryad (eds), *Transnational Islam in Interwar Europe: Muslim Activists and Thinkers*, pp. 181–209, New York: Palgrave Macmillan, 2014.
Bickford-Smith, Vivian, *Ethnic Pride and Racial Prejudice in Victorian Cape Town: Group Identity and Social Practice, 1875–1902*, Cambridge: Cambridge University Press, 1995.
Bowen, Patrick D., *A History of Conversion to Islam in the United States, Volume 1: White American Muslims before 1975*, Leiden: Brill, 2015.
Chopra, Pragha and P.N. Chopra, *Indian Freedom Fighters Abroad: Secret British Intelligence Report*, New Delhi: Criterion, 1988.
Dajani (Al-Daoudi), Amjad Muhsen S., '*The Islamic World*, 1893–1908', *Victorian Periodicals Review*, 47 (2014), pp. 454–75.
Davids, Achmat, *The Mosques of Bo-Kaap: A Social History of Islam at the Cape*, Athlone: South African Institute of Arabic and Islamic Research, 1980.
Everest-Phillips, Max, 'Colin Davidson's British Indian Intelligence Operations in Japan 1915–23 and the Demise of the Anglo-Japanese Alliance', *Intelligence and National Security*, 24 (2009), pp. 674–99.
Geaves, Ron, *Islam in Victorian Britain: The Life and Times of Abdullah Quilliam*, Markfield: Kube Publishing, 2010.
Gilham, Jamie, '"Upholding the banner of Islam": British Converts to Islam and the Liverpool Muslim Institute, c.1887–1908', *Immigrants & Minorities*, 33, 1 (2013), pp. 23–41.

BIBLIOGRAPHY

Khan, Mohammed Ayub, 'Universal Islam: The Faith and Political Ideologies of Maulana Barakatullah "Bhopali"', *Sikh Formations*, 10 (2014), pp. 57–67.

Nworah, Kenneth Dike, 'The Liverpool "Sect" and British West African Policy 1895–1915', *African Affairs*, 70 (1971), pp. 349–64.

Razvi, Shafqat, 'Mawli Barkatullah Bhopali: A Revolutionary Freedom Fighter of the Early 20th Century', *Journal of the Pakistan Historical Society*, 37 (1989), pp. 139–58.

Singleton, Brent D., 'Brothers at Odds: Rival Islamic Movements in Late Nineteenth-Century New York City', *Journal of Muslim Minority Affairs*, 27 (2007), pp. 473–86.

———— 'The *Moslem World*: A History of America's Earliest Islamic Newspaper and Its Successors', *Journal of Muslim Minority Affairs*, 27 (2007), pp. 297–307.

———— '"That ye may know each other": Late Victorian Interactions between British and West African Muslims', *Journal of Muslim Minority Affairs*, 29 (2009), pp. 369–85.

Chapter 8

Primary sources

Archives and private collections

Rasjid Skinner Private Papers: Daoud Rosser-Owen, 'The History and Organisation of the ABM', Draft confidential memorandum to ABM Council, 21 July 1987, Typescript, 12pp.; Shaykh Sharafuddin Murghanil [Daoud Rosser-Owen], 'Islamists and the British', Undated lecture to ABM (*c*. mid-1980s), Typescript, 7pp.

Interviews and personal correspondence

Author's interviews with: Daoud Rosser-Owen, January 2008; Fuad Nahdi, 7 November 2015; Rasjid Skinner, 21 October 2015.

Email communications to the author from: Batool Al-Toma, 14 November 2010 and 14 October 2015; M.A. Khan-Cheema, 7 October 2015; Abdurraheem Green, 8 October 2015; Ibrahim Hewitt, 7 October 2015; Atif Imtiaz, 8 October 2015; Shiraz Khan, 4 November 2015; Jamil Sherif, 9 October 2015; Adnan Siddiqui, 16 October 2015; Tim Winter, 7 October 2015; Yaqub Zaki, 7 October 2015.

Facebook communication to the author from M.A. Khan-Cheema, 14 November 2015.

Newspapers, newsletters and journals

Association for British Muslims Bulletin
The Crescent
The Independent

BIBLIOGRAPHY

Islamic Foundation Newsletter
Liverpool Echo
Meeting Point: The Newsletter of the New Muslims Project
Q-News

Books, articles and webpages

Abdullah Quilliam Society, 'The Sheikh Abdullah Quilliam Mosque and Heritage Centre' project brochure (January 2012), 21pp. [typescript], www.abdullahquilliam.com/wp/pdfs/Abdullah-Quilliam-Heritage-Centre-Brochure-JAN2012.pdf (last accessed 13 November 2015).

———— 'Abdullah Quilliam Mosque and Heritage Centre Progress Report' (13 August 2012), 3pp. [typescript], www.abdullahquilliam.com/wp/pdfs/ABDULLAH-QUILLIAM-MOSQUE-AND-HERITAGE-CENTRE-PROGRESS-REPORT-August–2012.pdf (last accessed 13 November 2015).

———— 'Obituary for Dr Mohammad Akbar Ali L.LD, MBE', Abdullah Quilliam Society website, July 2014, www.abdullahquilliam.com/wp/pdfs/Obituary-Akbar-Ali.pdf (last accessed 10 November 2015).

Al-Samarrai, Salih Mahdi S., 'Islam in Japan: History, Spread and Institutions in the Country', Islamic Centre of Japan website, 2009, www.islamcenter.or.jp/en/history-and-publications/history-of-islam-in-japan/ (last accessed 23 November 2015).

Alton, David, 'The Death of Akbar Ali', David Alton website, 8 July 2014, www.davidalton.net/2014/07/08/the-death-of-akbar-ali/ (last accessed 23 November 2015).

Asian Image website, 'Abdullah Quilliam Society Has Nothing to Do with Quilliam Foundation', 4 February 2014, www.asianimage.co.uk/news/north_of_england/10985951._Abdullah_Quilliam_Society_has_nothing_to_do_with_Quilliam_Foundation_/ (last accessed 12 April 2016).

Association of British Muslims, 'A Brief History of the ABM', Association of British Muslims website, 1998–9, www.members.tripod.com/~british_muslims_assn/briefhistory.html (last accessed 9 November 2015).

———— 'Our Team', Association of British Muslims website, n.d., www.aobm.org/our-team/ (last accessed 4 December 2015).

British Muslim Song website, 'Harmonia Alcorani & Audio Files', January 2010, www.britishmuslimsong.co.uk/?page_id=143 (last accessed 23 November 2015).

Chambers, Yusuf, 'Dawah: The Activism of the 21st Century', YouTube, 19 January 2012, www.youtube.com/watch?v=R5dfpHBp2Qc (last accessed 2 December 2015).

———— 'Great British Islam: The Lost Treasure', YouTube, 20 July 2012,

BIBLIOGRAPHY

www.youtube.com/watch?v=jrfjXLzlt1s (last accessed 6 November 2015).

Husain, Azim (ed.), *Mian Fazl-i-Husain: Glimpses of Life and Works, 1898–1936*, Lahore: Sang-e-Meel Publications, 1995.

Kelwick, Adam, 'The Life of Shaykh-ul-Islam of the British Isles, W.H. Abdullah Quilliam', YouTube, 15 June 2012, www.youtube.com/watch?v=Z-ANc3XaM30 (last accessed 2 December 2015).

———— 'Shaykh Abdullah William Henry Quilliam', YouTube, 1 September 2014, www.youtube.com/watch?v=z0yhNDpo3h8 (last accessed 5 November 2015).

———— 'One Man and His Da'wah (Abdullah Quilliam)', YouTube, 29 March 2015, www.youtube.com/watch?v=jQp5JSVCIJA (last accessed 5 November 2015).

Khulusi, S.A. (ed.), *Islam: Our Choice*, Woking: Woking Muslim Mission & Literary Trust, 1961.

Liverpool Muslim Society, 'Liverpool Muslim Society and Masjid History', Liverpool Muslim Society website, www.liverpoolmuslimsociety.org.uk/1/liverpool-muslim-society-and-masjid-history (last accessed 13 November 2015).

Masud website, 'British Muslim Heritage', www.masud.co.uk/ISLAM/bmh/bmh.htm (last accessed 23 November 2015).

Murad, Abdal Hakim [T.J. Winter], *Muslim Songs of the British Isles*, London: Quilliam Press, 2005.

———— 'British Muslims and the Rhetoric of Indigenisation', Masud website, 15 July 2014, www.masud.co.uk/british-muslims-and-the-rhetoric-of-indigenisation/ (last accessed 1 December 2015).

Muslim Council of Britain, 'Muslim Council of Britain Mourns the Passing of Dr Mohammad Akbar Ali', Muslim Council of Britain website, 2014, www.mcb.org.uk/dr-mohammad-akbar-ali-tribute/ (last accessed 11 November 2015).

Quilliam Press website, 'About the Quilliam Press', www.quilliampress.com/about/ (last accessed 23 November 2015).

Rosser-Owen, Daoud, 'A History of Islam in the British Isles: An Overview', Association of British Muslims website, 1998, www.members.tripod.com/~british_muslims_assn/history_of_islam_in_the_bi.html (last accessed 9 November 2015).

Thomson, Ahmad, 'The Life of Shaykh-ul-Islam of the British Isles, W.H. Abdullah Quilliam', YouTube, 15 June 2012, www.youtube.com/watch?v=Z-ANc3XaM30 (last accessed 2 December 2015).

Winter, T.J., *British Muslim Identity: Past, Problems, Prospects*, Cambridge: MAT Press, 2003.

BIBLIOGRAPHY

Secondary sources

Ally, Muhammad Mashuq, 'History of Muslims in Britain, 1850–1980', Unpublished MA thesis, University of Birmingham, 1981.

Ansari, Humayun, 'The Woking Mosque: A Case Study of Muslim Engagement with British Society since 1889', *Immigrants & Minorities*, 21, 3 (2002), pp. 1–24.

———— *The Infidel Within: Muslims in Britain since 1800*, London: Hurst, 2004.

Birt, Yahya, 'Abdullah Quilliam: Britain's First Islamist?', Yahya Birt website, 25 January 2008, www.yahyabirt1.wordpress.com/2008/01/25/abdullah-quilliam-britains-first-islamist/ (last accessed 12 April 2016).

Bougarel, Xavier, 'From Young Muslims to Party of Democratic Action: The Emergence of a Pan-Islamist Trend in Bosnia–Herzegovina', *Islamic Studies*, 36, 2–3 (1997), pp. 533–49.

Clark, Peter, *Marmaduke Pickthall: British Muslim*, London: Quartet Books, 1986.

Dyer, Richard, *White*, London: Routledge, 1997.

Geaves, Ron, *Islam in Victorian Britain: The Life and Times of Abdullah Quilliam*, Markfield: Kube Publishing, 2010.

———— 'Islam in Victorian Britain: The Life and Times of Abdullah Quilliam and His Contemporary Cultural Significance', REF2014 Impact Case Study, www.impact.ref.ac.uk/CaseStudies/CaseStudy.aspx?Id=42066 (last accessed 23 November 2015).

Gilham, Jamie, *Loyal Enemies: British Converts to Islam, 1850–1950*, London: Hurst, 2014.

Hamid, Sadek, *Sufis, Salafis and Islamists: The Contested Ground of British Islamic Activism*, London: I.B. Tauris, 2016.

Hobsbawm, Eric, 'Introduction: Inventing Traditions', in Eric Hobsbawm and Terence Ranger (eds), *The Invention of Tradition*, pp. 1–14, Cambridge: Cambridge University Press, 1983.

Kamran, Tahir, 'Husain, Sir Mian Fazl-i-', in H.C.G. Matthew, Brian Harrison and Lawrence Goldman (eds), *Oxford Dictionary of National Biography*, Oxford University Press online, www.oxforddnb.com/view/article/95339 (last accessed 9 November 2015).

Karčić, Fikret, *The Bosniaks and the Challenges of Modernity: Late Ottoman and Hapsburg Times*, Sarajevo: El-Kalem, 1991.

———— 'The Office of Ra'is al-'Ulama' among the Bosniaks (Bosnian Muslims)', *Intellectual Discourse*, 5, 2 (1997), pp. 109–20.

Khan-Cheema, M.A., 'Islam and the Muslims in Liverpool', Unpublished MA thesis, University of Liverpool, 1979.

Köse, Ali, *Conversion to Islam: A Study of Native British Converts*, London: Kegan Paul International, 1997.

McIntosh, Peggy, 'White Privilege and Male Privilege: A Personal Account of

Coming to See Correspondences through Work in Women's Studies', Working Paper no. 189, Wellesley, MA: Wellesley College, Center for Research on Women, 1988.

Mills, Charles W., 'White Supremacy as Sociopolitical System: A Philosophical Perspective', in A. W. Doane and E. Bonilla-Silva (eds), *White Out: The Continuing Significance of Racism*, pp. 35–48, New York and London: Routledge, 2003.

Moosavi, Leon, 'White Privilege in the Lives of Muslim Converts in Britain', *Ethnic and Racial Studies*, 38, 11 (2015), pp. 1–15.

Robinson-Dunn, Diane, 'Lascar Sailors and English Converts: The Imperial Port and Islam in Late 19th-Century England', *Seascapes, Littoral Cultures, and Trans-oceanic Exchanges*, 12–15 February 2003, Library of Congress, Washington DC, History Cooperative website, www.historycooperative. org/proceedings/seascapes/dunn.html (last accessed 29 January 2008).

Shearmur, Jeremy, 'The Woking Mosque Muslims: British Islam in the Early Twentieth Century', *Journal of Muslim Minority Affairs*, 34, 2 (2014), pp. 165–73.

Silverstein, Brian, 'Sufism and Governmentality in the Late Ottoman Empire', *Comparative Studies of South Asia, Africa and the Middle East*, 29, 2 (2009), pp. 171–85.

Stetkevych, Suzanne Pinckney, *The Mantle Odes: Arabic Praise Poems to the Prophet Muhammad*, Bloomington: Indiana University Press, 2010.

Tourage, Mahdi, 'Performing Belief and Reviving Islam: Prominent (White Male) Converts in Muslim Revival Conventions', *Performing Islam*, 1, 2 (2013), pp. 207–26.

Wolffe, John (ed.), *Religion in Victorian Britain, Volume V: Culture and Empire*, Manchester: Manchester University Press, 1997.

INDEX

INDEX

INDEX

INDEX

INDEX

INDEX

Society of London, 48; writes courtly love marriage poems, 66–7; joins lord mayor of Liverpool's 'state procession', 104

1908 works on Martha Thompson's divorce case, 18, 64; leaves Britain for Istanbul, xx, 18, 23, 42, 81, 97, 109, 112; found guilty *in absentia* of fabricating evidence, 18

1909 returns to Britain, 81; enters relationship with Edith Spray, 67, 69; death of Hannah; public marriage to Mary, 68–9

1913 death of Yarker; Meyer appointed head of APR, 36

1914 publication of *English-Manx-Gaelic Etymologies*, 42

1915 publication of *Geology of the Isle of Man*, 42, 48

1916 publication of *Sheikh Haroun Abdullah* and *The Haggadah*, 42

1917 publication of *Pipe Fishes* and *The Chellonia*, 42

1918 publication of *Two Sussex Parishes*, 42

1919 publication of *Memory Scientifically Considered*, 42

1920 publication of *The Excellent Name of God*, 42

1921 publication of *Ionization*, 42

1922 publication of *Influenza, Asbestos and Asbestiform Minerals* and *The Curiosities of the Calendar*, 42

1923 publication of *Sleep and the Psychology of Dreams*, 42

1925 publication of *Herbal Theurapeutics*, 42

1926 publication of *The Psychology of Oriental Peoples*, 42

1927 publication of *Der Prophet gleich Moses* and *Medicine and Physiology among the Arabs*, 42

1928 publication of *Arabian Poets* and *The Folklore of Herbal Theurapeutics*, 42

1929 publication of *The Celtic Discovery of America, Language of Afghanistan* and *Memory*, 42–3

1930 publication of *A Great Arabian Astrologer*, 43

1931 publication of *The Diffraction of Light*, 43

1932 death, 1, 69

Quilliam, Ethel Mariam, 109
Quilliam, Hannah, 11, 27, 67, 68
Quilliam, Harriet, 10, 58, 70, 109–10
Quilliam, John, 9
Quilliam, Lillian Ayesha, 109
Quilliam, Robert, 8–9
Quilliam, Robert Ahmad, 98, 104
Quilliam Foundation, 2, 142, 148–9
Quilliam Press, 141
Qur'an, 15, 46, 49, 50, 53, 54, 55, 57, 61, 77, 85, 108

race suicide, 72–3
racism, 12, 72, 123, 146
al-Rahma Masjid, Liverpool, 138, 139
railways, 47
Ramadan, 103
Rampur, India, 75
rationalism, 18, 21, 22, 49, 51, 84
Rawson, Albert, 34, 38
Razvi, Shafqat, 129
Rebuke of Islam, The (Gairdner), 85